A face smiles up at you from the pages of a Sunday theatre supplement or the sports section of the newspaper, and instantly you're transported ten, twenty, thirty years back in time.

"Is that who I think it is?" you ask. "I wonder what he's doing these days."

Between the covers of this book are one hundred faces we once knew and still remember: Jerry Lester, the first stalwart of nighttime television; Erik Rhodes, the dashing third corner of those great Astaire-Rogers musical triangles; Edd "Kookie" Byrnes, who combed his way into the hearts of every teen-ager on *Sunset Strip;* Kathryn Grayson, the dark little movie beauty with the larger-than-life voice; Sugar Ray Robinson, whose style and class in the ring have yet to be matched; Rosemary Clooney, whose recorded invitation to *Come On-a My House* swept the country—they and 94 others are here, as they looked then, and as they are today.

Along with 200 fascinating photos are the stories of what has happened to them over the years: the actors, the athletes, the starlets, the musicians, the TV superstars, the members of royalty. Let author Patrick Agan tell you where they've been, where they're at, and where they're going, for whatever your age, your interests, your likes and dislikes, you'll find 100 special people in this book who'll turn back your personal clock.

IS THAT WHO I THINK IT IS?

Vol. I

Patrick Agan

ace books

A Division of Charter Communications Inc.
1120 Avenue of the Americas
New York, N.Y. 10036

Is That Who I Think It Is? Vol. I

Copyright © 1975 by Patrick Agan

First Ace Printing October 1975

An ACE Book

Printed in the U.S.A.

This book is dedicated to the late Susan Hayward, a gutsy star who never let her fans down. Susan fought for the roles she believed in and because of that commitment to her craft, she's left us a legacy of ladies who'll shine as long as there's a movie screen.

ACKNOWLEDGMENTS: TO JON B. ARONEO for his help in researching and photographing sections of this book; to CHRISTOPHER YOUNG for his invaluable help; to EDDIE COLBERT for his long-distance patience and help in supplying photographs for this manuscript; and to JACK KUSTER, TONY DRAKE, BRIAN H. STEIN, ROZ STARR and her terrific staff, KEN SMITH, BAER FRIMER and the people at Pictorial Parade, JOHN CANEMAKER and The CON-TESSA, DONNA GOULD, and especially to all the gracious ladies and gentlemen who appear between these covers. A special thanks to editor EVELYN GRIPPO for her assistance and her assistants.

CONTENTS

Chet Baker in 1955

Jack Kuster

CHET BAKER

A movie producer once asked Chet Baker to star in a film about his life but the deal fell through. It's probably just as well it did since no one would have believed it anyway, it's that tragically bizarre. It started out to be a golden life of spectacular talent and equal reward but has since wound down, around and through every extended cliche a scriptwriter could dream up if he were creating the story from scratch. What Gene Krupa was to drums in the Forties, Baker was to the trumpet in the Fifties. Firm-jawed, handsome, with a rigid pompadour swooping over his forehead, Baker was the matinee idol of the jazz set, with the talent to make his title of the leading trumpeter of the times an understatement. Connoisseurs and fans alike swarmed to his concerts with Gerry Mulligan when they teamed to make a brand of music that's never been duplicated. He lived the life of the giants, only the giants he chose to imitate, Charlie Parker and Billie Holiday to name but two, unwittingly turned him on to a life that quickly became an endless quest for the next heroin fix.

He first tried the drug, he told Rex Reed in 1973, when he was a nineteen-year-old student at junior college in Glendale, California, "but I didn't get hooked until I was twenty-seven, although everybody thought I was on it when I was playing with Gerry Mulligan. 'He's gotta be high to play like that!,' they used to say." Dope was the fashion among musicians and if there was one thing Chet wanted, it was to be fashionable, part of the scene. Parker tried to talk him out of it when they worked together but Baker didn't listen and soon it was too late. At twenty-two he'd been busted for possession of marijuana and since then, until only very recently, he says his life has been one long jail cell. His career quickly fell apart, his record albums became collectors' items, twelve years disappeared from his life and he himself became an exile, hiding out in a Milan, Italy drug clinic where they tried a sleep cure.

2

Jack Kuster

Chet Baker in New York recently

He met his wife Carol while he was there. She was an actress appearing there in an English play. She's stuck by him ever since.

She nursed him for seven months when he was arrested again and spent over a year in a filthy Italian jail. To Reed again, "For fifteen months I lived in that cell working chess problems and playing my horn. I wrote a bunch of tunes and the guards drove me crazy asking me to play *Cherry Pink and Apple Blossom White*, one of his biggest hits.

After several more years of ups (scoring a Susan Hayward movie in London; briefly owning his own club in Milan; a new recording contract with RCA) and downs (thirty days in a British jail, then being deported to France) he was deported back home only to find that with his drug record he couldn't get a cabaret license to perform, "so I hocked my horn and ended up on welfare." He got into a Methadone program after deciding one friendless night that he'd either live life straight or not at all, and while he feels it's trading one addiction for another, he also says it saved his life.

At the Newport Jazz Festival in 1973 he made a comeback that staggered the surprised audience. The good looks were only a shadow of what they once were but the talent was as golden as it had been twenty years before. Physically, at forty-four, his coordination, diaphragm muscles, and general condition made it seem almost impossible that he could still coax that kind of sound from his horn, but he did. One old friend, of many, was Steve Allen, and Steve was willing to prove it by bankrolling him. Baker returned the favor by recording an album of Allen's songs. Though still on Methadone, he's winning his almost twenty-year battle with the hard stuff. In the winter of 1975 he gave a concert at Carnegie Hall and proved again that he could make music almost as good as ever. He and his family are based in California but he's often in New York, playing at small clubs wherever jazz buffs gather. To them he's still the greatest, and finally he is to himself too.

3

Barker and Susan Hayward in 1947
with sons Gregory and Timothy

Pictorial Parade

JESS BARKER

The story of the determinedly rising star married to the not-so-rising leading man is one that Hollywood practically cut its teeth on, yet seldom has it resulted in as explosive a union as that between Susan Hayward and Jess Barker. They met at the Hollywood Canteen—that oasis for servicemen during World War II—late in 1943 where Hayward would enter shouting "Anyone here from Brooklyn?", the rousing one-liner she used as a starlet when touring with the Louella Parsons stage show. Barker like her style and she his, and they began a stormy courtship that led to the altar on July 22, 1944.

She was just reaching full speed with her career in *And Now Tomorrow* and *The Hairy Ape* while he was also working steadily in things like *Cover Girl* and, at MGM, *Keep Your Powder Dry*. He was slender and handsome and she was vibrantly, red-headedly beautiful in a special way that wasn't flawless but which was infinitely more exciting than perfection. He was from South Carolina while she'd been born and bred in Brooklyn, and if it's true that opposites attract, these two proved it.

Stormy from the start, they separated in September of 1944 after a fight on board movie tough guy Steve Cochran's boat but reconciled two weeks later. She was quickly pregnant which further helped smooth things over at the time, and gave him twin sons, Gregory and Timothy, born prematurely on February 19, 1945. (To keep studio publicists and month-counting audiences happy, their marriage date was 'officially' amended to April 23, 1944 leaving her plenty of time to have the children.)

While he got lost in things like *This Love of Ours* (1945), a Merle Oberon starrer, and *The Time of Their Lives* with Abbott and Costello (1946), Susan moved upward in *Canyon Passage*

4

Jess Barker as he looks today

(1946) and *Smash-up, the Story of a Woman* (1947), steadily increasing her stature with *The Lost Moment* (1947) and *Tap Roots* (1948), finally blossoming into the full Hayward charisma in 1949's *My Foolish Heart.*

Their careers continued in opposite directions which added to the strain of two volatile personalities, in an industry and a town that stressed the individual. The Fifties saw her become one of Hollywood's most important stars but 1954 also saw the end of her marriage, and a very messy end at that. Suits and countersuits were filed and newspapers had a field day when one night he chased her around their Sherman Oaks swimming pool. She was nude at the time, reportedly shouting "Don't kill me!" Barker named Howard Hughes as a secret visitor and finally sued for divorce asking a community property settlement of their combined wealth. Susan, however, supposedly at the suggestion of her mother, had had Barker sign a marital agreement in 1944 which stated that their incomes would always be mutually exclusive. She made him a settlement offer of $100,000 but he said no, went ahead with his suit for half of everything and lost. He left the marriage with the family station wagon. The strain of the divorce took its toll on her and shortly after it, on April 26, 1955, she made a headlined attempt at suicide. She said "I'm divorced and I never wanted to be divorced. I did everything to make the marriage work."

Barker filmed *Shack Out On 101* in 1956 while Susan triumphed in *I'll Cry Tomorrow.* It wasn't that Hollywood held the marriage and its subsequently horrible publicity against him; he had simply passed his movie prime.

Today, son Gregory is a veterinarian and Timothy heads up his own public relations firm in Hollywood. It was he who handled the details surrounding his mother's tragic death in 1975 after a long illness. Barker himself was cut out of her will completely but has started working again, most currently on a movie in the Philipines. It's a character part.

5

Charlie and singer Sunny Gale backstage at New York's Paramount Theater in 1952

CHARLIE BARNET

One of the biggest hits of 1939 was *Cherokee*, recorded on the Victor-Bluebird label by a twenty-six-year-old society bandleader who, until then, was best known for his back-up work on Red Norvo's recordings. He was undoubtedly young for such a feat but also undeniably talented and committed to music, especially the jazz which was shortly to make him world famous. By age sixteen he'd had his own band and traveled with it back and forth across the Atlantic some twenty-two times, brightening up many otherwise quiet nights at sea. Born Charles Daly Barnet to a wealthy New York family on October 26, 1913, he was more commonly known to his fans and friends as Charlie. And after *Cherokee* he had thousands of them!

Barnet's family educated him at some of the finest private schools in the country and wanted him to fit his feet into the respectable shoes of a corporation lawyer, but he wasn't buying it. Somewhat of a prodigy, he'd mastered the alto, tenor and soprano saxophones by the time he had his transatlantic band and was so immersed in jazz that he even affected a New Orleans twang and didn't go overboard to deny that he came from there when people commented on it. After his sea-going career, which eventually took him to the South Seas and South America, he got a break on land when he started on the bandstand at New York's Paramount Hotel in 1932. By '34 his great talent was recognized by Norvo, the magician of the xylophone who was then known as 'Mr. Swing'. (Mildred Baily was Norvo's 'Mrs.' on-stage and off.)

After the success of *Cherokee*, Barnet and his band were very much on the map but he always went back to the roots of the music he loved, spotlighting in performances the works

Charlie recently in Hollywood

Pictorial Parade

of Duke Ellington and others. He not only recognized the origins of jazz but always scheduled appearances at black spots like Harlem's Apollo Theater on his tours (he'd first played there way back in '33) and was one of the first big band leaders to showcase black talent like Lena Horne, Trummy Young, 'Peanuts' Holland and Oscar Pettiford. After all, he said, "Jazz is the product of the black man. Why not pattern your music after the most inventive kind and try to go on from there?"

"From there" carried him into the Forties as one of that period's most colorful and popular musicians. In '41 he won the Metropolitan Jazz Poll and his records were solid sellers. Artists like Kay Starr, Fran Warren and Frances Wayne all occupied the band singer's chair with him at one point or another and all through the Swing Era he was one of its leaders.

When the Fifties killed off that colorful era in entertainment, Barnet kept working although the bookings got smaller and smaller. In 1958 he went into personal management in Hollywood but kept his music alive playing small gigs and recording with pick-up groups. He's kept his band together, forming and reforming it as the demand requires, still traveling to accommodate the current revival of the big band sound and the Forties in general.

A few years ago he went to a reunion in Hollywood that included Bob Crosby, Jo Stafford, Freddie Martin and many others who'd cut their teeth during the palmy days of fan-filled auditoriums and ballrooms and one-night stands across the country.

Ten times married, Barnet's personal life has been a hectic one to say the least. He lives in Hollywood and always has a bag packed and a telephone ready to gather up his musicians and hit the road. The fans are a little older now and the younger crowd needs a little education into the finer points of his music but he's happy to make new friends and get together with the old ones.

7

Bettina and Aly Khan in 1951

Pictorial Parade

BETTINA

The world expected the girl who was able to take Aly Khan away from Rita Hayworth to be something special, something spectacular. Something special she was, but while her beauty might have been called spectacular, she was in reality no match for the volatile Miss. H. It was this European fragility which made the difference for the 'playboy Prince' of the Forties who married Hollywood's greatest sex bomb. When he met Bettina, she was a model for Coco Chanel and he, for the first time in his life, was known as something else besides society's greatest lover—he was also known as Mr. Rita Hayworth and that didn't feel good. Their marriage in 1949 and the subsequent birth of their daughter, Princess Yasmin, was accompanied by constant headlines. They had to but discuss the choice of dinner wine in a restaurant and it was international news of a tiff. As the son of the powerful Moslem regligious leader, the Aga Khan, Aly was used to having all attention center on Him, and being married to one of the world's most publicized movie stars was a strain on his ego. Rita's movie career was peaking then and by the third year of their marriage it had all taken its toll. Aly was ripe for a change, and her name was Bettina.

They met in Paris when she was twenty-four and the toast of the Chanel salon. When it became apparant that he wasn't frequenting the place just to buy Rita a present the press went crazy, so much so that he was almost forced, gentleman that he was, to ask his famous wife for a divorce. He did, in 1951, and though everyone expected Aly and Bettina to instantly marry, they didn't. Instead they began a love affair that saw her stick through the thick (constant speculation as to whether on his father's death, he would become the new Aga Khan) and the thin (a widely reported liaison with Gene Tierney). It lasted until his death in May of 1960 in the Paris suburb of Suresnes when the Lancia carrying them both crashed head-on with another auto. His last words were "How is Bettina?"

Bettina today with escort, Italian playboy, Beppe Piroddi

Immediately the world speculated on two important questions: just how wealthy was the son of the man who'd been reputed to be the world's richest, and how would that fortune be disposed of? Surprisingly it totaled less than a million dollars, two-thirds of which he left Bettina, as well as leaving her his chateau in Chantilly. For several months the girl who'd given up her career to become one of the world's most famous unmarried women kept her silence. Finally she spoke, denying the rumors that she and Aly were on the verge of marriage when the crash occurred. She added, "It's also untrue that I am going to marry someone else. I will not marry now." And she didn't.

Later that same year she stood almost unnoticed on the crowded infield at Longchamps race track in Paris watching Aly's colors win the Grand Prix. Moments later she broke into tears and murmured, "Aly would have been so happy." His stables were his greatest passion besides Bettina. (Once, during a tiff, she flew to Dublin to see his horses race, disguising herself as 'Madame Graziano'. The impact of her interest wasn't lost on him as they reconciled soon after.)

After his death she was financially independent but without a purpose in life. In 1967, she underwent a strict routine of diet and yoga so she could return to modeling. In July of that year, she appeared in Chanel's annual show. Unfortunately for the forty-two year-old mannequin, it wasn't a successful comeback—even the highheeled shoes assigned her black outfit kept falling off.

She took a white villa at the Costa Esmeralda resort owned by the young Aga Khan, Aly's son Karim, and spent many hours lying on the beach watching the Jet Set go by. "Occasionally I go for a trip on Karim's yacht but mostly I just lie and read in the sun." A good friend of Elizabeth Taylor and Princess Soraya, she today lives a life of parties, movie openings and younger escorts. When one sees her in Paris and Rome, one can't help but think she's a woman who's known the best . . . and hopes she'll find it again.

Glamorous Joan in the early Forties

JOAN BLONDELL

If ever the phrase 'More Bounce To The Ounce' could be applied to a movie star, Joan Blondell would get that tag hands down. As she told designer Earl Luick when she first reported to Warner Bros. in 1930 (where he'd designed a corset to try and control her), "My can got me into pictures and my can's gonna stay in pictures!" It did too, but her body was only part of Blondell's appeal. An all-around actress, she was one of the original good-natured party girls in *Public Enemy* (1931), the chorus girl lost without an extra wad of chewing gum in Busby Berkeley's great *Golddiggers of 1933*—in which she sang the unforgettable *Remember My Forgotten Man*—and later even gave the Southern Belle route a new twist opposite John Wayne in 1941's *Lady For A Night*. She's been a survivor because she had more than just youthful good-looks and tapping feet to sell, and evolved steadily from leads to co-starring with other blondes (Jayne Mansfield in *Will Success Spoil Rock Hunter* in 1957, to richly textured character parts like the piano-pounding evangelist in '57's *Angel Baby* and her Sixties TV series *Here Come The Brides,* which had her as a happy-go-lucky bar owner in the North Woods. She's had a hectic personal life too, but was always strong enough to keep on going. She may have started out on screen as cheap champagne but today she's considered fine—and rare—vintage wine.

Joan came from a vaudeville family, and she grew up around show biz. She was part of the family's act almost from birth (New York City, 1909) and traveled all over the world with it. She got to Hollywood when Warner's bought her, Jimmy Cagney and the play they were starring in, and made it into *Sinner's Holiday* in 1930. After that she was on her way, churning out one film after another, wisecracking her way right up there. In 1932 she married cameraman George Barnes, who photographed in many of her early films. They split in 1935.

Joan's romance and marriage to Dick Powell in 1936 was

10

Eddie Colbert

Joan, caught off-guard in Hollywood, 197[

big news and they played it up on screen as well in *Colleer* and *Stage-Struck* (both in 1936)—the latter was very good Blondell as a tippling leading lady with a brass mouth. Warners didn't see them as a romantic screen team though, and although they made many flicks together, they usually played antagonists. When World War II broke out, Joan didn't wait for the USO to be formed but went out on her own to entertain the troops, a gesture that cost her lots of movie roles. She did make 1943's *Cry Havoc* and was terrific in it, as she was as Aunt Cissy in *A Tree Grows In Brooklyn* (1944), a part originally intended for Alice Faye. She and Powell split in 1944 after two children, Ellen and Norman, and that same year her career slowed too. 1945's *Adventure*—the famous "Gable's Back and Garson's Got Him" flick—saw her billed below the title for the first time in twelve years.

Her romance with dynamic producer Mike Todd blossomed into marriage in 1947 (she'd starred on Broadway for him in 1943's *The Naked Genius*) and she bore him a namesake, Mike Jr. A volatile pair to put it mildly, they battled royally—a habit with him—before splitting for good in 1950.

Back to work with a vengeance, she did *The Blue Veil* with Jane Wyman and Charles Laughton in 1951 and got an Oscar nomination for Best Supporting Actress. Then came the character parts, on stage in *Call Me Madam* and, later, *Bye Bye Birdie,* and on screen in *The Opposite Sex* and *Lizzie,* both 1957. In 1958's *Desk Set* she was heroine Katie Hepburn's pal, the same type of role she began her career with. One of her richest parts was as a card-dealing sharpie in *The Cincinnatti Kid* in 1965, sharing scenes with old friend and co-star Edward G. Robinson.

Since her divorce from Todd, Joan's never remarried and today lives in the San Fernando Valley with her four pet dogs. Her last TV series outing, a period cop drama, flopped, but don't be surprised if another one comes along. She's a lady who can still deliver the punch line like nobody else. Her autobiographical novel, *Center Door Fancy,* was very read-between-the-lines stuff.

11

The Spanish royal family in 1957 after Franco announced the eventual re-establishment of the monarchy. *Rear Row:* Don Juan's wife Maria Mercedes, Princess Pilar and Princess Margarita. *Front:* Juan Carlos, Dowager Queen Victoria Eugenia, and Don Juan.

DON JUAN OF BOURBON

Since the day his father, King Alfonso XIII, fled the throne of Spain in 1931, Don Juan of Bourbon, the Count of Barcelona, has lived in the dusty shadows of exile. The third son of the former king, he was named as successor to the throne shortly before his father's death in 1941, after his eldest brother had renounced his claims to marry a commoner and his second eldest brother, Jaime, born deaf and dumb, followed suit shortly thereafter. Since then he's waited for a call back to power. It hasn't come.

The history of the Spanish monarchy in the 20th Century has been a complicated one yet its royal remnants have always hung onto the belief that its restoration is imminent. Alfonso had ascended the throne in 1902 when he was sixteen. Later he married the British Princess Victoria Eugenia, but with the dictatorship of Primo de Rivera in 1923, began to lose power. He abolished the dictatorship in 1930 but it was too late. Within the year he and his family fled the country for Switzerland but without his formally abdicating the throne. The Second Republic was formed in 1931 which abolished the monarchy but that fell in February of 1939 when, after a bloody three year Civil War, Francisco Franco, the general of the Spanish troops in Morocco, became dictator. By the time of his death in Rome in February of 1941, Alfonso's citizenship and property had been restored by Franco but it wasn't until sixteen years later, in 1957, that the dictator committed himself to the restoration of the monarachy itself upon his own death. Naturally everyone assumed that Don Juan would be the eventual occupant of the long-vacant throne.

By then he'd had a family of his own: the Infanta Maria del Pilar, Princess Margarita and a son, Juan Carlos. When Don Juan announced his views on the royal reestablishment he said, "For a Monarchist there is no doubt. Therefore there

Don Juan and his wife on the balcony of their Estoril, Portugal villa

Pictorial Parade

is no question who should succeed. The Prince (Juan Carlos), my son, has been educated to the role of successor.'' It was a view with which Franco eventually agreed when he personally chose Juan Carlos as his successor and began a long period of close tutelage to make the eventual transition a smooth and popular one.

When Juan Carlos became engaged and later married the Greek Princess Sophia in a much-heralded ceremony in 1962, Franco gave his wholehearted consent. Even more public approbation came in 1968 when their child, Prince Phillip, was christened in Madrid, a ceremony that brought the dowager Queen back to Spain for the first time in 37 years. It was a day of triumph for her and when she died a year later, she did so knowing that at long last her issue would one day be king.

Don Juan, however, began to listen to his own coterie of advisors and had a change of heart, eventually concluding that when the monarchy is restored, he should be king not his son. Left to brood with his wife, Princess Maria Mercedes, in their villa in Estoril, Portugal, he subtly let his views be know.

In June of 1975 he gave a speech in Portugal that left no doubt as to his views, adding that his Son Juan Carlos was chosen by Franco without his consent. Within days the Spanish Ambassador to Portugal called up on him at his home to tell him that he was no longer welcome in Spain even as a visitor.

So now it seems the question of succession is settled and that Don Juan, a grandson of England's Queen Victoria, will live out his life in the 16-room, antique-filled mansion in Estoril that has been his refuge for many years now. He spends his time holding unofficial court with various other royal refuges who live there, such as Italy's ex-king, Umberto II, reading the newspapers and checking the news wire he had installed just in case the day comes when, by some quirk of fate or politics, he gets the job he now feels is legitimately and rightfully his.

13

Olympe in a pensive mood, circa 1938

OLYMPE BRADNA

Dark-haired Olympe Bradna had already lived by anybody's standards before Hollywood grabbed her in 1937 for *Souls at Sea.* Her life up until then was the kind backstage legends are made of, which, by the way, was where she was born—backstage at the Olympia Theatre in Paris (thus her name) on August 12th, 1920. She was the start of her family's fourth generation circus act and true to another cliche that you're never to young to get your feet wet, debuted with them at age eighteen months. The Bradna Family, as they were called, weren't selfish with her talent though, and at age eight she made a movie, *Roger la Hart,* which turned her into something of a Gallic Shirley Temple for a while.

When her beauty blossomed a bit, Olympe broke away from the family's circus heritage, after a stint as a bareback rider, to dance in the *Folies Bergere,* going on to success on the French stage in *Hit the Deck.* When the *Folies* came to America so did she, and once she was seen at the Century of Progress Exhibition in Chicago in 1934, she became an overnight sensation—the "darling of the columnists," Walter Winchell and Louis Sobel included.

She continued her acrobatic dancing with the *Folies* and went on with them to New York where, in 1937, everything started to happen at once. George Raft saw her act and quickly cabled director Henry Hathaway that he wanted her as a co-star in *Souls at Sea,* which he was about to make with Gary Cooper and Frances Dee. There was nary a dance sequence in it but Raft was persuasive, and once Paramount talent executive Oscar Serlin saw her he agreed with Raft's evaluation. A studio contract came next and Olympe was off to Hollywood. She was seventeen.

Souls at Sea was a success and she was fully launched in

Olympe Bradna recently

Jack Kuster

an A production. The studio built her steadily—in 1937 alone she was also in *Last Train From Madrid, Heaven on a Shoestring* with Pat O'Brien, and *High Wide and Handsome* with Randolph Scott and Irene Dunne.

There were small roles in things like *College Holiday* (1936) and *Three Cheers For Love* but her exotic name made her a more likely candidate for films like 1938's *Stolen Heaven* with Gene Raymond and *Say It In French* (1938) with newcomer Ray Milland. In 1940 she co-starred in *South of Pago Pago* with Victor McGlaglen and Frances Farmer, a Technicolor story of pearl thieves in the South Pacific, and a year later made *International Squadron* and *The Knockout,* a slick little story of a prizefighter (Arthur Kennedy) teetering between fame and folly (Virginia Field).

In 1938 Bradna made news when it came to light that she'd never been kissed! She replied she had indeed—on screen at least—and was prepared to make up for lost time when she turned eighteen. It was publicity fluff but it kept her name in the news. She and her studio also did the same when her former voice instructor sued them for $150,000 saying his story, *The Bird on the Flying Trapeze* had been incorporated into their *Night of Nights* movie.

In 1941 Olympe married for the first and only time. His name was Douglas Wood Wilhoit from a Montecito, Cal. society family, who had also made a stab at a singing career. When he came back from the war, she retired from films and they moved to Stockton, Cal. where he went into real estate. They have three children: Douglas Jr., Antoinette, and Jeanette.

She now lives in the rocky expanses of Carmel Highlands, California, in the Big Sur, and still comfortably lovely, she looks back at her movie career as just a phase of her life. Could she have continued had she wanted to? "I suppose so but then how many native girl parts were there?" She gets a kick whenever her name crops up on TV quiz shows.

Rossano Brazzi, 1960

Christopher Young

ROSSANO BRAZZI

The cult of the Continental Lover was created when Rudolph Valentino invented the type in the Roaring Twenties—and every era since has had its candidate for the title. For a while after Valentino's death there was Ramon Navarro one or two others, and then the durably charming Charles Boyer who held the title until Louis Jourdan eased it way in the late Forties. Then came Rossano Brazzi—on the arm of Jean Peters in 1954's *Three Coins In The Fountain.* The Italian actor had made another American film, *Little Women* in 1949, but at the time admitted he knew so little English that he could barely find his way through the script which cast him as a professor trying to instill culture into Liz Taylor, Margaret O'Brien, Janet Leigh and June Allyson—the *Women* in question. *Three Coins* was another story though, with Brazzi slipping into the movie mantle of European Charmer as smoothly and slickly as any of his predecessors.

Originally Rossano had wanted to be a lawyer and in fact attended San Marco University in Florence for this degree before ever dabbling in acting. Once he'd gotten his feet wet in a school play, the law books went back on the shelf and Rossano went to work, chalking up some 135 plays, radio and television shows plus several dozen Italian movies before attracting real attention in *The Life and Death of Socrates* in the late Forties. Born in Bologna, Italy in 1916, he was thirty-two when MGM brought him over for *Little Women.* After completing it he went back just as fast. It was another five years of undistinguished roles before Zanuck picked him for *Three Coins In The Fountain,* a romantic, made-in-Rome extravaganza that starred Dorothy McGuire, Clifton Webb, Maggie McNamara and Jean Peters. When he romanced Peters against the Roman backdrop, women all over the world got the message.

His next film, made in Spain, illustrates what happens when

A gloomy Rossano in *Frankenstein's Castle of Freaks,* 1974

an actor doesn't have studio minds behind him—his role in *The Barefoot Contessa* cast him as an impotent, war-wounded count who kills his wife, Ava Gardner, for her infidelity. In Hollywood he'd never have gotten that kind of part. He pulled the fat out of the fire though the following year when he made the near-classic *Summertime* with Katherine Hepburn, a glossily romantic travelogue of Venice that had schoolteachers everywhere-starting vacation accounts, and kept the fire going in 1957 when he traded overtures with no less a legend than Joan Crawford in *The Story of Esther Costello.* Luckily his age, then forty-one, made him an ideal co-star for the aging sirens of the Forties who were all winding down their major careers.

In 1958 he sparkled in the Ezio Pinza role in *South Pacific* opposite Mitzi Gaynor and its success made up for the lukewarm teaming of him and Joan Fontaine in *A Certain Smile.*

The Sixties saw him aging gracefully in *Light In The Piazza* (1961) with Fontaine's sister Olivia DeHavilland, and he was suavely elegant as usual with Maureen O'Hara in 1965's *Battle Of The Villa Fiorita,* a glossy soap opera. One of Shirley MacLaine's several male co-stars in *Woman Times Seven,* (1967) he also popped up in the earthquaker *Krakatoa, East of Java* in 1968.

In 1974 it was announced that he would star as Czar Nicolas in an Italian epic of the Russian Revolution which fancifully cast Joan Fontaine as his czarina and Victor Mature as Rasputin. It was never made though and subsequent credits have been a comedown, the most recent being *Frankenstein's Castle of Freaks.* Brazzi has remained married to the same woman throughout his years as a major hearthrob. An actress herself, Lydia Bartalini, who married him in 1940 has appeared in several of his films, most notably *The Christmas That Almost Wasn't* annually shown since its release in 1971. They live in Rome, still comfortably together.

17

Jack Kuster

Edd "Kookie" Byrnes

EDD "KOOKIE" BYRNES

"Kookie, Kookie, lend me your comb!" was one of the most plaintive pleas of the late Fifties, and when Connie Stevens crooned it into Edd Byrnes' ear on the highly popular *77 Sunset Strip* TV series, she was speaking for every teen-age girl in America. Actually she never did sing it to him face-to-face—except on TV variety shows—but the song became an instant hit, catapulting the pompadoured actor to the frenzied heights of bobby-sox heaven. New York-born Edward Breitenberger (July 30, 1933) had added an extra 'd' to his nickname and a new word to the vocabulary, and became a TV superstar. Unfortunately bobby-sox heaven proved only a temporary Valhalla.

Like most careers, Edd's was slow getting off the ground. His first real job was as a spear carrier in a New York production of *Hamlet* at $5 a night which wasn't much as he was helping to support his widowed mother, younger brother Vincent and sister Joanne. Whenever he did have an extra dollar he used it to buy a movie ticket, his favorite pastime and what turned him on to acting. Luckily New York in those days was the center of the television industry so when he did start looking for work, he didn't have far to travel. Nearness didn't guarantee success though and it took him several years to rack up any credits at all. And Hollywood wasn't much easier.

He did get signed by Warner Bros. for their talent program but it was a while before he got a part that attracted much attention—that of a gunman on the *Cheyenne* series. That led to his first feature, *Darby's Rangers* (also James Garner's first movie-starring role) in 1958 plus parts in *Marjorie Morningstar*, also 1958, and *Up Periscope* in 1959. The fan magazines picked up on him—mildly—and Warners decided to star him in *77*

18

Sunset Strip, a detective series with Roger Smith and Efrem Zimbalist Jr. As the fast-talking car jockey forever pulling his comb through his long brown hair, he became a sensation. He was Hollywood's number one cover boy and when he married actress Asa Maynor in 1960, the enthusiasm continued, which he accepted as evidence that he was a firmly entrenched star. Shortly thereafter he started asking Warners for better roles, even going on contract suspension for a time, and eventually left the studio after *publicly* asking Jack Warner for his release at a Women's Press Club luncheon! He got it in short order but also found that his actions had virtually blacklisted him at every other studio in town.

During the Sixties he went where the work was, Europe, and starred with Stewart Granger and Mickey Rooney in 1964's *Secret Invasion,* and tried a Clint Eastwood takeoff in 1967's *Any Gun Can Play* with Gilbert Roland.

The Seventies looked a little brighter and in 1974 he was up for the emcee spot on a new game show, *Wheel of Fortune.* The show eventually went on the air but he didn't. Now managed by Fifties starmaker Henry Willson— the man who put the Tab in Hunter and the Rock in Hudson—his most recent movie role was in the British *Stardust.* He played a television interviewer in it and got very good reviews. He also starred in a rather tepid late-night mystery movie for television, and in something called *Wicked, Wicked.*

Though he says he wants nothing more than to forget the 'Kookie' image, he capitalized on it with a series of TV commericals for a hair grooming aid. Divorced from Asa Maynor, he hasn't remarried and has no desire to. He and his nine-year-old son Logan divide their time between London and a house on the beach at Malibu. "I'm happier now than I've been in a long time," he says, adding, "Logan and I have a good life and I'm expecting some big things to happen soon."

Phyllis Calvert in 1949

PHYLLIS CALVERT

Of the handful of women who were considered cinema stars in Britain in the Forties, the one who seems to have survived it all with the most viable sense of humor is Phyllis Calvert. Though her popularity dimmed greatly in the Fifties, Miss Calvert managed to keep a tight rein on her common sense, and with the help of husband Peter Murray-Hill, developed other aspects of her personality besides the ones which her screen career made famous. She was second to Margaret Lockwood in the star sweepstakes, but when the title roles were no longer available, she made handy use of those that were, thank you very much.

Born Phyllis Bickle in 1915, Calvert was destined for the limelight from early childhood, and in fact made her stage debut in an Ellen Terry play at age seven. Her original ambition was to be a dancer and she was that during her teenage years until an accident forced her to turn to dramatic roles in order to remain on stage. There were years spent in various repertory companies refining her craft until, finally, she recieved an offer to appear in London at the Lyric Hammersmith in *Crossings*.

A long and varied film career followed with her screen debut in *They Came By Night* in 1940; *Let George Do It*, also in '40; *Kipps*, '41; *the Young Mr. Pitt*, '41; and *Uncensored*, '42. The following year she appeared in one of wartime Britain's most popular movies, a classic return to the sometimes inglorious days of their country's past in the swashbuckling *The Man In Grey*. Virtually everyone connected with this picture became a star—James Mason, Stewart Granger, Margaret Lockwood, and Calvert. A double-cross love affair among the royalty of yesteryear was just what the beleagured Britishers were looking for and they swarmed through the blackouts to see it—Phyllis was a major star. Her screen personality contained just the right amount of ladylike earthiness in a time that was demanding much of even the most genteel. Lockwood had the juicier part as the wicked Hester, who first steals Calvert's lover and then murders her, but Calvert remained memorable nonetheless. The

20

Phyllis Calvert in a recent film

very popular *Fanny By Gaslight* followed the next year, and then *The Madonna of The Seven Moons*, one of England's great camp classics, in itself a very strange story of a woman with a split personality—half lady, half gypsy temptress. Stewart Granger was the other half in her gypsy sequences.

In 1941 she'd married actor Peter Murray-Hill and they got a chance to work on screen together in her next film, *They Were Sisters*. Hollywood beckoned and she journeyed there for several pictures, among them *Time Out of Mind, My Own True Love* and *Appointment With Danger*. There were still star roles in England too, even though the postwar movie boom which spelled virtual death to her female fellows in the star ranks was in effect. Britishers weren't interested in seeing their wartime heroines around to remind them of those dark days, but she managed to pull off *The Woman With No Name; Mr. Denning Drives North* in '51; *Mandy;* and in 1955, *It's Never Too Late,* wherein she was a housewife turned novelist who has to face the consequences when her large family finds out—an idea that looked better on paper than on the screen.

She and her husband welcomed a son in 1954 so the gradual descent of her screen career wasn't as important to her as it could have been. She occasionally did stage work like *Escapade* and *A River Breeze* in 1956. When her husband died a year later she resumed working with a vengeance in something called, appropriately perhaps, *A Broken Journey,* and in 1958 produced and starred in *Lily Henry.* That year she also had a smallish part in the Cary Grant-Ingrid Bergman starrer *Indiscreet.*

Her late husband left her a thriving book shop business which she carefully ran between her occasional acting stints, finally selling it only within the past couple of years. Her son is now grown, she hasn't remarried and contents herself with the acting jobs that are available to her, which included a BBC TV series called simple *Kate.* This past year she had a reunion with *Man in Grey* co-stars, Lockwood, Mason and Granger, and though they've all gone their separate ways, the camaraderie was still there among them plus the memory that during Britain's time of crisis, they were all at least partially helpful in taking people's minds back to a simpler time far away from the buzz bombs and the ration tickets.

Rod in typical cowboy pose in the late Forties

ROD CAMERON

Western leading men have been cut from several bolts of cloth down through the years. The rugged go-get-itness of William S. Hart gave way to guitar-strumming cowpokes like Roy Rogers and Gene Autry, and they in turn gave way to the good-bad guy epitomized by today's Clint Eastwood. When Rod Cameron starred in westerns, though, you could still tell the good guys by their white hats, and while most of his dozens of in-the-saddle roles were far from A-class, the rugged Canadian-born actor gave them all the muscle he could muster—and that was far from inconsiderable.

Born in 1910, Rod originaly wanted to be a Northwest Mountie but an old back indury ruled that out. He got to Hollywood the hard way after a long stopover in New York where he earned his living any way he could with a string of jobs that included sandhogging on the Hudson River, hotel clerk and department store salesman. He saved what he earned for his trek West and got to Hollywood in 1938. Luckily the shy young man was able to make a few friends, and one of them, the Earl of Warwick who worked as a movie extra, got him an introduction at Warner Bros. They were impressed enough by his lanky good looks and deep voice to give him bits in *The Old Maid* and *Christmas in July* both in 1939. Paramount was looking for a stand-in for Fred MacMurray at that time and hired Rod away from Warners for the job. They also fulfilled his childhood ambition when they cast him as a young mountie in DeMille's *Northwest Mounted Police* (1940), which starred Gary Cooper, Paulette Goddard and Madeleine Carroll.

After several such minor roles and a stint of stunt-doubling for Buck Jones, Rod went over to Universal Studios who put him in rugged yarns like 1943's *Gung Ho!* a war-time adventure that had cowboys like Randolph Scott and Noah Beery Jr. out of chaps and into uniforms. After a dozen more small roles

22

Rod Cameron more recently

as in *Boss of Boom Town* in 1944, Walter Wanger picked up on him and starred him with Yvonne DeCarlo in 1945's *Salome, Where She Danced*. It was a hit and Wanger reteamed them the same year in *Frontier Gal.* By that time Rod was also making news off-screen, having been named in a paternity suit by Edgar Bergen's former secretary.

He was in *Pirates of Monterey* in 1946 and was back in the saddle in *Old Texas Trail* (1947), *Panhandle* (1947), *The Plunderers* (1948), *Brimstone,* (1949), and also that year, *Stampede,* a thoughtful Western which examined the murder ethic of the Old West, teaming him with Johnny Mack Brown.

After years in the saddle, Rod took a dive into television in 1953's *City Detective* series which ran two years. By then he'd married a Portuguese girl named Angela Alves-Lico and made news by honeymooning with her and her mother! It was a tempestuous union with front-paged fights and reconciliations, the most notable of which was when his mother-in-law had him put in a hospital claiming alcoholism. That same year his only child was born. Rod eventually solved his mother-in-law problem once and for all by divorcing his wife and marrying *her* in 1961!

He did another series, *Coronado 9,* in 1959, and still another the following year, *State Trooper.* Neither were very successful, causing him to remark, "I did three television series as a cop and a detective and the day the last one ended I was back on the big screen as a cowboy. I guess I'm eternally typed." After 1965's *Requiem For A Gunfighter* with Stephen McNalley, Rod went to Germany for one of their special brand of Westerns called *Old Firehand*. It was a big hit there but only ran in drive-ins here.

Currently living in Encino, California, he got good notices in 1971's *Evel Knievel* as a broken-down bronco buster. After 130 films, he's in another, *Redneck,* playing a modern-day sheriff for a welcome change.

Raphael Campos in the Fifties

Jack Kuster

RAPHAEL CAMPOS

The Blackboard Jungle—that 1955 expose of a 'typical' New York City slum high school was a groundbreaker in many ways. The students weren't all depicted as Judy Garlands and Mickey Rooneys; instead, the producers captured the true ethnic mixtures of an inner city school, digging beneath the ducktail-and-motorcycle-jacket surface to explore juvenile delinquency. Sidney Poitier, in his first real role, was one of the school's macho leaders and Raphael Campos appeared as his small-built Spanish-speaking classmate, a basically good kid who tried to joke his way to survival in the jungle. Campos' climactic scene comes when Vic Morrow commands him to stick teacher Glenn Ford with a disputed switchblade. He doesn't though, breaking the blade in the top of a desk as his gesture of independence. When Bill Haley and his Comets go into *Rock Around The Clock* at the fadeout, the viewer knows that Ford has won at least the first round in his attempt to instill decency into his surly class.

Raphael was the first of the new wave of authentic actors to be cast by Hollywood in ethnic roles as well he might be, having been born in the Dominican Republic in 1937. By age eight he was acting out sketches, by ten was learning to paint, and by twelve was working after school taking tickets and drawing posters for a small theater. He and his older brother Fernando formed their own small theater group and when he landed his role in *Jungle,* he'd been acting for nine years.

His family, including nine brothers and sisters, arrived in New York in 1949 where, after learning English, he attended the School for Young Professionals and eventually the High School of Performing Arts—a far cry from *Jungle's* North Manual High. He read that MGM was casting *Green Mansions* and since it was a favorite book of his, he decided to go see about a part. He walked right into a producer's office and was about to be ousted when the producer remembered that *Blackboard Jungle* was also being cast—and after testing, gave Campos a role in it.

A recent picture of Raphael with actress Edith Diaz

The gritty picture was a big hit and MGM was impressed. They put him immediately into *Trial*, (1955) again with Glenn Ford, as Angel Chavez, a Mexican falsely accused of murder. A tense melodrama, it was as controversial as *Jungle* had been. Campos was a one-man beleaguered minority group which prompted his mother to say that she wanted him "to play good boys."

In 1956 he co-starred with Victor Mature in *The Sharkfighters* —a title-tells-it-all meller—and a year later was very good as a busboy in *This Could Be The Night* with Jean Simmons and Tony Franciosa. Walt Disney grabbed him for the role of a Delaware Indian in his *Light in the Forest* and a year later put him in *Tonka,* another Indian role. He worked a lot on television but his image as the 'troubled youth' followed him along. He once said that psychology was the best weapon against juvenile delinquency "but the easiest way to stay out of trouble is to get into show business." But when he got too old for teens-in-trouble roles, he found it difficult to make the transition to grown-up parts.

He worked for Disney again in *Savage Sam* (1963) but it was far from the lead role. He did better in *Lady in a Cage* in 1964 as one of Olivia DeHavilland's brutish terrorizers (James Caan was another), and also popped up in *The Appaloosa* and *Mr. Buddwing* in 1967, and *Astro Zombies* in '70. He was last in '74's *Oklahoma Crude* with Faye Dunaway and George C. Scott.

In 1961 Raphael made headlines when he reportedly married blues singer Dinah Washington in Mexico but it didn't last and when he married actress Sally Boyd a year later there was no divorce filed which led many to believe it never legally took place. He and Sally had two daughters, Lucy and Mimi, whom he took custody of when they 'divorced' in 1965. He's recently appeared on television shows like *McCloud* but is more interested in an experimental film he's doing in Hollywood where he still lives. Physically he's not much changed from the days he flicked switchblades with Sal Mineo in 1958's *Dino*.

25

Gianna Maria when MGM starred her in *Go For Broke*, 1951

Pictorial Parade

GIANNA MARIA CANALE

When Steve Reeves burst upon the American movie scene in 1959's *Hercules*, his astounding musculature riveted females' eyes on him from coast to coast. Luckily male moviegoers had something to look at too. While the girls dropped their popcorn over Steve, the guys sat back and watched Gianna Maria Canale. Canale specialized in the type of hard-eyed temptress roles that hadn't been seen much on American screens since Hedy Lamarr's heyday and she gave them her all, for a time even tempting stalwart Steve away from his good-guy chores.

Like many girls in post-War Italy—Sophia Loren and Gina Lollobrigida to name two—Gianna used her looks to catapult her out of her poor background and onto the magic movie screen. Born in Reggio, Calabria, in 1927 to a simple, hardworking family, she realized early that there was no silver spoon waiting to dish up her future and that she'd have to forge it on her own. A natural beauty with her flowing dark hair and mysterious green eyes, she entered beauty contests seeking the instant fame of the picture magazines. She was a ripe twenty when the plan succeeded and she placed second in the Miss Italy contest.

In 1947 the Italian movie industry was just getting back on its feet and a producer saw her picture and thought she might be just the right support its sagging box office needed. She was signed, sealed and delivered to Rome where she immediately began to decorate the movies. She married Ricardo Freda, a studio unit man, and moved slowly from bit player on up, getting her big break opposite Van Johnson in 1951's *Go For Broke*, an unusual war drama with Johnson heading up a squad of American-Japanese soldiers.

In 1954 she starred with an aging George Raft in a made-in-Italy quickie called *The Man From Cairo*, and that same year

26

Gianna poses in a park near her home

Jack Kuster

starred in a giant epic entitled *The Sins of Rome*. Canale in costume was a sight to see and a year later got upped to title-roling it in *Theodora, Slave Empress*.

She signed a contract with a British studio and traveled there for *The Whole Truth* in 1959, starring with Donna Reed and Stewart Granger, and stayed there for *The Silent Enemy*. Before she left, though, she'd made *Hercules* and when it was released it started a landslide of demand for more sex-and-sandals pictures and prompted the international release of another film she'd done called *The Warrior and the Slave Girl*.

The offers rolled in and she was back in Italy, and into costume, before you could say *fettucine*. In 1962 she starred as *The Queen of the Pirates* and then made one for MGM called *The Secret of Monte Cristo*. Next came *The Mighty Crusaders* and then a re-teaming with Reeves in 1964's *The Slave*, another big international hit that blanketed virtually every drive-in screen in the world.

The bloom was beginning to fade for her though and she found herself unable to make the trasition to other roles. Though constantly working, her films became more and more forgettable and after one bomb called *Goliath and the Vampires*, she called her career quits. Luckily she saved her money so that she could continue to live like the movie queen she was—at least in her native Italy.

Today Gianna lives quietly in Rome in a house near the walls of Vatican City. She also maintains an island retreat where she can strip off the glamour and go fishing when she wants to. When in Rome she's very much into opera and the ballet, and occasionally comes over to America to catch up on stage shows. Now seen professionally only on the Late Show—although the recent re-release of *Hercules* cued another string of offers—she is as lovely as when she was a star in the Fifties and Sixties.

27

Sybil and Richard Burton in 1953

SYBIL BURTON CHRISTOPHER

History tells us that when Cleopatra barged down the Nile, Marc Antony trembled with passion, but in the 1963 movie version, he was supposed to be acting! When the world found out he, being Richard Burton, wasn't, front pages ignited from Cairo, Egypt to Cairo, Illinois and a pretty blonde lady who'd once acted briefly under the name Sybil Williams became the Debbie Reynolds of the Sixties. That was because Miss Williams had been Mrs. Richard Burton since 1949 and the public's memory was still fresh enough to remember the heralded romance and marriage of Elizabeth to Eddie Fisher just four years before, which had left Debbie Reynolds a 'Taylor widow', tarnished diaper pins and all. At first everyone thought the Taylor-Burton affair would be just that. After all, Burton was noted for his penchant for falling in love with his leading ladies but since, in the past, that had been just for the run-of-the-play or shooting schedule, Sybil had gotten used to it. This time was different though, as she and the world, not to mention Eddie Fisher, were soon to find out.

Sybil Burton quickly found herself in a very tricky position. A warm-blooded woman, the mother of two girls, Jessica and Kate, she'd seen Richard through the early years of stage recognition, the lionization by Hollywood after the success of *My Cousin Rachel* in 1953, and its subsequent rejection after flops like *Rains of Ranchipur* (1956), until finally he was back on the track as a serious actor. She chose to ignore the Roman circus swirling around her and retreated into dignified silence. Taylor announced she and Fisher were finished while Burton flew to Paris to visit Sybil and tell reporters there was no romance with Elizabeth. As we all know, however, there very much was and Sybil, after a divorce granted in Mexico, joined the ranks of Former First Wives. But she didn't keep that title long.

Sybil and Jordan celebrating his take-over as the lead in Broadway's *Sleuth*

A spunky lady, Sybil phased out Burton and eased into a new life in New York. She and several friends, including Roddy McDowell, opened a discotheque called Arthur. She also hired a rock and roll band called The Wild Ones. The club quickly became the hottest spot in town, the premiere party place of the Sixties, and Sybil was its queen bee. It was there that Judy Garland met a doorman named Mickey Deans and married him, and it was there that Sybil fell in love with the Wild Ones' lead singer, Jordan Christopher, and married him. He was twenty-four, she was thirty-eight, and the five minute wedding ceremony in her apartment overlooking Central Park was the second marriage for both.

Jordan shortly left the group, which eventually dissolved, to begin a career as an actor. He took over the male lead in *Black Comedy* on Broadway and held his own against Lynn Redgrave and Geraldine Page in the British farce. He made a movie, *The Return of the Magnificent Seven*, good, and a little comedy in Florida that was Jayne Mansfield's last film, bad. His career didn't take off though despite his talent and unquestionably handsome face, and ended with *Angel, Angel, Down We Go*, a sordid rock spoof that also starred Jennifer Jones.

The Christophers had a daughter, Amy, of whom Sybil said, "We're absolutely delighted with her." They seem to have a lot of fun together; he calls her Syb and she calls him Jord. They dressed up like Sonny and Cher for a typical Arthur party, and when that gathering place closed in 1971, they entertained at home, the higher echelons of what passes for contemporary society and the arts streaming constantly through their large living room. Jordan scored well on Broadway in 1973 when he took over the male lead in *Sleuth* opposite Patrick (The Avengers) MacNee, and occasionally takes a play on the road. They're as happy today as when they married in 1965 and are seen constantly at parties and openings. Through it all Sybil's emerged triumphant and complete. She took a chance on happiness and handily won the turn.

29

Pictorial Parade

ROSEMARY CLOONEY

One of the most popular songstresses of the 1950s, Rosemary Clooney sang out an invitation few people could resist—Come On-a My House! Her husky-sweet rendition of 1951's most famous come-on quickly became a Number One chart-buster and her musical invitation made her rich and famous as it sold some 300,000 copies in its first month of release! When she first heard the tune she wasn't crazy about it at all and had to be coaxed into recording it—but insisted on a faster tempo. Obviously the lady knew what she was talking about.

The Southern belle (born in Maysville, Kentucky, May 24, 1928) started her career as half of a sister act with Betty Clooney, but after radio shows while still in high school, she got an offer to go it alone as band singer for Tony Pastor. Joe Shribman, the band's manager, fired her though, and advised her to go to New York and try for a recording career—with him as her manager. They went, and in 1950 she appeared in the TV-er *Songs For Sale* which led to more appearances and the Columbia Record contract that resulted in her first big hit. In one year she shot from a $4,000 band singer to a quarter-million-dollar star.

In 1952 she had another hit, *Botch-a-me* and was nabbed by Paramount Pictures for a fat part in '53's *The Stars Are Singing*. She came off so well that the studio bosses cast her in *Here Come the Girls* with Bob Hope. Said an excited Rosemary, "If I'm acting, I think it's just wonderful!"

While critics sniped that her voice was "as innocent of training as a rosebreasted grosbeak," and she herself added that while she couldn't read music, "I can tell whether the tune goes up or down, but I can't tell how far," audiences loved her. And after completing *Red Garters*, (1954) an offbeat, stylized musical Western with Guy Mitchell, she flew to Dallas to join her boyfriend actor Jose Ferrer. Her studio bosses hoped she'd return single but she didn't—she returned as his wife, only a week after his second divorce had become final.

Eddie Colbert

A more recent Rosemary Clooney

During her brief stay there, Hollywood had taken Rosemary to its collective heart and she'd been generally warned against marrying Ferrer because of his turbulent private life. As the Ferrers began their life together, so many worried about her that a League of Clooney Protectors was founded by none other than Marlene Dietrich—a lady not usually too interested in any welfare except her own.

In 1954 Rosemary starred in the classic *White Christmas* with Bing Crosby, Danny Kaye and Vera-Ellen and gusted in Ferrer's *Deep In My Heart* the same year. Shortly after receiving a *Look* magazine award as Newcomer of the Year, Rosemary announced that she and Paramount were going their separate ways—by mutual agreement—and that she'd freelance in movies. She turned instead to television, becoming a fixture on shows like *Steve Allen* and *Perry Como*. In May of 1956, she was introduced on *Ed Sullivan's Toast of the Town* as one of Hollywood's Mothers of the Year. (She and Ferrer had two children at the time, with three more to follow.) In 1957 she had a show of her own on television which featured The Modernaires with Paula Kelly, but it didn't last long. On radio, she and Bing Crosby teamed up for a while.

Throughout the Sixties the Ferrers continually made headlines with their marital mix-ups. It seemed as though Hollywood's initial warnings to her were coming true and while she continued to work the best nightclub circuit—the Americana's Royal Box and the Waldorf—she made more news with her ups-and-downs with Ferrer. His career was stalling in the late Fifties and with his reputed ego, that fact must have added fuel to the fires. They filed for divorce in 1962 and were granted it. They reconciled shortly thereafter and Rosemary said the reconciliation had actually happened before the divorce was final. They divorced for good in 1967 and in '68 she petitioned for alimony and child support because she was too ill at the time to work. She still lives in the Beverly Hills mansion she shared with Ferrer and is currently working on a comeback. Everybody still likes her and wishes her success.

31

A 1944 publicity photo of Nancy

NANCY COLEMAN

The classic movie version of *King's Row* remains one of the screen's most riveting dramas—and Nancy Coleman's performance in it holds up equally well. As Charles Coburn's daughter who goes mad after learning her doctor-father has amputated Ronald Reagan's legs to keep him from marrying her, she shines even though she's frank to admit she's tired of hearing about it: "After all, I did make other pictures!" And so she did, until her studio turned against her and her movie stardom was stalled in mid-flight.

Born in Everett, Washington in 1917 to a family whose roots were in the newspaper business, Nancy wanted to be an actress from age eleven on. She never studied it formally but her innate ability won her the plum role of Gertrude Lawrence's daughter in *Susan and God* on Broadway, replacing Nancy Kelly, and when Warner Bros. beckoned with a seven year contract, Nancy smilingly—and confidently—said yes.

Those were the salad days at that studio, then chockful of stars like Davis, Flynn, Garfield, and Sheridan, and Nancy fitted in as smoothly as a fresh tomato. Her first major film was *King's Row* (1941) but before its release audiences saw her in *Dangerously They Live* (1941) as a would-be amnesiac rescued by Dr. John Garfield. Between that and *Row* she was fully launched and 1942 proceeded to be a busy year with *The Gay Sisters* with Barbara Stanwyck (the picture she remembers as being the most fun to make), and *Desperate Journey* with Flynn, Raymond Massey and Ronald Reagan.

When she heard of the upcoming *Edge of Darkness* (1943), Nancy set out to win a role in it by asking director Lewis Milestone at a dinner party one night to let her screen test. He okayed it and she won the heavy-breathing role of Helmut Dantine' mistress. It made her a full-fledged star.

Nancy at home in New York
with Julia, her cat

By the time she co-starred with Ida Lupino in *In Our Time* (1944) and *Devotion* (1945), she was equaling Lupino in the fan mail department and everything was looking up until love stepped in her path. When she married Warner's publicity chief Whitney Bolton—against the stern advice of studio heads who felt he'd have a natural conflict of interest—she was suddenly offered nothing but bad scripts, or worse yet, small scenes in bad scripts, and following several contract suspensions, she asked for her release and got it, after five years at that studio.

She freelanced a while in *Her Sister's Secret* (1947) and *Mourning Becomes Electra* (1948), but shortly afterwards decided to move back to New York. For two years she starred as daytime TV's *Valiant Lady* and in 1954 led a good Broadway cast in *The Desperate Hours*—menaced by a very young Paul Newman.

She opened the Sixties with a smashing tour of Europe and South America in a State Department-sponsored troupe and still gets letters from people remembering her and Helen Hayes' version of *Glass Menagerie,* one of the three plays in their repertoire. In 1964 she and co-star Roland Young took a very slow boat to South Africa (some seventeen days on the high seas!) for a successful tour of *Never Too Late,* another very happy experience.

Though her screen speciality was the timid neurotic, Nancy's nothing like that in real life. Her husband died five years ago after a career as a drama critic and columnist—a career he felt much more rewarding than movie publicity's—and since then she's lived alone in an apartment filled with antiques and memorabilia of an exciting life. Though she still gets and answers fan mail, she dwells firmly in the present, not in the past. An actress to her fingertips, she still studies with Harold Clurman at his New York workshop. When I asked her if she had a favorite leading man—Errol Flyn, Reagan, Bob Cummings, George Brent—she said she didn't. "They were all gentlemen and I got along well with them all." Which is only natural to a pro like Nancy!

Tim Considine as a teen-age
Disney star—off-camera

Jack Kuster

TIM CONSIDINE

The Mickey Mouse Club of the late Fifties shaped the dreams
of millions of America's youngsters, giving many an easy sense
of identity with their specialized programming which combined
singing, dancing, drama, games, and general fooling around.
One of its most popular features was *Walt Disney's Adventure
Time* which kicked off on the daily afternoon show with a serial
called *Spin and Marty*, about a rich little city slicker who spends
a summer on a boy's dude ranch and comes to grips with the
fact that money can't buy everything. David Stolley was Marty,
the rich kid, and Tim Considine played Spin, the well-rounded
outdoors type who gives Marty a few lessons in life. It made
them both pre-teen idols and cued *The Further Adventures of
Spin and Marty,* and for Tim, an extensive career.

Tim was born in Los Angeles in 1940, the son of movie
producer John Considine and the former Carmen Pantages, the
daughter of Alexander Pantages, the theater magnate. His father
had produced the last Valentino flick in 1926, *The Son of the
Sheik,* and when Tim was born he was at MGM where he'd
produced *Boys Town* (1939), *Young Tom Edison* (1940), and
A Yank at Eton in 1942, among others. In 1953, MGM was
looking for a lad to play Red Skelton's son in a picture called
The Clown, and Considine took his son in for a screen test.
He got the part in the poignant drama (which also featured
Jane Green), and got good reviews too. Next he was in *Miss
Baker's Dozen,* a picture that the studio hoped would revitalize
the public's interest in an aging Greer Garson. In this film she
played a teacher at a boys' school, and Tim was one of her
students; it was released in 1954 under the title *Her Twelve
Men.* That year he was also June Allyson's and William Holden's
son in *Executive Suite.*

Tim as he looks today

Tony Drake

Tim was in several more pictures including 1955's *The Private War of Major Benson* (1955) and *Unchained,* that same year, before leaving his career behind while he attended Notre Dame High School in San Francisco. When he graduated in 1958, he was ready to get back to work although he'd become increasingly interested in the business and creative side of moviemaking as well as acting. Disney signed him for *The Shaggy Dog,* which starred him with his future TV father Fred MacMurray in 1959, but it was the *Mickey Mouse Club* that made him a star. After the *Spin and Martys,* he did other serials on the show: *Annette,* which starred the queen of the Mouseketeers, Annette Funicello, and *The Hardy Boys,* teaming him with Tommy Kirk.

In 1960 he was reunited with Greer Garson when he played one of the Roosevelt sons in *Sunrise at Campobello,* and signed on as one of *My Three Sons,* an immensely popular series about a widower and his three sons. Tim and his older brother John Jr. (now appearing on the soap opera *Another World* after a stint on *The Young and the Restless)* worked on a script together called *The System* which they sold to *My Three Sons,* and in 1964, Tim took a hand at directing a few episodes.

Since the series ended, Considine has concentrated on writing and on studying all angles of the film business. A keen competitor under normal circumstances, the residuals from *Sons* has kept him from having to do just anything until the right project comes along. In 1965 he married actress Charlotte Stewart who he'd met on his series, but they divorced in 1970. Since then he's grown a beard and, visually at least, is a far cry from the embodiment of All-American youth that he started out being. Tim keeps busy on the Hollywood scene, a familiar figure in the Sunset Strip clubs, quietly working towards the day when he'll direct, act, or write again.

Cooper in training, 1959

Pictorial Parade

HENRY COOPER

The manly art of fisticuffs has its natural home in England where the sport was long ago legitimized by the Marquis of Queensberry. The English have always loved the sport and have given the world some great champions, but there's never been a greater one than Henry Cooper, the fighter who made history in December of 1967 when he won his third Lonsdale Belt—England's highest fighting honor. He came within inches of wresting the World Heavyweight Championship away from the then Cassius Clay on two occasions, in 1963 and 1966, and held British and Empire Heavyweight championships on and off for thirteen years before his retirement in 1971, after losing them to Joe Bugner in a brutal match that left him with his honor and reputation intact and an inspiring record for other young fighters to shoot for.

Born in May, 1934 in Camberwell, London, Cooper's roots were in the soil of the working class, his greatest fans, and he grew up among them, learning how to fight from necessity as much as from interest. He and his twin brother Jim decided at an early age that they'd seek their careers in the ring, and while Jim never made it (he was hurt in a fight against Chip Johnson in the early 1960s that ended his ring career, and then worked as his brother's trainer), Henry did, winning the British and Empire heavyweight titles by the time he was 25. It took him a total of 28 fights, of which he won 25 to do that—an incredible record. He won the titles by knocking out Joe Erskine, then considered World Champ Ingemar Johanssen's chief competitor.

In July of 1960, Cooper revealed that he'd married an Italian waitress named Albina Genepri in Clerkenwell Roman Catholic Church in a ceremony for mixed marriages. He shortly thereafter converted to her faith though, and they were remarried. Later

36

Cooper pulling the famous scowl at a recent London reception

that year his son Marco, also known as Henry Jr., was born.

The English approach boxing differently than the Americans, and throughout the Sixties, Cooper defended his titles against virtually all comers, retaining them until 1969. He fought World Heavyweight Champion Cassius Clay (now Mohammed Ali) twice but couldn't manage to take him. (He sustained a severe eye injury during the initial 1963 bout, but put up such a good fight that he won the admiration of millions, including Richard and Elizabeth Burton, who sent him a congratulatory wire.)

In 1965 he purchased a produce store in Wembley High Street, London, and was for a time the country's most famous greengrocer. Henry always displayed a good sense of humor which he confirmed when he went to Rome in 1969 to defend his European heavyweight title against Piero Tomasoni, by posing in the Coliseum with a gladiator's helmet and sword. He won the bout and went home to receive the Order of the British Empire from the Queen. He gave up his titles later that year after difficulties with the British Boxing Board, but won them back a year later in a smashing fight against Jack Bodell. That fight won him his 10th Lonsdale Belt in eleven years—a record yet to be beaten.

In 1971 he fought contender Jack Bugner and lost to him. The fight made him decide that perhaps he'd had it in the ring and he retired right after it to raise his son and help tend the family business. He's written an autobiography in the meantime, and also keeps up with his youthful hobbies of rebuilding automobiles plus a daily vigorous workout to keep in shape. After slugging his way to a record that should stand for years in international boxing circles, it's very unlikely that Henry will ever join the ranks of the retreads who come out of retirement to fight again. He and wife Albina live quietly outside London, and while he was able to invest much of his fighting money, they live a simple life. Marco, now 14, has no plans to follow in his dad's footsteps although at times the temptation must be great.

Cornell in 1950

Pictorial Parade

DON CORNELL

After racking up Gold Record hits like *So Rare, Love Letters* and *This Is The Beginning of the End* during the Fifties, Don Cornell's swooning appeal was judged so potent that someone said he could make girls faint "if he sang the phone book!" One wonders how he would have done if he'd pursued his original desire to be a prizefighter!

Bronx, New York-born (1921) Dominico Franciso Connello got so far with fighting that in high school he won the school championship. That was great by him but not by his mother, who pleaded with him to drop it, which he did. He took up the school glee club instead and got interested in singing as a career when again, the approval of his schoolmates bolstered him up. Through an audition he was heard by Sammy Kaye who liked the handsome Italian teenager enough to offer him a contract as singer with his band—after graduation, of course. Cornell took him up on it but left in 1941 after Pearl Harbor to join the Air Force. After the War he came back and Kaye was waiting. The partnership lasted until well into the Fifties.

His first hit with Kaye was *It Isn't Fair*, in 1950, and over the next few years he chalked up several more including *I'm Yours*, and, dueting with Teresa Brewer, *This Is The Beginning of the End*. A constant TV guest, Don also moonlighted on the nightclub circuit. An engagement at New York's famous Paramount Theater lasted five weeks—a record, and a great one, when you consider that that had been Sinatra's showcase.

His relaxed sexy baritone crooned more hits—*So Rare, Love Letters*, the bouncy *White Sports Coat*—but he was also smart enough to throw a few one-liners in so that folks wouldn't take him too seriously. His light way with a lyric and on-stage magnetism made him a top TV-guester and he hit them all from Arthur Godfrey to Perry Como to Ed Sullivan. In 1955 he had

The Don Cornell the public sees today

three hits in the Top Ten at one time including *I'll Walk Alone* and something called *Hold My Hand*, which was the first recording to be featured in a movie, *Susan Slept Here*, with Dick Powell and Debbie Reynolds. That Top Ten record stood until the Beatles came along ten years later!

The Beatles and the avalanche of new music they brought with them loudly ground out many careers and Don's admittedly was one that slowed down. He was smart, though, and professionally knew the oldest trick in the book—give 'em something new. In 1967 he decided to try the stage and picked a good showcase role as male lead in *The Pajama Game*. He opened in Kansas City to loud reviews, setting a box office record that still stands. He hit the strawhat circuit with a vengeance then, starring in *Redhead, Bells Are Ringing* and *Say Darling*, all solid shows that displayed the Cornell voice and charm to its best advantage.

For the past five years or so Don has centered his singing career around the Las Vegas-Reno-Lake Tahoe entertainment axis, spending about forty weeks a year playing clubs in those desert resorts. He invested all that gold record money wisely and lives in Mahwah, New Jersey, on an eleven acre estate complete with swimming pool (the day I spoke to him he was lounging by it), horses and a small golf course.

Golf is in fact his favorite pastime, besides singing, and he's picked up a few trophies along the way, teaming with Gene Sarrazen to capture the Italian Open in Chicago and the Bill Harrah Invitational in Lake Tahoe. His favorite trophy is the one presented him by Bob Hope when he won the Tony Lema Memorial Tournament in Las Vegas.

Married for thirty-four years to a former schoolteacher from Kansas City whom he met on one of his first band tours, they have a twenty-one-year-old daughter and sixteen-year-old son. Cornell's style has survived many music changes, "and I plan to be around through a lot more."

Mary as she looked
to millions of TV viewers in the Fifties

MARY COSTA

After spending even a few minutes with Mary Costa, one finds it unbelievable to think she was ever the shy, retiring type she claims to have been before becoming one of television's most glamorous salesladies for *Chrysler*'s Forward Look cars in the mid-1950s. Her glamour plus Bill Lundigan's good looks and sales pitch made them every bit as popular as the two shows they 'commercialized' on, *Climax* and *Shower Of Stars*. But according to Mary, "All through my early years in Knoxville (Tennessee, her home town) whenever anybody would come upon me singing, I'd just shut right up." Later, after a disastrous Glendale, California high school production of *The Prince of Pilsen,* she thought she'd never act either. "They worked for a month trying to get my Southern accent to sound British. After that I just wasn't sure of myself. I was too timid." But when she strode around those shiny new cars, pointing out their finer points, she always looked the picture of calm and competence—and her own finer points didn't go unnoticed in the process!

After trying her hand writing a soap opera called *The Dark Veil* for KEIV in Glendale and acting in it, Mary came to the attention of agent Ben Medford who had her audition for Edgar Bergen as a singer, but "the very first thing that I did was when Susan Hayward did *With A Song In My Heart* on the *Lux Radio Theater.* I sang the song for the commercial and I had Lux for a whole year. I was the cleanest person in town."

Medford also introduced her to the man who helped mold her career and her life when in 1953 he introduced her to Frank Tashlin, a director and writer (*Son of Paleface* with Bob Hope among many others) at Paramount Studios. "My mother and I and three lady cousins all lived together in Glendale and he started to come out for dinner. We had immediate rapport. That's how it started. We had eleven years of a very, very happy marriage and he was always encouraging through the

Mary on a recent New York visit

diversity of careers I had.'' The Tashlins separated in 1964 but weren't divorced until three years later. ''It was a very amicable divorce. He died of a heart attack in 1972 when I was in Europe making *The Great Waltz* and I thought how strange it was that the day he died I was in front of the cameras and he wasn't directing anymore.''

The *Forward Look* campaign made Mary a household word *and* figure but her real love remained singing. In 1953 she was signed by Walt Disney to sing the role of *Sleeping Beauty* in his animated fairy tale. The job lasted six years but never once did Disney lay eyes on his 'star'—''He wanted to hear the personality through the voice and not be affected by their appearance. I finally met him shortly before he died and he told me he had a live-action film for me but I never found out what it was.'' Her Prince Charming in that was Bill Shirley whom she hasn't seen since the movie finally opened in 1959.

She was twenty-four in 1957 when she made *The Big Caper* with Rory Calhoun but laughs a lot about that one today. ''I was a totally different person then. It's so funny to see it now.'' The Chrysler shows ended in 1958 which finally gave Mary a chance to get her singing act together properly. Since then she's performed with virtually every orchestra in the world from New York's Metropolitan Opera to symphony orchestras in the mountains of Colorado with a repertoire that includes opera and popular standards. As long as she can sing, she's happy.

While *The Great Waltz* wasn't a big success over here, it was a huge hit abroad, especially in Japan. When Mary sang there last year with the Metropolitan Opera she went at that country's specific request. She personally feels she learned a lot by making the Andrew Stone production and would love to do more films, especially a re-make of *The Merry Widow* with Vincente Minnelli directing. She lives in a large apartment in Westwood, California and would like to marry again—''there's nothing like the excitement of a romance.'' And when she sings, audiences say there's nothing as exciting as Mary Costa.

Les as he looked in 1964

LES CRANE

In November of 1964, a brash young radio announcer made his late-night TV talk show debut with the *Les Crane Show* amid a network flurry of noisy hopes and noisier publicity. Expected to be stiff competition for the *Tonight Show,* its primary ingredients were surprise attack and frank outspokenness as personified by host Crane, who sat perched on a high swivel chair swinging this way and that at his often speechless guests. It was Allan Burke's rudeness and Mike Wallace's insight carried several steps further, with Crane coupling his glib tongue with undeniable good looks for a total effect that quickly labeled him 'Peck's Bad Boy of late-night television.' ABC thought it had a winner and sat back to wait for the high ratings to roll in. They never did.

Crane had worked up his controversial image over the years, specializing in those telephone call-in radio shows that were always controversial since it was his job to make them so. He started in San Francisco and made his initial leap to the tube via an afternoon show in L.A. His nocturnal rescheduling was the next logical step. He immediately became Topic A among TV critics, touching off more debate than any performer since Jack Paar. Unfortunately he often opened up subjects about which he had little knowledge, prompting one reviewer to say, "Any light moments of fun which were provided were too far outweighed by the appalling spectacle of watching a man struggle beyond his intellectual depth without knowing how to dog-paddle." The show's producer quit after the first week and smoke signals were quickly floating over the network relaying the information that the show was in trouble.

On February 24th, 1965, Crane announced over the air that ABC had cancelled him and as his loyal studio audience booed that decision, said he'd "had more fun, more laughs and more tears on the show than ever before in his life." Off-camera,

Les Crane more recently

when he'd gotten the news, he'd been more outspoken saying, in effect, that he'd conducted the show exactly as he'd been *told* to.

Since his exposure and the resultant publicity following his cancellation had at least made him famous, the network gave him another chance later in 1965 with *Nightlife.* Announced as host for only the first four weeks, they hoped to stimulate viewer interest with a 'see him quick or not at all' campaign and added Nipsey Russell to beef up the cast. "I've turned down a multi-million dollar, five-year deal with Universal for TV and movies, and that's no lie—I turned down seven figures from Universal just to do these four weeks. That's how much it means to me," Crane said. Defanged, he was lighter, happier, non-controversial, and, unfortunately, not what people expected. Hip California had replaced the *enfant terrible* and after the four weeks he was dropped again.

The following year he married sometime sex symbol Tina Louise *(God's Little Acre)* at her Beverly Hills home and began a television debate show on a local Los Angeles channel in October of 1967. In 1968 he kicked off a syndicated talk show—no more networks for him—prompting one detractor to comment that it was obviously the year of two-time losers what with Crane back on TV and Nixon back in the running for the presidency!

Les did get a chance at a movie career in *I Love a Mystery* with Ida Lupino. It was hoped it would spread into a series but instead wound up on the rerun circuit. He invested in real estate in Palm Springs and for a while things looked stable if a far cry from the superstardom he tried so hard for. When he and Tina split (they have a daughter Caprice, born in 1971), though, the accumulated frustrations drove him through his emotional roof. He was felled by an overdose of pills but was saved after being rushed to UCLA Hospital. Today he lives quietly in Beverly Hills and it's not inconceivable that one day he'll take still another stab at the bigtime.

43

Bob Cummings and Hedy Lamarr share a hatful of something in a 1948 publicity shot

Pictorial Parade

ROBERT CUMMINGS

Bob Cummings' forte was always light comedy—at least he's best remembered for that, especially because of his 1950s TV series—but he was also an accomplished young dramatic lead. Pictures like *King's Row, Flesh and Fantasy* and the haunting *Lost Moment* with Susan Hayward prove that point. Yet when you think of him, he's almost always smiling.

Missouri-born Cummings (Joplin, June 10, 1908) dropped his first name of Clarence when he started grade school in favor of his second name, Robert. He never even considered his third name, Orville!

He engineered another name-change years later when, after graduating drama school, he found himself unable to get a job. Taking himself to England, he soaked up a little atmosphere and then returned home with the very tweedy name of Blade Stanhope Conway. Status-conscious Broadway let him crash the party for a role or two but Bob soon realized the grass was greener out Hollywood-way. He pulled another fast move by successfully getting Western enough to land his first big role in 1935's *Virginia Judge,* after a smallish role in *So Red The Rose.*

Married in 1933 to actress Vivian Janis, Bob quickly became one of Tinseltown's most properly handsome young male leads in films like 1937's *Souls At Sea,* as a noble young seaman, and a follow-up to Deanna Durbin's *Three Smart Girls,* appropriately called *Three Smart Girls Grow Up.* Fox gave him the Betty Grable-in-Technicolor routine in *Moon Over Miami* with Carole Landis and Don Ameche, and in 1941, Universal took him back for another outing with Deanna in *It Started With Eve.*

King's Row in 1942 gave him his first serious role and he handled it with a hesitant subtlety that was just right. His soft-spoken, gentle charm when he talks to Nancy Coleman in the bedroom scene after her breakdown, blended a standout mixture of compassion and talent.

44

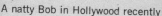
A natty Bob in Hollywood recently

Eddie Colbert

In 1945 a childhood injury came back to haunt him during the filming of *You Came Along* with Lizabeth Scott. A severed nerve in his left cheek resulting from being hit by a flying bat during a sandlot baseball game caused that side of his face to droop occasionally when he smiled, and the cameraman noticed. Since then he's been careful to be photographed from the right side except when he's moving.

Divorced from his first wife since 1943, Bob wed Mary Elliot in 1945. For years theirs was one of Hollywood's most durable marriages and they had seven children. Cummings worked steadily during the Forties but it was television that gave him his greatest stardom. *The Bob Cummings Show* (originally called *My Hero*) teamed him with Rosemary De Camp, Ann B. Davis, Dwayne Hickman and glamor girl Joi Lansing, and cast him as a bachelor photographer in perpetual heat. It lasted from 1952 to 1961 but unfortunately strapped Cummings with the image of the ever-young man-about-town, an image he relentlessly pursued in private life and which, movie-wise, Alfred Hitchcock made the most of in 1954's *Dial M For Murder*. He wrote a book, *How To Stay Young and Vital*, and practiced what he preached. A health food and vitamin addict, he was constantly interviewed on how he stayed so young until, in 1970, he gave the classic American explanation—he divorced his wife of twenty-five years for a younger woman.

She was Regina (Gigi) Fong and they had met in 1966 when she was the script girl on a picture he made in Hong Kong called *Five Golden Dragons*. She came back to America as his secretary and on March 27, 1971, after careful plotting by several Hollywood astrologists, she became his third wife. It seems she'd had a crush on him since her father had taken her to one of his movies when she was eleven.

He and Gigi have dabbled in everything from 'mind dynamics' to a rejuvenation therapy which included injections from lamb fetuses, and their Hollywood home is testimony to the fact that if there *is* a way to stay young, Bob Cummings will find it.

45

Howard as he looked in the Forties—menacing!

Pictorial Parade

HOWARD DA SILVA

Over the years there have been many fine actors who have made their reputations as screen 'heavies', but hardly a one has left such a rich backlog of movie menace as Howard Da Silva. DeMille used him wonderfully in his epic *Unconquered* (1947) as the wicked slavemaster out to get bondservant Paulette Goddard at all costs, and Hollywood used him routinely to threaten, tease and otherwise torment its lady stars from Veronica Lake in *The Blue Dahlia* to Maureen O'Hara in *Tripoli*. His exceptional gift as a straight dramatic actor was amply showcased in 1945's *The Lost Weekend* in which he played the bartender trying to keep Ray Milland away from the bar, but Hollywood always opted for the obvious.

Despite his image he proved to be only too human himself when in 1951 the House Un-American Activities Committee pounced on him and he refused to testify. He quickly found out that life was as full of moral inconsistencies as any movie script. Once the blacklisting started, he said simply that "I felt like I'd fallen off the edge of the Earth," so complete was his ostracism. Luckily he had the stage to return to.

The stage is where his career began in 1929. Twenty-year-old Howard Silverblatt, a former mill worker from Cleveland, Ohio, first trod the New York boards with the Civic Repertory Theater. He started at fifteen dollars a week but within a few years commanded much more as he hopscotched from show to show—*Golden Boy, Casey Jones,* The Mercury Theater Production of *The Cradle Will Rock,* until finally he got the role of Jud in *Oklahoma.* That was 1943.

Hollywood had picked up on him earlier and he'd already been seen in films like *Abe Lincoln In Illinois* (1940), *The Sea Wolf* (1941), and *The Big Shot* (1943), but after *Oklahoma* the parts got better—and the best was *Lost Weekend.* Partially filmed on location in a bar on New York City's Third Avenue, he was superb and should have been Oscar-awarded, but was overlooked.

Howard Da Silva today

Throughout the rest of the Forties he was Tinseltown's Number One Menace, in *Two Years Before the Mast* (1946), *Blaze of Noon* (1947), *They Live By Night* (1948) and many others. After *Tripoli* in 1951, he starred in *Slaughter Trail* with Brian Donlevy and Virginia Grey but after his appearance before the Un-American Activities Committee, his name was omitted from the cast list when it was released. He didn't film again until 1962's *David and Lisa,* for which the British nominated him for their Academy Award.

He and twenty-two other actors and writers whose careers were trampled by the blacklist—Dalton Trumbo, Anne Revere and Gale Sondergaard to name a few—attempted to sue the major studios because they were being deprived "the liberty to work," asking individual damages of $250,000 apiece. California courts dismissed the suit since none had been contracted to studios, but they took it to the Supreme Court who awarded them a victory, in name only, however. Non-employment by the movie industry continued.

Luckily Da Silva's impressive talent was not overlooked by the New York theater establishment, and in 1953 he directed *The World of Shalom Aleichem* and also co-produced and starred in it. Later he was the prosecuting attorney in *Compulsion,* and in 1959 appeared in *Fiorello,* directed 1961's *Purlie Victorious* and triple-threated again as actor-director-producer of *The Zulu and the Zayda* in 1965. He's also concentrated on off-Broadway productions because "you can afford the luxury of possible failure with something you feel deserves to get a hearing without danger of bringing on a heart attack, an ulcer or the psychoanalyst."

In 1975 he commuted to the Professional Theater of Queensborough Community College in New York where he starred in *The Caucasian Chalk Circle.* He also went back to Hollywood for the highly acclaimed *Missiles of October.* He and his wife live quietly in Ossining, New York, which is how he likes it.

47

Dagmar in her TV heyday

Pictorial Parade

DAGMAR

The Golden Age of live television produced many stars but there was only one Dagmar—the small screen's own Mae West. When she butted up to Jerry Lester on *Broadway Open House*, a legend was born that all the subsequent versions of the show, including Johnny Carson's, haven't dissipated. When she first came on the show in June of 1950, her introduction was brief, to say the least. The show's producer simply said, "Just sit there by the band and look dumb. Oh, your name is Dagmar!" She did more than that though and by the end of her first year had tripled her salary to $1250 a week. Her and Lester's comic antics caused millions of Americans to lose sleep and for the next few years they were the talk of the towns all over the country.

Dagmar's real name is Virginia Ruth Egnor but she changed it to Jennie Lewis when she embarked on an acting career in Olson and Johnson's *Laffin' Room Only*. When they asked what her acting credentials were the buxom blonde merely shrugged and said, "Oh I don't want to go into all that!" and got the job.

After *Open House* hit, she spread herself into other activities like her appearance in 1951 with Frank Sinatra at New York's Paramount Theater. She also spent a good deal of time writing her own material which, when coupled with her awesome dimensions, got her quickly dubbed 'America's most prominent literary talent'. That year she also wed comedian Danny Dayton whom she'd been dating for several years since their initial meeting on the *Cavalcade of Stars* TV show.

She broadened further with appearances at the Steel Pier in Atlantic City and hit the strawhat trail in *Loco*, a comedy which she quickly redubbed *Personal Appearance*. 1956 saw her nominated as one of New York's favorite pinups.

In 1957 she appeared on *The Mike Wallace Show*—the grand-daddy of today's anything-goes talk shows—and spoke out in

Dagmar today

favor of tranquilizers, an almost unheard of topic in those days. When queried about it later she denied having taken any before hitting Wallace's 'hot seat'. "Hot Seat? It wasn't even warm!" Dagmar had the kind of fame that was largely based on exposure and when she stopped getting as much of it, people wondered what happened. "I'd rather they'd say that than for me to do rotten shows and have 'em say *look* what happened to Dagmar!"

A regular panel member of TV's *Masquerade Party* from 1953 until 1957, she left it to go on the road in a musical called *The Amazing Adele.* The public didn't find it very amazing though and it closed before making Broadway. As a result of the Wallace interview, Dagmar got offers to appear in England, but turned them all down because she'd have had to leave her poodle, appropriately named Shakespeare, behind and "I'd go crazy without him." That same year she made more news when one week after winning a jitterbugging contest on the *Arthur Murray* TV show she entered a New York hospital to have a pregnancy ended which, according to hubby Dayton, "constituted a threat to her life."

In 1961 she and the comic split—and she shortly thereafter married her business manager, Richard Hinds. Though she hasn't been seen much on television recently, she's toured constantly in plays in summer stock, among them *The Women* with an intriguing cast which included Gloria Swanson, Marge Champion, Marilyn Maxwell and Elaine Stritch. In 1967 she jumped on the burlesque-revival bandwagon when she joined Lili St. Cyr in *At The Drop Of A Fan*—which she tastefully renamed *Bravo Burlesque.* That same year she authored her first book, a highly successful spy-spoof called *The Spy With The Blue Kazoo.*

Currently Dagmar lives stylishly in New York and is preparing a new nightclub act like the ones she wowed Las Vegas with in the Sixties. The sense of humor is better than ever—and so is everything else!

Lil in the Twenties

LIL DAGOVER

In the early days of the Talkies, the studios knew that talents had to be developed to make up for the casualties that Mr. Microphone had caused, and, as was often the case they looked across the seas for it—especially in the glamour department. There was nothing more tempting to them than an established foreign actress, preferably beautiful, who had some of the allure that an already popular Garbo or a newcomer like Dietrich had in such obvious abundance. Lil Dagover had first caused a sensation in the classic 1919 film *The Cabinet of Dr. Caligari* and throughout the Twenties her German-made pictures, like 1926's *Tartuffe* and *The White Devil* in 1929 had been good box office—good enough to convince Warner Bros. that she might be just what they were looking for. They imported her for *The Woman From Monte Carlo* in 1931 and reviewers did indeed call her Warner's "own entry in the Garbo-Dietrich race," placing her briefly up there with the two of them and Tallulah Bankhead as a Silver Screen Vamp, Talkie-style.

Unfortunately audiences didn't see her quite that way despite support from co-stars Walter Huston and Warren William, and in fact it wasn't much of a picture. Called *The Captain's Wife* while in production, the story line was tired even in '31 and Dagover had little to work with to help create any sort of real impression. Like Bankhead, Hollywood misused her and when the box office results came in she returned to Germany, quickly regaining her place as their pre-eminent movie star.

She'd been born in 1897 on the island of Java as Marie Antonia Siegelinde Seubert and came to Germany with her family in 1903. Her marriage to actor Fritz Daghofer gave her both a new career and a new name—after a bit of editing—both of

Lil in the Seventies

which she displayed in her first film *Harakiri* in 1918. *Caligari* was next and it was a monument in many ways. Her role as the beautiful woman beset by nightmares after being raped and having her lover killed was only part of the dark story set in a mental institution. Conrad Veidt was the somnambulist used by Dr. Caligari (Werner Krauss) to commit acts of violence, and the story, coupled with the expressionist sets and art direction, mirrored the frustrations of a post-war Germany in an eerily eccentric way that quickly made it the often-imitated high water mark of German cinema. Sam Goldwyn presented it to American audiences in 1921.

During the Thirties, Dagover starred in pictures like *The King's Dancer,* '32; *Johannis Nacht,* '35; and *Das Maedchen Irene* in '37. Her beauty, coupled with her athletic prowess in tennis and swimming, kept her a fixture in the German film world until it disintegrated in World War II.

She went back to work after the war, and in 1958 got great reviews for *The Big Barrier*—''the veteran Lil Dagover, still one of the screen's great beauties, easily outshines much younger competition.'' That year she was also visible in the acclaimed *Confessions of Felix Kruhl,* which launched Horst Buchholz into international stardom. Most recently she was in *The Pedestrian,* nominated for an Academy Award as Best Foreign Language Picture of 1973, which starred and was produced by Maximilian Schell. Another Hollywood survivor, Elisabeth Bergner, was also in it.

As befits a star of her rank and another example of European chivalry when it comes to aging actresses, Dagover's reputation has stayed constantly bright over the years. She still appears often on the pages of German women's magazines and lives in a small cottage on the grounds of the Bavaria Filmplatz movie studio outside Munich, greeting fans and old friends with the grace that has made her a legend in her own country.

Dennis and Jack, off-screen friends

Pictorial Parade

DENNIS DAY

For more years than we'd probably care to remember, Dennis Day served as Jack Benny's live-in *Henry Aldrich*-type character on both radio and television. Their comedic affair was an instantaneous meeting of minds, each appreciating the other's ability. Like two springs in a fine watch, they meshed perfectly. Actually it was Benny's wife, Mary Livingstone, who is the unsung hero of their partnership since it was she who first heard Day, one afternoon in 1939, at a recording studio where he was making a demo record. The nineteen year-old New York-born law student was named Eugene Denis McNulty at birth and had cut his Irish tenor vocal chords on folk songs of the Old Sod, one of which he was recording that day as a hoped-for introduction to a full-time show business career. Up until then his experience had consisted of family parties and a one-night stint with Ray Block's orchestra for which he'd sung two songs and got paid scale—then $21. (Actually show biz was Dennis' *third* career tryout. In 1934 he'd attended New York's Cathedral College in preparation for the Catholic priesthood but switched to pre-law after two years.) Mary liked what she heard and sent the recording to Benny, and, talent spotter that he was, Benny too was captured by the clear vocal magic of the youngster. As Dennis Day, Eugene McNulty debuted on the Benny show in the Fall of 1939 with a long-term contract following early in 1940. College never saw him again as he quickly made radio millions forget Kenny Baker, the singer he replaced on the show.

Day's little-boy charm and squeaky speaking voice made him the natural butt of Benny's humor, but he also injected a lot of his own into the proceedings until 1944, when he left for a two-year hitch in the Navy. He was welcomed back much as any son was welcomed back from the war, and the fun started all over again.

Credit: Eddie Colbert

Dennis Day today

In 1948 he married Margaret Ellen Almquist and they started on one of Hollywood's most whopping families—ten children in all. (Dennis' brother, Dr. James McNulty, has long been married to Ann Blyth and they have four.) That year he also had his own radio show as well as keeping up with Benny. Also that year he used his unique vocal talents in the Walt Disney picture *Melody Times* as the voice of Johnny Appleseed. In 1949 he was in *The Secret of St. Ives* and in 1951 got a big break opposite Mitzi Gaynor in *Golden Girl,* a biopic of the life of frontier entertainer Lotta Crabtree.

When Jack Benny went into television, Dennis did too, and in 1952 he got a crack at his own series alternating a Friday night at 8 spot with Broadway and The Metropolitan Opera's Ezio Pinza. Critics called it overproduced and lacking warmth, though, and it got switched to a Monday night time slot before eventually fading away.

An astute businessman, Dennis invested wisely from the day he first started making big money, choosing property that would bring in an income, and eventually taking over part of a half-million dollar restaurant business. In 1953 he gave an interview stating how happy he was every year when it came time to write out his income tax check. He added that he was more than happy to part with the lion's share of his half-million per year earnings to keep America strong and free.

1958 saw him take time away from his TV chores for the Broadway lead in *Pardon My Glove* but it didn't take off.

When his mentor, Jack Benny, died in 1974, Dennis appeared on several talk shows with Mel Blanc and others who'd shared the great days of the Benny troupe. "He was like a father to me," is the way he puts their association. He and his wife live in Hollywood and he works only when he wants to. One thing that did interest him though was doing a television ad in 1975 for an album of Irish folk songs. Obviously the modest man hasn't forgotten his roots.

Gloria in her starlet days

GLORIA DE HAVEN

One of the prettiest of the young MGM ladies of the late Forties, Gloria De Haven had an interesting career. She was either the girl-next-door or the sultry troublemaker down the block. Her vibrant red hair made her a Technicolor natural and she sparkled in several of the Mighty Metro Musicals like *Three Little Words* and *Summer Stock*. In the latter she was devilish to sister Judy Garland (in her last MGM picture) but delightfully so. You got a little mad at her, so she was obviously doing a good job. After her stint at MGM she went over to 20th Century Fox for a while but when the musical boom ended in the Fifties, Gloria's career was left high and dry.

The daughter of the well-known stage and movie actor Carter De Haven, she was born in Hollywood with the entertainment industry right in her back yard. Her father worked steadily in character parts and it was only natural that when it came time for her to choose a career, she picked the movies. She started early too, making *The Great Dictator* with Chaplin in 1940 when she was only sixteen. From that film she went right to MGM and grew up there along with girls like Judy Garland, Ava Gardner, Lana Turner, and Kathryn Grayson. Her first flick there was *Susan and God* in 1940, followed by 1941's *Keeping Company,* a suitably juvenile outing; *Two-Faced Woman,* Garbo's last movie (1941), and two years later was apple-cheeked and bouncy in *Best Foot Forward* with fellow-gamin June Allyson, and Lucille Ball.

She could sing and she could dance so Metro put her into musicals like *Thousands Cheer* (1943), *Broadway Rhythm* (1944), *Two Girls and a Sailor* (1944), and *Step Lively* (1944). She worked hard—often, as Garland did, skipping from film to film with hardly a week's rest inbetween.

54

Gloria De Haven as she looks today

In 1944 she married John Payne, *not* a Metro star, and managed to sandwich in two children, Kathleen and Thomas, between more films such as *The Thin Man Goes Home* (1944) and *Between Two Women* (1945). Off-screen for several years, she returned in a Micky Rooney epic, *Summer Holiday* (1948), but her best part, an imaginative Arabian Nights dream sequence, was dropped from the final print.

After *Scene of The Crime* and *The Doctor and The Girl* (both 1949), she went to Universal for *Yes Sir, That's My Baby* with Donald O'Conner. Reviewers remarked on her "verve!" Her marriage to Payne broke up in 1950 but she managed to forget about it by making four movies that year: *The Yellow Cab Man* with Red Skelton; the very good *Three Little Words; Summer Stock;* and her first for 20th, *I'll Get By.* After that she freelanced at RKO in 1951's *Two Tickets to Broadway,* then 20th's *Down Among the Sheltering Palms* with Bill Lundigan, and back to Universal for a Tony Curtis starrer, *So This is Paris.* After 1955's *The Girl Rush,* for yet another studio, Paramount, her major career ended. (Her *Rush* co-star, Rosalind Russell, went to character parts after this one too.)

Briefly married to Martin Kimmel (1953-4), De Haven moved to New York where in 1957 she married Richard Fincher and settled down to being a Westchester housewife. She hosted a daily movie show on a local New York channel and charmingly gossiped about the films and the stars in them, many of whom she'd worked with. She and Fincher, with whom she had a son, Harry, divorced in 1963 after a move back to the West Coast.

Since then she's had another marriage and has tried to resuscitate her career. There have only been a couple of potboilers though, as far as movies are concerned, but she occasionally pops up on television in dramatic parts. One of the best she did was as an overweening mother on a *Marcus Welby* episode in 1973. Still red-haired, she's often seen around Hollywood with Henry Berger, who was married to the late Anita Louise.

A formal Daphne in the early Forties

DAPHNE du MAURIER

England's Cornwall, with its rugged coastline and stretches of wild, unspoiled moors, still retains much of the flavor of the days when smuggling was a way of life and horse-backed highwaymen rode the narrow country lanes by night in search of hapless travelers. And lucky for the reading world that it does since it's been a constant source of inspiration to one of this century's most romantically prolific writers, Daphne du Maurier, who lives there in regal seclusion in a mansion like those she's written of in books like *Rebecca* and *My Cousin Rachel*, to name but two of her long list of successful novels.

The London-born writer (1907) comes by her talent for the dramatic honestly. Her father was Gerald du Maurier, one of the most famous actor/managers of the London stage at the time, and her mother was a well-known actress, Muriel Beaumont. Educated privately, Daphne was 'finished' at Versailles in homage to her partly French heritage and then studied further in Paris. Her writing career began with a number of short stories that she wrote at her parents' home in Fowey, Cornwall, where she returned after finishing school abroad. In 1929 she used the family home for the setting of her first novel, *The Loving Spirit.*

Three years later she completed *I'll Never Be Young Again* and then married a handsome major in the British Army, Frederick Browning. She traveled with him when he was sent to Egypt but she carried with her the memories of her home, which resulted in *Rebecca*. This time the setting was a 17th Century mansion called Menabilly located near her home in Fowey. She fictionalized it as Manderly in the dark tale that in 1939 became a stage play with John Gielgud (and Margaret Rutherford as Mrs. Danvers) and a year later became a sensational film with Joan Fontaine, Orson Welles and Judith Ander-

Daphne and her two daughters, Flavia and Tessa

son. Eventually du Maurier bought the sixty-room house and made it her home, using it again in a novelized setting in *The King's General.*

Digging once more into local history, she used the authentic headquarters of a smuggling gang for *Jamaica Inn*—an old coach stop built in the 1600s. It was one of several of her works which have been made into movies, getting the film treatment by Charles Laughton and Maureen O'Hara in 1939. In 1944 Paramount made the wonderfully entertaining *Frenchman's Creek* into a Technicolor extravaganza with Joan Fontaine, and two years later Valerie Hobson and Michael Redgrave starred in a version of *The Years Between.* (Not to be outdone by sister Joan, Olivia de Havilland starred in the 1953 adaptation of *My Cousin Rachel* opposite a youthfully virile Richard Burton, augmented by a haunting Franz Waxman score.) Even Alfred Hitchcock got into the act when he bought a short story from a collection called *Kiss Me Again, Stranger,* which became *The Birds!*

Daphne has constantly interspersed biography with her fiction, concentrating largely on her own family. *The Glass Blowers* was about her French ancestors while *Gerald* was a study of her matinee-idol father and *The du Mauriers* emerged as a three-generation biography of her family's colorful history. Her books have been translated into thirty languages, making her one of the most-read women in history.

In 1971 she published *Don't Look Now* and at age sixty-eight shows no signs of letting up. In 1969 she was honored with the Order of the British Empire and throughout all her years of success has raised three children, Tessa, Flavia, and Rupert. Her husband was treasurer to the Duke of Edinburgh, Prince Philip, and had risen to the rank of Lt. General at the time of his death in 1965. She has kept Menabilly as it has always been and by her work has almost insured that it always will be. Her 1973 book, *House On The Strand,* hauntingly combined it and the area's history with experimental drug use. For Daphne there's not only yesterday but tomorrow as well.

Don interviewing Welterweight Champ Emile Griffith before his title bout against Benny "Kid" Paret in 1962

DON DUNPHY

The sports world has always needed articulate translators, those firm-voiced men who sit in the press box and make it all that much more exciting for the rest of us huddled around a radio or a TV set. One of the all-time greats in that department was Don Dunphy, and the good news is that he's currently working on a book which will explore many of the most exciting sports events of all time—from his personal bird's-eye view.

Don is a native New Yorker, born there in 1909, and was interested in sports from grade school on. By the time he graduated from Manhattan College he'd chalked up a notable school career as a track star and also as the campus sports correspondent. The next step—becoming a sports writer for the Bronx Coliseum—was a natural and in 1933 he started his broadcasting career on a New York radio station, WBNX. A year later he joined the local Hearst station, WINS.

His break into general broadcasting occurred in 1939 when newsman Arthur Brisbane hired him after tracking him down from an unsigned sports story in the New York Times. The result was a thirteen week football series; and as sports director for the local station, he did his first boxing commentary in 1940—a five hour stint at the old Queensboro Stadium. He was so good at it that a year later the Gillette Safety Razor Company picked him from a small army of sports reporters for the singular job of calling the boxing matches they had just signed to sponsor. It was what is known in the business as a long run as he worked for Gillette for the next twenty years, thrilling millions who heard the fights broadcast over 164 stations in the United States and Latin America plus 26 other countries, the biggest boxing hookup of its time.

Don didn't limit himself to just boxing though, and in 1944 announced the World Series between the St. Louis Browns and the St. Louis Cardinals and eventually began covering

Don in a recent publicity shot

everything from basketball to bowling to harness racing and even a few St. Patrick's Day Parades!

Among the highs and lows he covered boxing-wise was the classic 1946 Tony Zale-Rocky Graziano Middleweight bout—one of the most exciting in ring history. The dullest was when a disenchanted Madison Square Garden crowd broke out in a chorus of *Let Me Call You Sweetheart* over the poor in-the-ring performers. The most personable boxer Dunphy's ever known outside the ring was Fritzi Zivic—"He had class and lots of it. Mind you, I said *outside* the ring." Inside, especially with Fred Cochrane, it was another story. Remember when the Pittsburgh Welterweight went into a clinch with Cochrane during the title fight so he could listen to Dunphy's commentary?

Don broke into television in its early days and stayed there until the Saturday Night Fights were finally dropped in 1963, ending a twenty-three year tenure as boxing's leading interpreter. He'd called more than 900 fights during his career. A devoted exponent of the sport, he was once asked if, because of its viciousness, shouldn't it be outlawed? He replied that if you outlawed boxing then football would have to go too, as well as mountain climbing and anything else that had inherent danger in it—virtually every sport on the books, in other words.

Don's still broadcasting, having recently completed two years as host of a Home Box Office cable-TV fight show which originated from Madison Square Garden's Felt Forum. His eldest son, Don Jr., is now executive producer of a popular New York news show and his younger son Bob is a producer in the CBS Sports Department. Both graduated from Notre Dame University. Don and wife Muriel, whom he met when she was a secretary at NBC, live on Long Island and between lectures and television appearances he's working on that book which "is going very well so far. There's a lot of interest." Not surprising since it'll be some story.

In 1975, Don traveled to Malaysia to call the heavyweight bout between Mohammed Ali and Joe Bugner.

Jimmy in the classic Durante pose

JIMMY DURANTE

America's been having a love affair with Jimmy Durante's nose—not to mention the rambunctious comedian attached to it—for almost fifty years now. His slouch hat-framed face with the hotcha grin is recognizable all over the world and as far as the entertainment world itself is concerned, well, he's simply one of the greatest, most respected comedians of them all.

New York City-born in 1894, Durante was a child of the streets. His Italian parents were newly arrived in America and it was a rough life, so rough in fact that he had little time for attending school. One reason for his preoccupation with things other than book-learning was that he was constantly teased about the size of his nose. It may have been an easy source of laughter to his friends but to him it was a source of constant pain. "Even if they said nothin', I'd just shrivel up and think they were sayin', 'What an ugly kid! What a monster!' And then I'd go home and cry." But while he was crying, he was also thinking, and came to the conclusion that if people were going to laugh at him anyway, he might as well try getting paid for it.

Jimmy got his first job in show business as a piano player at Coney Island, throwing in a few jokes along with the music. Next he formed his own five-piece Dixieland band which played all over New York, and along the way he met the two men who'd team up with him in one of vaudeville's all-time great acts, Lou Clayton and Eddie Jackson. The act—Clayton, Jackson and Durante—got together in 1923 but it took many years of knocking around from one small club to another before they got a big break, the biggest, in fact, with Flo Ziegfeld. He hired them for his 1929 Broadway presentation *Show Girl*.

They were a hit in it and later that year slaughtered sophisticated audiences at *Les Ambassadeurs* nightclub with the frenetic routines that became their trademark.

60

Jimmy at a Hollywood tennis tournament, 1974

The act broke up in the Thirties and, among other things, Jimmy sought work in the movies—*Roadhouse Nights* (1930), *Cuban Love Song* (1932), *The Passionate Plumber* (1932), *Joe Palooka* (1934), *You're In The Army Now* (1941)—but didn't hit it big until MGM signed him as a speciality act, showcasing him in many of the lavish musicals of the Forties. The one that made the difference was 1946's *It Happened In Brooklyn* with Frank Sinatra and Kathryn Grayson. The following year he starred with Esther Williams in *On An Island With You*, and the high point was when he and his white piano sank to the bottom of a pool in mid-number! Perhaps the best of them all was 1950's *The Great Rupert* which co-starred him with Terry Moore and a squirrel.

After guesting on everyone else's TV show, he started alternating as a host of the Four Star Revue in 1950. (The other hosts were Jack Carson, Danny Thomas and Ed Wynn.) He had a show entirely his own during the mid-Fifties and the ending was always most poignant with the star walking from one pool of spotlight to another ending with "Goodnight Mrs. Calabash, wherever you are!" Everyone suspected that he was referring to his late wife, Jeanne Olson, with this trademark goodbye, which might have been the case since after he married again in 1960, he no longer used that farewell.

He and Margie Little, an actress, had one of the longest courtships in Hollywood history before finally tying the knot. They have two adopted daughters and live quietly in Beverly Hills, Cal. During the Sixties Jimmy made occasional TV appearances, including a short run on *Jimmy Durante Presents The Lennon Sisters* in 1969—and was on the big screen in 1962's *Jumbo* with Doris Day and Martha Raye, and 1963's star-filled *It's A Mad Mad Mad Mad World*.

Recently his friends celebrated his recovery from a stroke by throwing a party in his honor hosted by Milton Berle. Wearing his battered hat and horn rim glasses, he sang a chorus of *Inka Dinka Doo* from a wheelchair. . . still a great trouper.

Sunny backstage at the Paramount Theatre with Nat "King" Cole in 1952

SUNNY GALE

The songstress who helped get the Fifties off the ground with her huge hit *Wheel of Fortune* is currently getting it all back together with a down-home country sound and when *Variety* reviewed her latest album, *Sunny Sings Dixieland Blues*, they attested that her voice still conveys the same "bright and bouncy sound" that made her a star.

Sunny was born in Clayton, New Jersey, (a Pisces) but didn't stay there long. When she was two her family moved to South Philadelphia, that Golden Ghetto of such talents as Mario Lanza, Eddie Fisher, Al Martino and Joey Bishop, all of whom Sunny knew while growing up. She started singing as soon as she knew she could carry a tune and performed at weddings, bar mitzvahs—wherever she could. Also while growing up she worked every week with the U.S.O., singing constantly at all the naval installations and hospitals that surrounded Philadelphia from Fort Dix to Tinicum Barracks. They were so pleased and impressed with her dedication that they gave her a testimonial dinner at Philadelphia's swank Bellevue-Stratford Hotel, hostessed by no less a lady than Madame Chiang Kai-shek herself.

In early 1951 Sunny began singing as the star vocalist with the Hal McIntyre Band and began her spectacular rise to fame and fortune on her talents alone. (I say that because she had won the Miss Philadelphia title in the prelude to Miss America but wanted to sing more than she wanted to just stand there and look good!) Within the year, though, Sunny decided she wanted a crack at New York and went there, where she was discovered by talent agent Gary Romero. He too was vastly

Sunny's latest publicity shot

impressed with the Philadelphia songbird and got her her first recording contract as well as finding the song that would make the difference, *Wheel of Fortune.*

Romero, a mystic-of-all-trades who's also a songwriter and playwright, fanned the fire and her record quickly topped the charts. Interestingly enough it managed to head up the Rhythym and Blues charts too—a field then totally dominated by black singers. 1952 was a banner year that saw Sunny appearing twice at New York's Paramount Theater as well as on the *Ed Sullivan Show*—which showed America the blonde singer for the first time, a surprise to black record buyers who quickly decided they liked her whatever color she was!

Nightclubs came next and Sunny played them all from Las Vegas to Paris to London and even the Far East: Japan, the Phillipines, and Taiwan (where she renewed her acquaintance with Mme. Chiang Kai-shek). After her marriage to Noel Cramer, Romero dropped out of the picture, but after her divorce (she has a daughter, Beth, who's sixteen) he came back to the fold and has her career off and running again.

Her new album was cut on a small label but she and Romero have plans for moving on to a larger one shortly. The reviews warrant such thinking too—*Record World,* for instance, picked it as an Album of the Month for November, 1974, calling it a "Christmas charmer"—and they both feel it's only a matter of time.

She lives in Forest Hills, a plush section of Queens, New York, with her mother and daughter and when she has the time for it, indulges in cooking Italian food, a favorite means of relaxation along with shopping and fishing. Like most people born under the sign of Pisces, she's a romantic, confessing her favorite song is *When I Fall In Love.* From the way the future looks, she'll be too busy to relax once the Gale-Romero re-partnership really gets rocking!

63

Peter and the late Carol Haney in the sensational "Steam Heat" number from *Pajama Game*

PETER GENNARO

Broadway's whiz kid choreographer of hits like *The Unsinkable Molly Brown* and dancing master of the Perry Como and Ed Sullivan television shows is currently working on an entirely new phase of his career, nightclub performing. Despite his steady work producing the stage shows for Radio City Music Hall, he's put together an act with two girls that has had New York clubgoers looking for new adjectives—"I guess I've got a lot of fans who remember me from way back when, the Como show and everything. They dig what I do and frankly I like to perform more than anything in the world." And Peter's the kind of guy who's been lucky enough to be albe to pull that ideal off most of his life.

He left his hometown of Meterie, Louisiana to join the army in World War II, ending up in India where his natural talent for dancing (he'd studied tap a while as a kid) was quickly snapped up by a Special Services Unit headed by Melvyn Douglas. He joined a group of eight other hoofers and they traveled up and down the Burma Road, through all of India, the top of Ceylon—anywhere there was an Army base with soldiers who needed entertaining. He did that for his last eight months in the service and was then mustered out to return home and to his family's tavern. Then a letter came six months later telling him that Melvyn Douglas was mounting a musical for Broadway and would he like to try out for it, that was all he needed. He came immediately "but I didn't get in it. I was rather untrained so I decided to go to school, the American Theater Wing, and studied very hard, eight, ten hours a day, learning every kind of dance. I've been dancing ever since."

His very firstt job was with the San Carlos Ballet in Chicago and it was there he met Jean, the girl he married three months later. Back in New York he worked on the 'subway circuit'— which extended, naturally, to any theater within subway range from Manhattan to the Bronx to Long Island—joining other newcomers like Michael Kidd and Carl Reiner. "We did anything to dance." He made the national company of *Make Mine*

Peter with Ethel Merman and author after his nightclub opening at The Grand Finale in New York in March, 1975

Manhattan and hit Broadway in 1951 in the classic *Guys and Dolls*. His son Michael, now also an actor, was born then, and his wife quit dancing for good. They have a sixteen year-old daughter, Lisa, who's also a dancer. He stayed with *Guys and Dolls* for four years and then went into teaching, one of the first jazz dancing teachers in town and his students were people like Chita Rivera, Merv Griffin, Grace Kelly, Joel Grey and Farley Granger. Through his classes he landed his first choreography job, a musical version of *Seventh Heaven* with Gloria De Haven, Ricardo Montalban, and Bea Arthur, who replaced Fifi Dorsay in it as a French madam! He'd quit the hit show *Pajama Game*, in which he did the unforgettable *Steam Heat* number with the late Carol Haney, for *Heaven* and when it ultimately flopped he returned but only as a member of the chorus, not the lead dancer. "People thought I was crazy but I had to work!"

Things were happening fast though and in 1955 he worked with Jerome Robbins on the choreography for *West Side Story*, primarily the *America* number with Chita Rivera. Then came *Fiorello, Mr. President,* and *The Unsinkable Molly Brown,* both the stage version with Tammy Grimes and the movie with Debbie Reynolds. Hollywood wanted Peter to stay and even dangled another picture called *Sound of Music* in front of him but he wanted to get back to New York.

America got to see lots of Peter when for three years he choreographed and regularly performed on the *Perry Como Show.* When it ended he did the *Kraft Music Hall* and then the final three years of the *Ed Sullivan Show.* His dance routines were winners and since he started working as a producer at Radio City, the Rockettes have never kicked so high or so well.

He almost went into Bob Fosse's *Chicago* but instead decided to embark on the nightclub act which he put together during off hours in just a few weeks. "It's a whole new world and I love it." And it shows!

65

Gloria looking serene
but cautious in the Fifties

GLORIA GRAHAME

Gloria Grahame's performance as the oh-so-Southern wife of Dick Powell in 1952's *The Bad and the Beautiful* won her an Oscar for Best Supporting Actress but the part was the kind of change-of-pace role that often wins awards when an actor steps out of a basic character and takes a swing at something different. Up until then Gloria was the baddest girl on the screen, even holding her own against DeMille's elephants in 1951's *Greatest Show on Earth.* She had a well-traveled beauty and an upper lip that was constantly curled in a half-sexy, half-mocking sneer signaling the innate wariness of a girl who's had to call her own cab once too often. In a classic life-imitating-art triangle, her personal life began more and more to resemble her screen roles—at one point she became her own mother-in-law when she married her former stepson!

Gloria Grahame Hallward was born in Pasadena, California in 1925. Nineteen years later, after an up-and-down acting career that saw her finally reach Broadway, only to be discovered by Louis B. Mayer's minions and sent right back West, she debuted on-screen in *Blonde Fever* as a sultry competitor with Mary Astor for the affections of Philip Dorn (now living in Westwood, Cal. and firmly retired). She was terrific but got only a smallfish reward for her troubles in *Without Love,* A Tracy-Hepburn vehicle in 1946.

Then, as he did for so many others, Frank Capra came along to give her career a little class as his platinum blonde in *It's A Wonderful Life* (1946). Her next, as a saloon singer in *Crossfire* (1947), got her an Academy nomination. MGM used her in 1947's *It Happpened in Brooklyn, Song of the Thin Man* and *Merton of the Movies* with Red Skelton but she didn't film at all in 1948, what with her divorcing actor Stanley Clements (whom she married in 1945) and marrying maverick director Nicolas Ray.

He directed her in her next, *A Woman's Secret* (1948) with Melvyn Douglas, and after a low-budget Western called *Roughshod,* he directed her again in 1950's minor classic *In A Lonely*

A more recent Gloria, at home
with "Oscar"

Place with Humphrey Bogart. Her hard-lipped cynicism matched Bogie's to a T and it was a successful venture. In 1951 she took over the role of the elephant trainer's girlfriend in DeMille's *Greatest Show on Earth* from a pregnant Lucille Ball and helped it earn its Best Picture Oscar. After *Macao* and *Sudden Fear*—both moll doll roles—Gloria got a crack at her own in Vincente Minelli's great *The Bad and the Beautiful* in 1952. As Dick Powell's sexy wife she stole every scene she was in and walked off with the Best Supporting Actress Award. It was an up-and-down year as she also divorced Ray after bearing him a son, Timothy.

Full-fledged stardom eluded her though, and her follow-up roles were mostly co-starring ones, with the ludicrous exception of *Prisoners of the Casbah* (1953) with Turhan Bey. Two other exceptions, both of which are now considered classics of their kind, were the films she did for Fritz Lang, *The Big Heat* in 1953 and *Human Desire* a year later, both of which teamed her with Glenn Ford. (The *Desire* role, by the way, was originally intended for Rita Hayworth.)

In 1955 she appeared in *Not As A Stranger,* the *Peyton Place* of hospital movies, and then sang as Ado Annie in *Oklahoma,* a definite change of pace and virtually her last major film.

In 1954, Gloria married writer Cy Howard but they divorced a few years later after having a daughter Mariana. In 1961 she married again and stunned Hollywood in the process as she picked Tony Ray, her former husband's son and her former stepson, becoming her own mother-in-law. She left the screen shortly thereafter to raise her children but in 1965 chose to comeback in a brutal—and bad—western, *Ride Out For Vengeance.* She's made several low-budget flicks abroad and a couple of TV movies, the most interesting of which was *The Girl On The Late Late Show,* appearing briefly—amid many film clips of her old movies—as a long disappeared star. Many thought it a bit too autobiographically close for comfort but it wasn't. She and Tony live quietly in Van Nuys raising their set of children and while she remembers vividly every stage of her career, she told Rex Reed, "I don't want others to remember the details, just the images." As if we could forget them!

Farley at the height of his career in 1952

FARLEY GRANGER

In his years of young stardom, Farley Granger was one of the handsomest stars on the screen. He was discovered when he answered a newspaper ad for actors and commandeered the attention of Samuel Goldwyn. Goldwyn thought he had star quality after debuting him in 1943's *North Star* but didn't get around to trying to prove it until later in the Forties. When he did, he pulled out all the stops but a doubting public never caught his enthusiasm. Granger's peak of popularity was the years after World War II, before the Fifties (Tab Hunter, Rock Hudson, Tony Curtis, etc.) got started. It was an in-between time for Hollywood and its stars, and unfortunately Farley didn't fare too well with the public.

Farley was born in San Jose, California in 1925 and was only seventeen when he did his first picture, followed quickly by the third lead in the excellent prisoner-of-war drama *The Purple Heart* in 1944. Then he went into uniform for real (the Army) and when he got out had to start all over again pounding on studio doors. Nicolas Ray opened RKO's a crack with *They Live By Night* in 1948. Howard Hughes, then RKO's chief, held it up a year but when it was released it got critical acclaim. By then Granger was in the middle of *Rope* for Alfred Hitchcock, a drama about two homosexuals who play at murder, (John Dall was the other one) and had been signed by Goldwyn to a five-year contract.

Farley's first for Goldwyn was *Enchantment* (1948) with Evelyn Keyes, but the biggie was *Roseanna McCoy* (1949), of the feudin' Hatfields and McCoys, which was supposed to launch him and co-star Joan Evans as America's two brightest new stars. The Goldwyn publicity mills ground out story after story about the two of them and the film but no amount of puffery could sell the public, and it flopped. Not discouraged, though, Goldwyn lent Farley to MGM for *Side Street* (1949) while two

Farley Granger at fifty. Still a handsome man.

more vehicles were prepared for him and Evans. The first, *Our Very Own* (1950), was a soap opera-ish account of an adopted girl (Ann Blyth) with Farley as her boyfriend and Evans as her mean sister, and the second was *Edge of Doom* (1950), a murky slum-set melodrama in which he kills a priest. They too fizzled at the box-office, and a third picture, *All For Love,* was quietly shelved.

After *Strangers on a Train* (1951) for Hitchcock—as the tennis player, and very good too despite Hitchcock's later criticisms—Farley made *Behave Yourself!* (1951) with Shelley Winters, and fan magazines had a field day speculating whether their relationship extended off-camera as well. It didn't. After *I Want You* in 1951, and *O'Henry's Full House* and *Hans Christian Anderson* in 1952, he went back to MGM for *The Story of Three Loves* (1952). His sequence, *Mademoiselle,* with Leslie Caron, was one of the best in it but all Metro could then come up with was *Small Town Girl* (1953) with Jane Powell.

The turning point came in 1953 when he went to Italy to make *Senso* for Luchino Visconti. Teamed with Alida Valli, it was the best work Granger ever did. He stayed until he came back to Hollywood for *The Naked Street* with Tony Quinn in 1955 and *Girl in the Red Velvet Swing* (1955) with Ray Milland and Joan Collins. It was his last big American movie.

Despite his movie failures, Farley has always taken his acting career seriously and has stage-played all over America, including Broadway in *The Carefree Tree.* He found new fame in Italy during the Sixties, starring in many popular pictures which seldom made it across the water, including one of the successful Western series based on a Clint Eastwood-type character named 'Trinity'. He's never married and relishes his free-floating status, returning now and then to Hollywood for things like the disastrous TV version of *Laura* with Lee Radziwill, and the recent comedy-shocker *Arnold* with Roddy McDowell and Elsa Lanchester.

69

Dolores made up for the Hollywood cameras in 1955

Pictorial Parade

DOLORES GRAY

When Ethel Merman decided not to do *Annie Get Your Gun* in London in 1947, Dolores Gray, a wide-mouthed hand grenade of energy, got the part. It wasn't easy either as her first audition flopped because the producers thought she was too glamorous. However, she dressed down for her call-back, walked off with the role, and kept it for three applause-filled years, which prompted one sage of the British stage to call her "the greatest leading lady of musicals ever seen in London."

Back home she starred in *Carnival In Flanders* and though it only lasted six performances, she managed to sing her way right into a Tony Award as Best Actress with the help of a song called *Here's My Rainy Day.* The movies grabbed her for 1955's *It's Always Fair Weather,* a Stanley Donen-directed confection with Gene Kelly, followed quickly by *Kismet* (1955) in the part Joan Diener originated on Broadway. In that she vamped down the soundstage walls opposite Howard Keel and was so much woman on-screen that in her few scenes with Vic Damone, she easily overwhelmed him. *Kismet* was one of the last of MGM's glossy tuners and was directed by that studio's resident genius, Vincente Minelli. Dolores gave it her all and if that happened to be too much for even the Cinemascope screen, it wasn't her fault!

Chicago-born (June 7, 1926), Dolores shook the breezes of the Windy City at age three when her mother moved to Hollywood. A dozen years later Rudy Vallee heard her singing and put her on his radio show and before you could say 'Vo De Oh Do', she'd been heard by the owner of New York's *Copacabana* nightclub and signed to sing there.

Billy Rose was her next 'discoverer' and he promptly placed her alongside Bea Lillie and Bert Lahr in his 1944 show *The Seven Lively Arts.* As of then, the show, as they say, was definitely on the road!

70

Dolores, off-guard,
in the Seventies

There were two more Broadway shows, *Are You With It* and *Sweet By and By,* before *Annie* in London, which firmly established Dolores as a talent to contend with. Hollywood seemed a natural for the high-stepping blonde and she arrived there for *Weather* with Momma, 36 pieces of luggage, a French maid and seven poodles. She said she loved Lana Turner movies, unsalted peanuts, and Bugs Bunny, and set up housekeeping in a glass-walled bungalow with an Oriental swimming pool. After *Weather* and *Kismet,* though, producers weren't quite sure what to do with the 5'7" blonde. She got the Roz Russell part in a remake of *The Women* (called *The Opposite Sex*) and in 1957 did her best to vamp Gregory Peck away from Lauren Bacall in *Designing Woman.* But after that nothing so she trekked back east—36 suitcases and all—to star on Broadway in *Destry Rides Again* with Andy Griffith. One night during a performance a fire broke out in the theater but the crowd was kept from panicking by Dolores' soothing way with a love song. She got a "Cool Head" award for her act.

The Sixties saw her more on the front pages rather than the entertainment section. A former fiance was brought to trial about some $400,000 worth of phony land deeds and she had to testify. Later she sued him for the return of her engagement ring, a $55,000 diamond he'd taken back and given to another girl. She fought hard but lost in 1968.

The musical version of *The Man Who Came To Dinner* starring her and George Sanders looked like a sure thing. Called *Sherry,* it wasn't. Sanders pulled out before it opened—which was just before it closed. She was up for *Mame* but Angela Lansbury got it, but since she'd married wealthy businessman Andrew Crevolin, the loss didn't overly shake her. Ironically, in 1974 she replaced Lansbury in the London run of *Gypsy* and found reviewers as glad to see her as they'd been twenty-eight years before. In the Spring of 1975 Dolores got her act together and opened at a small New York club, *Brothers and Sisters,* (later a showcase for another pro, Vivian Blaine) and showed that while the figure was a little heavier the voice was as dynamic as ever.

71

Kathryn in her Hollywood heyday

KATHRYN GRAYSON

The motion picture industry has always had a knack for making silk purses out of sow's ears but in the case of Kathryn Grayson, her lovely voice and proper beauty justified her screen reputation and for a few years she reigned supreme as the Numero Uno of movie sopranos. For a while America had a new Jeanette MacDonald and even though her 'Nelson Eddy' alternated between Mario Lanza and Howard Keel, the total effect was one of Technicolor gorgeousness whether she was cinched into *Showboat's* girdles or let loose to shout in MGM's stagestruck version of *Kiss Me Kate.*

MGM originally pacted her after it lost Deanna Durbin to Universal (who took no chances and also signed Susanna Foster and Gloria Jean in an attempt to corner the sweetheart-soprano market!) and then decided—or rather Metro kingpin Louis B. Mayer did—that it needed one of its own. They quickly nabbed Katie, born in Winston-Salem, North Carolina in 1923, without even making a screen test. They coached her for a year and then debuted her in *Andy Hardy's Private Secretary*—in the title role no less. Next came small parts with Frank Morgan in *The Vanishing Virginian* in 1942 and with Abbott and Costello in *Rio Rita* the same year.

MGM then fashioned *Seven Sweethearts* (1942) for her in hopes that it would do for her what *Three Smart Girls* had done for Durbin. It didn't but she did get lots of good notices for her next, *Thousands Cheer* (1943) with Gene Kelly. They were a good team and worked again in 1945's *Anchors Aweigh.* Next came a guest spot in the star-filled *Ziegfeld Follies* in '46 and then she teamed with another Metro cutie, June Allyson, for *Two Sisters From Boston* with Jimmy Durante. Interestingly she next did another guest shot in *Till The Clouds Roll By* (1946), dueting with Tony Martin in a musical sequence of *Showboat,* the film version of which she was to star in several years later.

After her next film, *It Happened In Brooklyn,* with Frank Sinatra, Metro teamed them again in 1948's *The Kissing Bandit,* a notoriously bad movie that both stars would like to forget

Kathryn at the wedding of the late Mario Lanza's daughter, Lisa, and Bobby Bregman

ever happened.

Since Metro had already tried her in something old (the remake of *Rio Rita) and* something borrowed *(Seven Sweethearts)*—there wasn't anything blue in those days—they finally tried something new, teaming her with their newest discovery, Mario Lanza, in *That Midnight Kiss* (1949), and *The Toast of New Orleans* (1950), both of which were big hits. After the mediocre *Grounds for Marriage* (1950) with Van Johnson, she hit her peak as Magnolia in *Showboat,* one of the most richly realized and grandly stylish of all MGM's monumental musicals. Howard Keel played the ne'er-do-well gambler who loves and leaves her, and Ava Gardner was astonishingly good as the tragic Julie. Agnes Moorehead and Joe E. Brown lent high quality support and the film was one of 1951's biggest successes.

Metro teamed her again with Keel the following year in *Lovely To Look At* but she didn't much like the results or the other scripts the studio was coming up with and went to Warner Bros to do *The Desert Song* with Gordon MacRae. It was fine but her follow-up, a biopic of opera singer Grace Moore called *So This Is Love,* hardly did her, the subject, or her fresh young leading man, Merv Griffin, justice.

Metro called her back for *Kiss Me Kate*—yep, with Keel—and for a while it looked like a whole new career ballgame. They announced projects like musical versions of *Camille* and *Trilby* but her contract had been completed with *Kate* and she didn't re-sign. Instead she went to Paramount for *The Vagabond King* (1956) opposite their singing white hope Oreste (Kirkop) but it disappeared quickly after its release—as did Oreste! The age of the movie musicals was over and Kathryn seemed one of its casualties. Like Jeanette MacDonald, she walked away from her screen career with dignity—and reputation—intact. No black and white B pictures for her.

Though she's been twice divorced (actor John Shelton, 1940-46, and singer Johnny Johnston, 1947-51 by whom she had a daughter, Patricia), she's considered a bachelor girl. Over the years she's remained close to the family Mario Lanza left behind and occasionally tours in summer stock, most notably a recent reteaming of her and Howard Keel in *Man of La Mancha.*

Beauteous Hope in 1938

HOPE HAMPTON

Hope Hampton has been many things to many people. A sequin in the public's eye for almost sixty years, she ricocheted back and forth from the silent screen to the opera stage, back to Hollywood again and onward to New York where, in 1962, no less than the Encyclopedia Britannica named her The World's Fastest Twister, referring to the dance craze of the time. Is it any wonder that for several generations people remarked on how Hope springs eternal?

The blonde beauty entered silent films when she was only thirteen and was a star by 1920, after *A Modern Salome*. She was nineteen at the time. In those days stars were expected to publicize their movies and Hope went on the road. Rather than just stand there and look gorgeous, she decided to sing a number or two for the audiences and hit upon *At Dawning* which ended with the phrase 'I love you.' She shortly became known as 'The I Love You Girl'. Sigmund Romberg heard her one day and was so impressed he wrote an operetta for her, *My Princess*, which she starred in at the Schubert Theater in New York in 1927. After that, and a follow-up, *My Golden Girl*, Hope decided to give up movies in 1928, and launched a career as an opera singer, gradually racking up credits in *Manon, La Traviata* and other romantic roles with the Philadelphia Grand Opera, the Paris Opera Comique and the Chicago Grand Opera.

In 1938 she went back to Hollywood for *The Road to Reno* with Randolph Scott, a satire on divorce which obligingly included an operatic sequence so she could stretch her by then well-trained pipes. When one interviewer referred to the film as a comeback, she replied, "Comeback? I am *going* back, as a full-fledged prima donna. They (Universal) have hired me for my singing just as other studios have hired Pons, Grace Moore and Gladys Swarthout." By then, however, America's

Hope springs eternal on a recent date with Tony Carlyle

movie-opera quotient was already being well filled by Jeanette MacDonald.

In 1923 Hope had married Jules Brulatour, described as "one of the country's richest men drawing royalties on every foot of motion picture film sold by Eastman-Kodak," so it didn't really matter that her renewed movie career was a short one. He died in 1942, and Hope has remained a merry widow ever since.

The Forties saw her capture the title of New York's 'Queen of Firstniters', attending every Broadway opening on the arm of one titled man or another. In 1951 she was robbed of $336,000 worth of jewelry the day after she'd canceled its insurance, and in 1954 she was in *Hello Paree,* a low-budget flick whose publicity referred to her as the "Marilyn Monroe of the Twenties." A year later she opened at New York's swanky *Versailles* nightclub wearing a form-fitting sequinned gown that quickly became her trademark. And she didn't have to warble a note to get yearly front-page coverage of her annual entrances at the opening of the Metropolitan Opera. Occasionally, if coaxed by the shutterbugs, she did a little two-step on one of her several floor-length chinchillas.

When the rock group, Joey Dee and the Starliters opened at the Peppermint Lounge in 1961, Hope was there and became entranced with the Twist—so much so that when Paramount made *Hey, Let's Twist* with Dee and Chubby Checker in 1962, she consented to appear briefly as a New York society woman (typecasting?) in the noisy goings-on. She expanded her terpsichorean efforts to include the Swim and the Watusi, learning them from dancemaster Killer Joe Piro who also coached such celebrities as Jackie Kennedy and Sybil Burton.

Today Hope is still the Duchess of Park Avenue even though her appearances of late have been infrequent. Her 12-room Park Avenue townhouse is an opulent treasure trove of antiques, paintings, and the movie queen touch of a leopard carpeted staircase. She's lived a life full of exclamation points and is to New York society what Mae West is to Hollywood's—the indefatigable Queen Bee.

Sterling Hayden,
Hollywood Golden Boy in 1941

STERLING HAYDEN

Dubbed the Most Beautiful Man in the Movies after pictures like *Bahama Passage* with then-wife Madeleine Carroll in 1942, Sterling Hayden was stuck with that image until the mid-Fifties turned him into a mach-male character actor. The marriage to Carroll was more publicity than true love and ended without a whimper in 1945 as her star was setting in Hollywood and his was rising. In fact dialogue was imitating life when they made *Passage* and she asked him to make love. "No, let's fish," came his blond-and-bronzed reply and the public roared.

Born in Montclair, New Jersey in 1916 to a socially prominent family, Hayden made his movie entrance in 1941's *Virginia* but put the whole thing on the shelf when he enlisted in the Navy—one of the first stars to do so. Afterwards he had to start his career over again but *Blaze At Noon* (1947), helped him get right back in gear. One of the screen's original rebels, he didn't get much of a chance to show it in things like *El Paso* (1949), and *Manhandled* with Dorothy Lamour, also that year, but in 1950's *Asphalt Jungle* the true Hayden came through and the box-office verdict was that it was quite something! He was called before the House UnAmerican Activities group in Washington but emerged a good guy, having been unwilling to testify against any co-workers in the movie industry. This stalled his career but he kept going in action pictures like *The Golden Hawk,* with Rhonda Fleming, and *Flat Top,* an aircraft carrier drama, both in 1952.

He had a chance to share the screen with Bette Davis in *The Star* but mostly all you saw of him was the back of his neck—the same fate that awaited him when he worked with that other screen legend, Joan Crawford, in the acclaimed *Johnny Guitar* in 1954.

A bearded Hayden in a recent movie

He married Betty DeNoon later in 1945 after his divorce from Carroll, and when they split in 1955, she kept custody of their four children. He kept working in things like 1955's *The Last Command* and 1958's *Terror In A Texas Town* to keep up the alimony and support payments.

In 1963 Hayden had his autobiography, *The Wanderer,* published, which exposed the reasons for his up-and-down career. Besides bad scripts, there was also a drinking problem plus an insatiable desire to roam the high seas. In 1959 he defied a court order by sailing off to Tahiti with his four children. He admitted most of his money had gone into the various sailing ships he'd owned over the years—eighteen in all.

In 1955, Hayden had been in Stanley Kubrick's *The Killing*, and nine years later worked for him again in *Dr. Strangelove,* that blackly comedic dissection of military overpreparedness dominated by Peter Sellers. He married again and apparently settled down but after finishing *Strangelove* he left his wife Kitty and went wandering—"I just didn't want to face another movie camera; I had to drift, just drift." Drift he did but Kitty and their two sons, Andre and David, stayed behind.

Hayden admits he never had a head for money and has always been just able to keep up with his debts. "I used to make $160,000 a year but I never had any stocks or bonds. Every time I've made a few thousand bucks I've spent it quickly on a ship or to pay off debts. I made $25,000 for five days work on *The Godfather* and that lasted me a few months." He was also in Elliot Gould's *The Long Goodbye* and insisted on being paid in cash so he could make a quick exit.

Back in Europe he's worked in minor films like *Last Days of Man On Earth,* a British attempt at science-fiction with Jon Finch and Hugh Griffith, but hasn't yet been able to rekindle leading-role interest. Which is too bad as indeed he gave the screen a great deal of natural excitement long before Paul Newman and Brando made the scene. His home base is Wilton, Conn., where he's completing a novel set in the 1890s. He also says he's currently "on my greatest adventure—searching deeply for my inner self." We hope he makes it.

Richard Haydn, handsome in repose

RICHARD HAYDN

Richard Haydn's constant adenoidal condition has as much to do with his long success as a character actor as anything else. Coupled with his prissy character of Professor Carp, the bespectacled buttinsky that made him famous on New York and London stages long before he made movies, the results have been hilarious. One image that jumps to mind was when he pitched his brand of humor against the caustic wit of Clifton Webb in *Sitting Pretty* and lost—but sidesplittingly so. Haydn has been camp so long that he's undeniably one of the great comics who helped write the definition of the word.

British-born (1905), he was a dancer in his youth and starred in many London revues—those song-and-dance-and-comedy spots that also made Bea Lillie and Gracie Fields stars. His standard character, Professor Carp, the ultimate absentminded professor complete with butterfly net, was always an endearing one and he went from show to show steadily convulsing audiences on both sides of the Atlantic.

In 1940 he came to New York to star in Noel Coward's *Set To Music,* and while here finally decided to take up one of the many movie offers he was constantly getting. If there was ever a chance for him to expand his character, this film eliminated it. As Professor Oddly in Howard Hawks' *Ball of Fire,* he crossed wits with some of Hollywood's most venerated funny character men—Oscar Homolka and S. Z. "Cuddles" Sakall for two—in the zany story of a professor (Gary Cooper) who runs into a stripper on the lam (Barbara Stanwyck) while researching a book on slang. Haydn's character was constantly eulogizing the *anemone inamoratus,* his love flower, to Cooper between Coop's numerous bouts with Barbara. It was an impressive first impression—and one so good that Hollywood casting men never forgot it!

Richard Haydn
in *Young Frankenstein*

He immediately got so many offers that Hollywood became his second home—*Charley's American Aunt* (1941); *Forever and a Day* (1943); *Ten Little Indians* (1945), the Agatha Christie classic in its first Hollywood outing; *Cluny Brown* (1946), as the wonderfully droll pharmacist Jennifer Jones almost marries; and *Forever Amber* (1947), in a change of pace role as Linda Darnell's much older husband who tries to kill her during the Great London fire. He was excellent in all and others too.

In 1948 he directed his first movie, *Miss Tatlock's Millions*, an original comedy about a Hollywood stuntman (John Lund) who makes a fool of himself to help heiress Wanda Hendrix. Veteran actors Monty Wooley, Dorothy Stickney and Barry Fitzgerald were also in it. Haydn acted in this one too as he did in his second time out as director the following year, in *Mr. Music*, with Bing Crosby, Nancy Olson and Groucho Marx. (In 1950 he directed *Dear Wife* but did not appear in it.)

In 1954 he helped flesh out one of Esther Williams' last big screen outings in *Jupiter's Darling* and in '60 supported Doris Day and David Niven in *Please Don't Eat The Daisies*, once again the absentminded professor. Also that year he was in *Lost World*, and traveled to Tahiti with half of Hollywood for *The Mutiny On The Bounty* (1962) with Brando. He worked constantly on television too but always found time for big pictures—*Five Weeks In A Balloon* (1962) and that all-time whopper, *The Sound of Music* (1965).

It was only natural that sooner or later he'd join Walt Disney's cast of characters, and he worked for him in 1965's *Clarence The Cross-Eyed Lion*, and the following year in *Bullwhip Griffin* with Roddy McDowell, a takeoff on *Ruggles of Red Gap*, the proper butler out West. One of his TV high spots was playing an Oriental suitor to "Aunt Clara"—Marion Lorne—on *Bewitched*.

Today Haydn lives quietly in Pacific Palisades, California, near the homes of Eddie Albert and Ronald Reagan. He's appeared in plays in Los Angeles at the prestigious Mark Taper Forum and last year was coaxed back in front of the movie cameras by Mel Brooks for *Young Frankenstein*—as gem-like a performer as ever.

Wanda in a typically wistful pose, 1948

WANDA HENDRIX

Wanda Hendrix was one of the prettiest girls of the post-war period in the late Forties. Hers was the kind of face one might stumble upon in an Italian museum etched onto an ancient canvas—it has that kind of purity. When she faced rascally Tyrone Power in *Prince of Foxes* to defend her tiny kingdom and aged husband, she was every inch the noble lady caught up in events that she might not be able to handle but that she nevertheless understood. In that flick it was the old story of virtue versus vicissitude—and Hendrix's virtue won by a mile!

When fifteen year-old Dixie Wanda Hendrix took a lead role in a Jacksonville Little Theater production in her hometown of Jacksonville, Florida in 1943, the furthest thing from her mind was Hollywood. Yet that's just what it got her when a Warner Bros. talent scout spotted her in it. With her parents' consent, she went there shortly thereafter, signing a contract with Warners and being, as they used to say, "groomed for stardom", a torturous course for many screen hopefuls, in manners, morals, camera angles, behavior in general and possibly an acting lesson or two. She passed with flying colors, and her debut role was in *Confidential Agent* (1945) with Charles Boyer and Lauren Bacall.

Warners was pleased but unfortunately when they went to their script department they found no roles available for the young beauty. After keeping her on ice two years, they let her go to Paramount. She quickly did *Welcome Stranger* (1947) with Bing Crosby there and then was personally chosen by Robert Montgomery in 1947 for his *Ride The Pink Horse,* a moody classic of its kind with Montgomery a baddie who swtiches tracks at the sight of Hendrix. A year later she became a full-fledged star with *Miss Tatlock's Millions*, directed by Richard Haydn. Next was *The Prince of Foxes* (1949), an epic of the underhanded Borgias in which she shone.

Wanda Hendrix in today's Hollywood with her dog, Lady

After a heavily fan-magazined romance with war hero-turned-movie actor Audie Murphy, they married in 1949. She asked her studio to loan her to Universal to co-star with him in *Sierra* (1950) and says it was her greatest thrill when they let her do so. The new marriage was already on rocky shoals and she hoped the picture might help them overcome their difficulties. It didn't work. They divorced in 1950 and she's currently writing a book about their romance—a subject she's never spoken of before. (He died in a tragic plane crash in 1971).

After pictures like *Captain Carey, U.S.A.* (1950) and the poignant *The Highwayman* (1951) with Philip Friend—yes, as the girl in the poem who warns her lover away from danger by shooting herself!—and *Last Posse* (1953), she married Robert Stack's very social brother James and retired from the screen in the mid-Fifties. A rare outing away from home was 1961's *Boy Who Caught A Crook.*

When they divorced she tried to resume her career but it hasn't been easy. In 1965 she was in *Stage To Thunder Rock,* hardly star-material, and appeared on television. She also took to the boards, touring summer stock circuits in plays like *Critic's Choice* and others.

Lately, though, things have been looking up careerwise. She did a *Police Story* segment last year and also made two films in Canada—*Oval Portrait* and *One Minute Before Death*—which haven't been released in the U.S. yet.

She and her third husband, Steve La Monte, live in the exclusive Toluca Lake section of the San Fernando Valley (they were wed in 1969) in a house that befits a movie star, and is happier than she's been in years. She still tours in plays—recently *For Love Or Money*—and is set to star in *The Legend of Frank Leahy,* a biopic of the famous coach. She seems to be personally debunking the Hollywood myth that a star just doesn't 'come back'.

Hillary in mufti for his
1956 Antarctic expedition

Pictorial Parade

SIR EDMUND HILLARY

When Sir Edmund Hillary became the first man to conquer the 29,028-foot peak of Mount Everest on May 28th, 1953, he became an instant hero, larger than life—the stuff of which legends are made. The monumental feat was actually his second try at the mountain—in 1951 he was part of the unsuccessful British Everest Expedition led by Eric Shipton—but that fact only added to the portrait of him as a superhero, a man who fights back at impossible odds until he's successful. The journey up the treacherous peak, battling the ice, sub-zero temperatures, lack of oxygen and fierce winds that made the last thousand feet almost impossible, was the important part to him, the proving that it could be done. When the expedition, this time led by John Hunt, descended the face of now-conquered Everest, they were flabbergasted to find the world waiting for them with wide-open arms and banner headlines. Sir Edmund describes with amusement his reaction on finding out that he'd been knighted for his achievement—"My God, I'll have to get a new pair of overalls!"

His personal world changed overnight with a flood of lecture offers, commercial propositions and lionization by people everywhere. He wasn't sure about those but he was positive about marrying the girl he loved, a twenty-three year-old student at the Sydney Conservatorium of Music, named Rose Louise. They faced the world together until her tragic death in March of 1975 in a plane crash while en route to visit him in Nepal.

Born in New Zealand in 1921, his early life on his father's honey farm in Aukland was quiet and more than a little isolated. It wasn't until World War II that he left its safe confines and joined the world. His decision to enlist in the New Zealand Royal Air Force was a painful one since he was and is an

Sir Edmund Hillary, Lady Hillary and a Sherpa guide in Nepal two years before her death

outspoken critic of war and killing of any kind. It wasn't until the Japanese began attacking the northern islands off Australia that he decided to enlist.

This was also when he discovered mountain climbing, a natural outlet for the personal mixture of solitariness and curiosity that characterizes him. Yet Everest has not been his only triumph for in 1956 he became the first man to lead an overland party to the South Pole. It was Nepal, however, which fully captivated him. The Everest achievement brought huge publicity to that country and Sir Edmund began to work to bring it some of the benefits of modern science but without changing its ancient ways. A humanitarian and conservationist, he triggered a Herculean effort to build hospitals, schools and bridges in some of the most remote regions using only the methods and materials which could be found and used by the villagers in their own environment. It has been back-breaking labor but intensely worthwhile, mirroring Hillary's personal pride in achievement and adherence to the strict code of conscience instilled in him by his fiercely independent parents. It's given him the satisfaction of paying back the people who helped him reach his goals in a coin that neither spoils nor threatens their own ideals and lifestyles.

Though this work has constantly engaged him, he's found time to be generous in disseminating his mountain climbing experiences and techniques. "I've always kept diaries more for the information of other alpinists and for journals. I've always hated the danger part of climbing but there is something about building up a comradeship—that, I still believe, is the greatest of all feats—and sharing in the dangers with your company of peers." He's recently finished his autobiography, *Nothing Venture, Nothing Win,* explaining that the thought of death was always a close and constant presence too. Its lifelong familiarity has helped him cope with his recent loss of Lady Hillary and his teen-aged daughter Belinda. Their plane crashed en route to a hospital site on the side of Everest, one he's building for the Sherpa guides who helped him in his famous climb.

Valerie in *Blanche Fury*—at
the height of her career

VALERIE HOBSON

Valerie Hobson was for years the movie screen's perfect
lady. Her long-boned grace and softly modulated voice coupled
with her never overt smile combined for a quality best defined
as good breeding—and breeding will out every time.

The daughter of an English Army commander, she was born
in 1917 on the island of Larne off Northern Ireland, and as
a teen-ager followed the standard route that led to the Royal
Academy of Dramatic Arts. Her first venture was on Drury
Lane in *Ball at the Savoy* with the curtain barely down before
the movies beckoned her. After one small part, she was given
the lead in *Two Hearts in Waltztime* and Hollywood offered
her the role of Estella in *Great Expectations*. Valerie's expectations were cut rudely short however when she got there and
found that her part had gone to Jane Wyatt. (Much later in
1947, David Lean directed her in *his* version of the Dickens
classic and she proved ideal in the same role that Hollywood
decided not to give her.)

Since she was already in Hollywood and Universal wanted
her to sign with them, Hobson stayed. She had gentility to
sell on screen, but the only way Hollywood used it was in
a series of thrillers such as *Bride of Frankenstein* (1935), *Mystery
of Edwin Drood* (1935), *Rendezvous at Midnight* (1935), and
Werewolf of London (1935) among others. She screamed and
fainted a lot but always in a very lady-like way. Universal let
her go during a studio power shift and she eventually returned
home, prepared to start her screen career from scratch.

Instead she played the lead opposite James Mason in something called *Street of Stamboul* (1936), did an air adventure
called *No Escape* (1937), and finally *Jump for Glory* (1937),
directed by Raoul Walsh—the film that established her star
image and her career. The next year she made *This Man In*

Valerie today in the garden
of her English home

Paris and eventually married its producer, Anthony Havelock-Allen. They stayed married until 1952.

After her marriage, she worked steadily for a few years more until 1943, when she decided to take some time off. That lasted until *The Years Between* made in 1946.

The perfect lady was now the perfect movie star, firmly planted at the top of the British female star list. Proof of it was the obligatory star vehicle, in her case the heavy-breathing *Blanche Fury* (1947) opposite Stewart Granger, followed by the brilliant *Expectations.* The role she's probably most remembered for is in *Kind Hearts and Coronets* (1949), the super-zany comedy that launched Alec Guinness into international stardom. A classic, it was unfortunate that she couldn't follow it up with another but she went ahead with minor films until her marriage in 1954 to John Profumo, a Conservative member of Parliament. On stage she did *The King and I* and after it closed she quit acting altogether feeling it was unlikely she'd ever have that good a role again. Her last film, made before the West End run, was a good one, though, *Knave of Hearts* (1954) opposite Gerard Phillippe.

The quiet life of a country lady seemed to be her future, and indeed was for almost ten years until her husband became involved in Britain's flashiest and most sensational scandal in years. Throughout the months of headlines, Valerie Hobson stood quietly by her husband with all the reserve and appeal she'd evinced on the screen, going about the small duties required of her and smiling bravely. The world greatly admired her composure and courage. After the hullabaloo died down, there were a few separation rumors but they proved just that. She still lives with her husband, quietly and elegantly, in Hertfordshire. (Incidentally, in June, 1975, John Profumo was awarded the O.B.E. for outstanding service among the poor of London.) When we first discussed this book she said simply, "I cannot remember the exact sequence of my various films. I have not, as you may know, appeared professionally for a number of years." And it's a shame she hasn't.

Howe lining up a shot in the Forties

JAMES WONG HOWE

The man behind the movie camera has been the maker—and salvation—of many an actor's career, yet it's been only in recent years that this power position has been fully realized, thanks in large part to the durable genius of James Wong Howe. During the Golden Days of Hollywood he made the beautiful look gorgeous (Mary Astor in *The Prisoner of Zenda*) and the gorgeous look stupefying (Hedy Lamarr in *Algiers,* the original "Come With Me To The Casbah" flick), and most recently came out of retirement to do his best for Barbra Streisand in *Funny Lady,* but more about that later.

Born Wong Tung Jim in Kwantung, China in 1899, his family emigrated here when he was four years old. In his late teens he embarked on a career as a professional boxer but after a few years turned his life and sights completely around for a career in the brand new industry of making movies. He got a job as assistant to DeMille's chief cameraman, Alvin Wyckoff, at the Jesse Lasky Studios.

His first big break came when Mary Miles Minter let him do a still photograph of her. "In those days blue eyes came out white because of the film. But when I photographed her they came out dark. She was so excited she asked me to be a cameraman on her next picture," which was *Trail Of The Lonesome Pine* in 1922. His days as a studio camera carrier were over but the experience, five years of it, had served him well.

Under the name James Howe, he worked steadily throughout the transition years from silent movies to sound, photographing classics like 1924's *Peter Pan* with Betty Bronson, 1928's *Laugh Clown Laugh* with Lon Chaney, to the sophisticated talkie, *The Thin Man* in 1934. MGM started publicizing his Chinese nationality about this time and the Wong went back into his name.

Eddie Colbert

As he looks today

His films during the Thirties and Forties include many of the very best of the period: *Fire Over England* (1936), Leigh and Olivier's first film together; *Abe Lincoln In Illinois* (1939); *Dr. Ehrlich's Magic Bullet* (1940); *King's Row* (1941); *Passage to Marseilles* (1944); *Confidential Agent* (1945), and the one that's considered by many to be his best work, 1947's *Body and Soul* with John Garfield. The final fight scene was shot with a handheld camera with Howe on roller skates in the ring.

In 1946 he filmed a Chinese sequence for *God Is My Co-pilot* and desperately wanted to use his talent as well as his heritage in a film called *Rickshaw Boy,* and indeed two years later began work on it in China but it had to be abandoned.

He finally got his crack at directing with *Go, Man, Go* (1954), the fast-moving feature about the start of the Harlem Globetrotters basketball team, and in 1957 directed *The Invisible Avenger.* Over the years Howe has chalked up a total of eleven Academy Award nominations for Best Cinematography and has won two of them, for *The Rose Tattoo* (1955), and *Hud* (1963) with Paul Newman and Patricia Neal. (He should have won also for 1958's *Sweet Smell of Success.)*

Acknowledged as the king of black and white cinematography, he proved Technicolor was no obstacle with the classic *Picnic* (1955); *Bell, Book and Candle* (1958)—Kim Novak never looked lovelier!—and the flick that gave the world Capucine, 1959's *Song Without End.* 1967's *This Property Is Condemned* with Natalie Wood and Robert Redford was his last major film before his retirement. It took Barbra Streisand herself to coax him back out for her *Funny Lady,* perhaps the most mammoth production he ever did. One reviewer said it is as full of microscopically loving close-ups as a nature film about the life of a queen bee, an appropriate comparison to the movie's star. It was an exhausting project though, and shortly after it was completed he was hospitalized for a heart condition.

Married to novelist Sanora Babb since 1949, Howe lives in a lavish Spanish hacienda in Hollywood, as befits a man who's contributed so greatly to making the world enjoy itself at the movies. He still teaches a cinematography course at UCLA.

Martha in 1959

MARTHA HYER

The girl with the heart-shaped face and the structured blonde hairdo hails from Texas. And you know what they say about Texas girls—they know what they want and how to get it! Martha, for instance, knew she wanted to be an actress, and a good one, and as soon as she graduated from Northwestern University she enrolled in the Pasadena Playhouse for just that purpose. The daughter of a Fort Worth attorney (born there August 10, 1924 or '29 depending on what studio bio you read), she'd already been to Europe where she developed her liking for art. In short, Martha was a classy dame, although she was well into her career before she began getting classy parts.

After graduating from the Playhouse she snagged her first role in a murky meller starring Laraine Day and Robert Mitchum called *The Locket* in 1946. It didn't do much except bring her to the attention of low-budget Western producers who thought her looks—and her naturally dark hair—was just right for good girl-schoolmarm roles, which she played almost exclusively for the next few years.

Happily, in 1953, Billy Wilder picked her for a juicy part as William Holden's society fiancée in *Sabrina*. He lightened her locks, pulled them back, dressed her in stylish clothes and the new Martha Hyer was born. She kept up the good work in *Kelly and Me* (1956), *Battle Hymn* with Rock Hudson (1957), and played comedy opposite the master, Bob Hope, in 1958's *Paris Holiday*.

Her really big break came in 1958's *Some Came Running*, a steamy drama of post World War II disillusionment in the South and won an Academy Award nomination for Best Sup-

Martha and husband Hal Wallis today

porting Actress—again as the girl who knew what she wanted. In *The Best of Everything* a year later she was very good once more in a small, waspish part.

Married briefly to Ray Stahl (1951-53), Martha was one of Hollywood's most publicized bachelor girls throughout most of her career. She designed her home around her growing collection of paintings and once even made headlines by having possession of a few that were 'warm', not to say hot. Her career alternated between good roles and terrible ones (*Desire in the Dust*, 1961) but the good seemed to start all over still again when she got picked for *The Carpetbaggers* in 1964. Even though Carroll Baker got most of the press coverage, Martha landed lots of her own, especially in the scene where she wears nothing but a black mink stole.

Unfortunately her follow-up films were B-minus but nobody could say she wasn't working; *Pyro, Bikini Beach, First Men On The Moon,* all in 1964 alone! *The Sons of Katie Elder* (1965) was a juicy John Wayne Western but 1967 saw her wallowing along with Anthony Quinn and Faye Dunaway, in her movie debut, in *The Happening.* She made a European Western, *Massacre at Fort Grant,* and a poor comedy—and Buster Keaton's last picture— *War, Italian Style.* In 1968 she went to the Orient to co-star with Bob Cummings in *House of 1,000 Dolls.*

After a romance of several years, she married super producer Hal Wallis in 1966. He'd been formerly wed to silent screen comedienne Louise Fazenda who died in 1962. Since then Martha has appeared in only a few pictures like *Crossplot* (1969) preferring to remain at home or accompany Wallis on his many globe-trotting production trips. She's regarded as one of Tinseltown's tiptop hostesses, definitely on what Rex Reed calls the A List, subheaded under "group recluses" since she and her husband are private people. They live lavishly and thanks to the ease of her life, she's as lovely as ever.

89

Brenda in her first outing as Jane, 1945

BRENDA JOYCE

Brenda Joyce is best remembered for her role as Johnny Weissmuller's Jane in four *Tarzan* epics—and once as Lex Barker's in *Tarzan's Magic Fountain*—but when she started her career her fresh-scrubbed blonde beauty promised more than that. A personal discovery of 20th Century Fox's longtime kingpin Darryl F. Zanuck, she was chosen for the role of Fern Simon in *The Rains Came* as a result of one of Hollywood's greatest talent searches, but instead of going on from that to A stardom, she soon became bogged down in B pictures where she stayed until her retirement in 1950.

Born Betty Leabo on February 25th, 1915 (later upped to 1920 by studio publicity people) in Kansas City, Missouri, she grew up in Los Angeles where her family moved while she was very young. Those were the movie-crazy years of the Depression but Brenda wasn't star-struck. After high school she went on to college, one semester at the University of Southern California and three more at the University of California at Los Angeles. Money problems forced her to leave which is when she first thought of show business—or at least that phase of it called modeling. Her 5'4", 112 pound, well-rounded body highlighted by her fresh blonde prettiness brought quick response from photographers, and a group of fashion illustrators voted her the Typical American Girl—which was just what Zanuck was looking for.

When he came across her picture in a magazine he was already well into his search for Fern Simon. He saw in Brenda just the right amount of beauty and level-headed naivete that the part called for; the fact that she'd never had an acting lesson in her life didn't deter him. The film was one of 1939's biggest successes and she was quickly starred in *Maryland* (1940) with John Payne and Walter Brennan—a Technicolor ode to horses, and also a popular picture.

Brenda as she looks today

But the studio started using her in B pictures almost immediately and in 1940 alone she appeared in *Am I A Stranger; Public Deb Number One* (presumably they meant debutante); and only one biggie, *Little Old New York* with 20th Queen Alice Faye, Fred MacMurray, and Richard Greene as the man who invented the steamboat.

1941 started off even busier with her marriage to Lieutenant Owen Ward, a high school sweetheart and college suitor. Her studio was furious as she'd broken Hollywood's oldest rule for matrimony by marrying an unknown who couldn't advance her socially, professionally, or economically. (They had a daughter in November of 1942 which cost her the lead in Laurel and Hardy's *A-Haunting We Will Go.* She was replaced by Sheila Ryan.) This marriage as much as anything accounted for her quick relegation to the B ranks. *Marry the Boss's Daughter* that year was a feeble comedy and poorly received—the same fate that happened to her other flicks that year, *Private Nurse, The Postman Didn't Ring* and *Whispering Ghosts* with Milton Berle.

Throughout the Forties her All-American charms were menaced by a wide assortment of evildoers, from the Nazis in 1944's *Strange Confession* to Gale Sondergaard in the *Spider Woman Strikes Back* in 1946, with even Lon Chaney getting a crack at her in *Pillow of Death,* also 1946. Tarzan was quite a relief when he showed up with *Tarzan and the Amazons*—her debut in the classic role of his jungle frau. She ably helped Weissmuller through *Tarzan and the Leopard Woman* (played by Acquanetta), 1947's *Tarzan and the Huntress,* and lastly *Tarzan and the Mermaids* which showcased a young Linda Christian. She finally hung up her jungle duds with *Tarzan's Magic Fountain* (1949) with Lex Barker—and her career as well.

She and Ward made their home in Laguna Beach, California and when their marriage finally ended she stayed on, listing herself in the phone book as Betty Ward. A shy woman, she has no regrets about her career or marriage. She wed for love and didn't regret it, in itself a rare feat in Hollywood.

Ed as Commander Buzz
Corey on *Space Patrol*

ED KEMMER

For a kid growing up in the early Fifties, Saturday morning didn't get started until *Space Patrol* came on. In retrospect it was a naive concept of the universe but at the time it was chock full of as much science fiction as any seven-year-old could handle. The leader of the *Patrol* was Commander Buzz Corey, played with rockjawed sturdiness by Ed Kemmer and ably assisted by his sidekick, Happy, acted by Lynn Osborn. The duo battled foes in space, primarily Prince Bacaratti (Bela Kovacs) who lived in a castle on his own dark planet and was forever trying to gum up the inter-galactic works with his evildoing. He never, ever, triumphed for long but he sure tried hard. Every week in fact.

Patrol started out as a local show in Los Angeles in 1950 and at the time there was no union for TV actors. Kemmer and Osborn got paid eight dollars per show, the rest of the cast five. Ed hung in there though as the show's popularity increased, knowing that network presentation was inevitable. (He was, by the way, a member of the first actors' committee that evolved into AFTRA, the current television actor's union.) The show did build in popularity, so much so that at one time the cast was doing the network half-hour on television, two weekly half hour radio versions, plus five fifteen minute daily versions for Los Angeles radio. There were tie-ins like decoder rings and T-shirts which no self-respecting kid could do without! "There were no teleprompters in those days; it was all done live." Terrific experience for the young actor who had just graduated from the Pasadena Playhouse acting school. It was his first job.

Born in Reading, Pa., Ed got into acting in a bizarre way. "I learned to act in a prison camp in Germany. After being shot down on my forty-seventh mission I was put into a British prison compound—the same compound pictured in *The Great Escape*. When I finally left they were still digging the tunnel—

92

Ed Kemmer (right) with author in Ed's New York apartment

and those guys had built a theater. I joined the band right away and when they decided to put on an American play they picked *The Front Page* and I played Hildy Johnson and liked it. By chance when I got out I met Percy Kilbride and after talking he suggested the Playhouse so I decided to give it a try." Osborn suggested he audition for *Space Patrol* and he was on his way.

When the series ended in 1955, Ed went into movies playing in things like *The Spider* and *The Giant In Devil's Cave.* His best was as Dorothy Malone's alcoholic young husband in *Too Much, Too Soon* in 1958. Malone played Diana Barrymore with Errol Flynn as her father, John. "If the word charisma can ever be used, Flynn had it. He'd come on that set and everybody else would fade away. Magnetic."

Ed did his first soap opera, *Clear Horizons,* in 1964. When it was canceled he was brought to New York for a lead on *Edge of Night.* "That was where I met my wife Fran. We were married on the show and several years later got married for real." When that part ended Ed was ready to return to the West Coast but got on *The Doctors* and after that a long-running role on *As The World Turns* as an attorney. "So I've been doing soaps for ten years now. Never did get back West."

For several years Ed starred as Ben Grant on the excellent *Somerset,* playing opposite Georgeann Johnson. When the producers decided that because of its late-afternoon time slot the show should have younger characters, he was one of several who quickly "died off." (He 'died' while on a business trip to Germany.) It was a very dark day for viewers when *that* happened! He returned to *As The World Turns* in his old part and will shortly be back there for good in its new hour-long format.

He and Fran, who's semi-retired now to raise their family, live in a comfortable New York high-rise. They wed in 1969 and have two sons, Johnathon, three, and Todd, almost two. He's come a long way since his ray-gun days and seems a very happy man for it.

Tommy Kirk at a Hollywood
premiere in 1961 with
actress Sally Boyd

Eddie Colbert

TOMMY KIRK

Walt Disney made almost as many famous movie stars as
he did cartoon characters and one of the biggest and brightest
was Tommy Kirk—the round-faced, straight-haired All American Boy who debuted for Walt in 1957's *Old Yeller*—the classic
boy-and-dog tale. Disney demanded the same kind of off-screen
image as on, and until Kirk gave him reason to worry, he was
one of Disney's stable of young actors that included squeaky-
clean types like James MacArthur, Tim Considine, Annette
Funicello, Kevin Corcoran and Hayley Mills.

Tommy hailed from Louisville, Kentucky where he was born
in 1941, but from 1945 on lived in California after his family's
move there. He took part in school plays and showed enough
talent to land a small part in a Pasadena Playhouse production
—fertile ground for talent scouts—where a Disney agent saw
him and nabbed him for the *Hardy Boys* series a *Mickey Mouse
Club* serial with Tim Considine. It was enormously popular
with the afternoon subteen TV set and Disney knew he had
another young winner.

After *Yeller* came *The Shaggy Dog* (1959) which gave Tommy
his first chance to play himself and, through Disney magic,
the title role as well! In quick succession he made *Swiss Family
Robinson* (1960); *The Absent-minded Professor* (1960) with Fred
MacMurray, who was to fathers what Kirk was to sons in
Disney-ese; *Babes in Toyland* (1961) with Annette Funicello,
Ray Bolger and Tommy Sands; and *Bon Voyage* (1962) with
MacMurray and Jane Wyman.

Tommy would have liked more powerful roles but Disney
just didn't make that kind of movie so he continued in *Son
of Flubber* (1963), a sequel to *Absent-minded Professor,* and
The Misadventures of Merlin Jones, in 1963. Kirk ran afoul
of the Disney commandments after completing *The Monkey's
Uncle* (1965), a sequel to *Merlin,* when police found some pills
in the glove compartment of his car after a Hollywood party.

Tommy as he looks today

The studio hushed the whole thing up but scandal—or even the breath of it—and Disney didn't mix, and Kirk was let go. There was talk of another film plus appearances at Disneyland but neither came off.

Tommy was up a tree career-wise until American-International came to his rescue with their highly successful *Beach Party* pictures. Those teen-age epics of the Sixties were the salvation of several careers—Frankie Avalon and Annette Funicello for instance—and they were that for Tommy too. In 1965 he made *Pajama Party*, then *Ghost in the Invisible Bikini* in 1967, and *It's A Bikini World* in 1968. The roles weren't much different from his Disney days but he got a chance to work with character stars like Elsa Lanchester, Jesse White, and Buster Keaton.

Tommy knew too that the films weren't exactly establishing him as any kind of actor of repute, and he started to become a bit balky and temperamental. The studio wasn't having any part of that though, and he was let go, not working after completion of *The Catalina Caper* in 1968 until he got a small part in *Downhill Racer* two years later.

Tommy has never married and was rumored to have come out in favor of various underground causes before he left Hollywood in 1974. Since the movie industry didn't take him seriously he's decided to perfect his craft as an actor on his own. He's currently settled in Ohio—he doesn't want it known exactly where—and is working at a regional theater there experimenting by playing roles that Hollywood would never have given him a chance to do. Something, as he says, with a few teeth in them—which is a long and far cry from his tousle-haired Disney days (he did a total of twelve movies for Walt plus numerous television dramas on the Disney show), and the sexless and often witless beach party movies with their Technicolor vision of a life that was never even close to the real thing.

95

Frankie Laine calling out "Mule Train!"

FRANKIE LAINE

Singer Frankie Laine is a man who's lived to see the American Dream come true both for himself and his family. He was born in Chicago, March 30, 1913, as Frank Paul Lo Vecchio. His parents were immigrants to this country from Monreale, Sicily, and he was brought up to appreciate how lucky he was to have been born here. His father worked as a barber to support the family and had a few plans mapped out for his son too. He wanted him to become a pharmacist or an architect, but Frankie had other ideas. He was already singing in the choir of the neighborhood church, Immaculate Conception, and he liked the sounds that came out even if the material was a little ecclesiastic. Luckily he followed his head instead of his dad's advice and carved out one of the most distinctive popular singing careers in the process.

After graduating from Chicago's Lane Technical High School, Frankie headed West to California—talk about the American Dream—but landed lots of nothing jobs such as office boy, dancing instructor, bookkeeper, auto salesman and shipping clerk instead of singing engagements. His luck changed one day when he met Hoagy Carmichael at *Billy Bergs,* a musicians' hangout on Vine Street. He gave an on-the-spot audition for Carmichael who in turn was impressed enough to arrange a test record. That 'test record' turned into Frankie's first hit— *That's My Desire,* 1947. Its success put to rest many tough memories for Frankie, one of the toughest of which was when he and partner Ruth Smith danced for 3501 hours—the all-time marathon dance championship—from May 26 to October 18, 1932 in Atlantic City, New Jersey. They split a thousand dollar prize for their troubles!

Frankie broke into movies in 1950 with *When You're Smiling,* following it with 1951's *The Sunny Side Of The Street, Rainbow Round My Shoulder* (1952), and the bouncy *Bring Your Smile*

Frankie Laine today—a classy gent!

Along in 1955. He never quite clicked on the screen but was so busy getting out one hit record after another that it really didn't make much difference (*Mule Train, Swamp Fire* and others). In 1956 he attempted a straight dramatic role in *He Laughed Last,* but it didn't break his mold as a pop singer. He did much better singing the theme songs for movies like *Blowing Wild, Man Without A Star, Strange Lady in Town,* and *Gunfight at the OK Corral.* In fact he recently did another one, a takeoff on his old Mule Train image for Mel Brook's *Blazing Saddles.* (Brooks was looking for a Frankie Laine-type voice and got the real thing when Frankie showed up!)

In 1950 Frankie married former screen star Nan Grey (*Dracula's Daughter,* 1936; *Three Smart Girls,* 1936, etc.), and they have two daughters, Pam and Jan, by her previous marriage. In 1961 he and Nan hosted a lavish party in Las Vegas to help celebrate his parents' golden wedding anniversary, which was packed to the walls with every celebrity in town.

The couple and their family live in San Diego, California in an oceanfront house less than one hundred yards from where he keeps his boat docked. He's an avid boatsman after Nan introduced him to the sport and they spend a good deal of time sailing. In 1971 they expanded their hobby into a business venture by securing commerical fishing licenses.

Still a deeply religious man—besides singing in the church choir, he was also an altar boy—Frankie has promoted an annual *I Believe Day* in May as a day to reaffirm one's faith in God and the future. In many cities across the country it's become an annual event.

Around San Diego, the Laines are admired and respected for their interest in the arts. They collect silver and rare coins and have a growing painting collection. Frankie is also working on the organization of a San Diego Music Composers Festival in which new music writers will get a chance to showcase their compositions.

P.S.: If that *Manhandler's* soup commerical on TV sounds just like Frankie Laine, there's a good reason. It is.

Our Lady of the Sarong

DOROTHY LAMOUR

In camp movie circles, Dorothy Lamour will forever be our Lady of the Sarong—her signature costume in what seems like dozens of movies in the 1930s and '40s. A blue-collar goddess, she wasn't unattainable like counterparts Lamarr or Veronica Lake, but projected a wholesomely feminine sexiness, a breath of fresh air to a generation recovering from the silence of Garbo and the steely-eyed gaze of Dietrich. Sarong or no sarong, Dorothy was basically a good old-fashioned American girl, even if audiences didn't see her as such until well into her career.

Dottie was a radio singer with her own Los Angeles show when Paramount Pictures signed her for *The Jungle Princess* in 1935, having already been, among other things, an elevator operator at Chicago's Marshall Field department store and a singer with Herbie Kay, to whom she'd been briefly married. *Princess* was originally a B-budgeted programmer but after preview audiences started spreading the good word about Lamour, Paramount gave it A treatment, if not its star. After several years of mostly decorative parts, Sam Goldwyn picked her in 1938 to star in his gigantic *Hurricane* opposite Jon Hall, and in it she held her own nicely with pros like Mary Astor, Raymond Massey, C. Aubrey Smith and Thomas Mitchell. It was definitive sarong stuff and she followed it with *Her Jungle Love*—in this case Ray Milland—and others like *Spawn of the North*, 1939, with Henry Fonda; *Man About Town* with Jack Benny, 1939; and a part that played her up as a sulky moll with Tyrone Power in 1940's *Johnny Apollo*.

That was also the year she hit the *Road to Singapore* with, of course, Crosby and Hope. Much has been written about the comic chemistry of this trio and almost all of it is true. To watch the boys double-dealing each other for her favors while she languidly watches it all, an amused smile warming her lips, is still funny stuff. They made good music *and* good box office and over the years all three made successful trips on the

Dorothy in Hollywood recently

same roads to *Zanzibar* (1941), *Morocco* (the funniest) (1942), *Utopia* (1945), *Rio* (1947), and after a rest stop, *Bali*, in 1952.

She was in other films, too, like *Typhoon* (1940), *Chad Hanna*, with Fonda and Linda Darnell (1941), and lots of musical comedies which mainly called for her to look good and sing—*The Fleet's In* (1942); *Beyond the Blue Horizon* (1942), and *Rainbow Island* (1944) to name a few. Lamour was also one of World War II's most popular pinups, vying for barracks space with Betty Grable and Lana Turner. Little Dorothy Kaumeyer had come a long way since her reign as Miss New Orleans in 1931!

Later in the Forties script pickings became leaner and flicks like *Wild Harvest* (1947) with Alan Ladd, *Lulu Belle* (1948), a heavy-breathing costume outing with Otto Kruger, and *Slightly French* with Don Ameche in 1949, did little to add to Lamour's luster. After *Road to Bali,* she finished her main career with a small but starry part in DeMille's *Greatest Show On Earth*—doing the ultimate sarong parody as she sang *Lovely Lua Wane Lady,* "don't you ever be a-fraidy"—dressed in a plastic grass shirt and backed up by the entire Ringling Brothers, Barnum and Baily Circus!

She'd married businessman William Howard Ross in the Forties and decided that 1952 was a good year to retire and raise their sons, living quietly outside Baltimore, Maryland, until Hope and Crosby called her back for still another journey —the lukewarm *Road to Hong Kong* in 1961. The actual femme lead went to Joan Collins but critics agreed it should have been all Lamour.

When her sons were grown, Dottie and Bill moved back to California, settling in the San Fernando Valley near Bob Hope's home, where she expected to resume her career. In 1963 she was in *Donovan's Reef* and even appeared in a Beach Party flick, but otherwise the offers have been negligible. She was the best thing on a recent TV special about the making of a starlet and outshone all the nubile ladies in one scene alone, kiddingly putting her hands back into the cement prints at Grauman's Chinese Theater and smiling her warm smile—with not a sarong in sight!

Jesse Lasky Jr. and his first movie idol, Antonio Moreno, 1923

JESSE LASKY JR.

Being the son of one of the founders of the motion picture industry has not made life especially easy for Jesse Lasky Jr. Luckily he's been able to prove over the years that he has talent enough to 'overcome' the handicap a famous name can be and has etched his own corner in movie history as a screenwriter, primarily with the late Cecil B. DeMille. For *Samson And Delilah, Reap The Wild Wind, The Ten Commandments* and others, he's put the words into some of Hollywood's greatest stars even though his personal views on the place and the moguls who peopled it are a far cry from DeMille's florid vocabulary.

Lasky was born in New York in 1910 but grew up in the adolescent Hollywood that exists now only in the faded photographs of legendary people either dead or long forgotten. His father, Jesse Lasky Sr., made the first movie ever produced in Hollywood in 1913, *The Squaw Man,* in partnership with a failed New York actor, Cecil B. DeMille. That film virtually founded the multi-billion dollar industry of dreams known as Hollywood. Famous Players-Lasky Studios grew with the industry and as a child Jesse Jr. knew them all: Mary Pickford, Douglas Fairbanks, Charlie Chaplin, Gloria Swanson—all the people who helped create the definition of 'movie star'.

His own initiation into the movies was as an extra in the Fairbanks spectacle *The Thief of Baghdad* in 1922—holding a camel's reins! When he grew to young manhood he traveled extensively, envisioning a career as a poet—only to return to Hollywood in the late Thirties to find his father's empire, which had evolved into Paramount Pictues, crumbling. He struggled awhile and then went to see DeMille and was promised a job as a writer after supplying a line of dialogue for *The Buccaneer* (ironically the film marqueed in John Schlessinger's production

100

Jesse Lasky Jr. today

of Nathaniel West's black-eyed view of Hollywood, *The Day of the Locust*).

In 1939 he worked on the screenplay for *Union Pacific; Northwest Mounted Police* with Gary Cooper the following year; and in '41, *Reap The Wild Wind* with Ray Milland, John Wayne, Paulette Goddard and a budding star named Susan Hayward.

Throughout the Forties he scripted many films, most notably *Unconquered* in '48, and *Samson and Delilah* in '49—two blockbusting successes. In 1950, after a rift with the man who made movies for "De Millions", he went to Italy where he scripted Maria Montez' last film, *The Thief of Venice*. DeMille called him back to "wade in the Red Sea" with him in *The Ten Commandments* in 1956, and he did. But the industry had changed and after *Seven Women From Hell*—which started as an epic and ended up being shot in a public park with ten extras—he left Hollywood for good.

He and his third wife, Pat Silver, also a writer, live in London, where she is a partner in an antique miniature shop where, "if everyone's busy, I'll come out and take the stand." They recently partnered on *Ace Up My Sleeve,* a flick with Omar Sharif and Karen Black.

In his novel *Naked In A Cactus Garden,* Lasky Jr. gave a scathing inside look at Hollywood moguls and their machinations which, he admits, "was a composite of DeMille, Louis B. Mayer and my father." He also has a new one in mind based on letters between Lasky Sr. and DeMille—"one's father is always a ghost that must be exorcised." Partial exorcism at least has been accomplished with *Whatever Happened To Hollywood?,* an intimate glimpse into the lives, loves and laughs of the Golden Era of Movieland. On a recent trip to Hollywood, a news camera followed him around as he visited once-familiar landmarks of his life. At Malibu he kicked aside some refuse in a now-vacant lot and uncovered a portion of the tile floor that used to be the entrance to the family mansion—the legendary estate where Chaplin clowned, Pickford smiled and Valentino did the tango.

101

Frank and Jeanne Crain from 20th's *In The Meantime, Darling*

FRANK LATIMORE

Frank Latimore's classily lean good looks made him a favorite of the fan magazines and their bobbysoxed readers for several years during the Forties. Luckily for him most of the big male stars were still off to war in 1944 when he started his movie career, and he had a chance to shine in a movie uniform with Jeanne Crain in the pleasant hit *In The Meantime, Darling*. He was happiest—and most at home—out of uniform though, and until his departure for Italy several years later was 20th Century Fox's resident young-man-about-town.

Born Frank Kline on September 28th, 1925, he attended a series of proper New England schools during his youth, graduating from the Cherry Lane School in Darien, Connecticut. His first job in the theater, though, came by accident when after forgetting his wallet in a telephone booth on his way to New York, he arrived there with only two dollars to his name. The first work of any kind that he could land was in a tiny stock company where a talent scout happened to see him, giving him the 'in' he needed to continue his happenstance career. (His faulty memory was something even stardom didn't cure though—once he turned up to escort co-star June Haver to a premiere wearing a tuxedo and bedroom slippers!)

In The Meantime, Darling was a comedy directed by Otto Preminger which cast him as a soldier with Crain the 'rich girl' who has to make some heavy adjustments to the rough and tumble of Army barracks life after their marriage. Also in the cast was a young actor named Blake Edwards—shortly to leave that career for a more successful one as a producer and eventually as Julie Andrews' husband.

Fox liked the reaction Latimore received and cast him next in the lavish Technicolor biography of *The Dolly Sisters*, which

102

Frank Latimore today

starred Betty Grable and June Haver. It was the usual stuff of Hollywood biopics—over-glamourized and oversimplified in favor of a happy ending—but he was good as *Sister* June Haver's wealthy young husband. 1946 was his biggest year with roles in *Three Little Girls in Blue* (Vera-Ellen, Haver and Vivian Blaine), a let's-pool-our-money-and-pretend-one-sister's-rich comedy, and the powerful if wandering *Razor's Edge* with Tyrone Power and Anne Baxter.

Latimore went to Italy in 1947 to make *13 Rue Madeleine* with Jimmy Cagney and Annabella, and quickly fell in love with the country. While making *Black Magic* with Orson Welles, he found further reason to stay there when he met Valentina Nikitina, a Russian girl who'd worked as a nurse during the war and had joined her sister in Italy to study singing. They returned briefly to America to be married in Stamford, Connecticut, in 1948, but then went back to Rome where they made their home.

The post-war Italian movie industry was just then getting back on its feet and Latimore never lacked for work although his absence didn't help him in Hollywood. He didn't care though, and starred in numerous films including *Three Forbidden Stories* in 1950. When American productions started 'running away', he rejoined Hollywood moviemakers, most notably in 1959's expansive—and expensive—*John Paul Jones.* The closest he's gotten to a classic though was a role in the fascinating French thriller *Purple Noon,* the film that launched Alain Delon. He played O'Brien, one of Delon's victims.

If you looked closely, you could have seen Latimore in '67's *Cast A Giant Shadow;* 1969's *The Sergeant,* a muddled tale of homosexuality in the Army, which starred Rod Steiger and John Philip Law, and which featured Latimore as an Army captain; *If It's Tuesday This Must Be Belgium* in 1970; and *Patton* in 1972.

In 1975, back in New York, he was part of the original *Ryan's Hope* soap opera.

103

Jerry in his top TV days

JERRY LESTER

America's original late-night companion with his *Broadway Open House* show in the early Fifties, Jerry Lester's been keeping people chuckling ever since he turned to comedy after tearing a leg ligament which ruled out his original career of ballet dancing! He'd started studying ballet when he was thirteen and had also trained with operatic vocal coach Alexander Nakutin but after his accident, high class became low—and riotous—comedy, a lucky break for the Insomniac Set who brought him his greatest fame.

Chicago-born (1910) Lester's father was music critic for New York and midwest newspapers. Lester's original ambition was to pursue a classical career. While attending Northwestern University, though, he took whatever work he could find and started ad libbing at local fairs, gradually putting together the patter that earned him the tag of 'the talking comic'. He got so good at it that he once ad libbed through ten curtain calls and when Gus Edwards saw his takeoff of Ted Lewis, the university lost a student.

Radio was where the stars were being made in those days, and Jerry got a big break when in 1934 he started emceeing the *Rudy Vallee Show*, broadcasted from the old Hollywood restaurant. He guested on NBC's *Shell Chateau* and in 1940 got a show of his own, as summer replacement for Bob Hope. In 1941 he was back as a featured regular on the *Kraft Music Hall*. When he had the time, Jerry played all the top nightclubs from New York's Copacabana to the Chez Paree in Chicago and on to Ciro's in Hollywood. His rubber face and comic antics had reviewers creating new adjectives—just as they did again in 1950 when he started *Broadway Open House*.

Still pulling funny faces in 1975

Open House's zany cast of characters included Dagmar, of course, plus David Street, Wayne Howell, Ray Malone and Milton DeLugg and was, as Lester agrees, a far cry from its contemporary grandson, *The Tonight Show*. "I don't think you can compare it to *Broadway Open House*. I had a permanent cast that was more or less a comedy rep company. *The Tonight Show's* success is predicated on who shows up. Of course the band is fine, Johnny Carson is fine and so are most of the guests but actually as a unit they don't 'perform' together." For the next few years Jerry reigned supreme in his late-night spot, one of the few clouds on his horizon occuring in 1951 when his wife divorced him saying succinctly, "He's no joke."

But the changing complexion of the new industry bothered him. As it grew, his freedom as a performer came more and more under fire. In 1960 he was in the movie *The Rookie* with Peter Marshall and Tommy Noonan, but in 1963, when interviewed, reiterated the fact that television frustrated him—"you're an industry, not an act." For a while he had a production company in Canada and videotaped shows for broadcast there and abroad, but after *Open House* ended he didn't want another regular series.

In 1965 he toured the summer stock rounds in *A Funny Thing Happened On The Way to The Forum* and at 55 had amassed a tidy fortune in Florida real estate and Oklahoma oil. He and his second wife traveled among homes in Miama Beach, Oklahoma and Los Angeles, while he continued to turn down TV offers. In 1968 he toured with Ann Corio's *This Was Burlesque* and a year later worked with Guy Lombardo in his giant production of *South Pacific* at New York's Jones Beach.

His home base these days is North Miami, Florida and in 1974 he and Mickey Rooney partnered in producing and starring in *The Godmothers*. When I contacted him he was on the run as usual, this time to his place in the Ozark Mountains, but after saying it would take hours to tell all, added, "but to quote Steve Sondheim's score from *Follies*—'I'm still here'—and moving!"

Lilo at the time of *Can-Can*

LILO

When Lilo landed in New York in January of 1953 to star in Cole Porter's *Can-Can,* the press called her France's best export since champagne and the most fascinating lady since the Statue of Liberty! "At the time I was very happy about it," she says today. "I didn't speak a word of English so I thought it was very nice. Champagne, I knew what it meant and it was very lovely to be compared to it." At first glance her lack of English made it seem dubious casting, but some of Broadway's biggest brains got together to make one of the Mainstem's all-time hits. "Abe Burrows (who wrote the book and directed the musical) spoke Yiddish and I spoke high school German to him. That's how we got the show together. I was in Paris at the time of the liberation yet I never met an American until I got my visa to come here!"

Though unknown here the Parisian-born actress was already a star in France, appearing in *Chanteur De Mexico* when she got the call "from a Monsieur Fooyah (producer Cy Feuer) backstage one night. I thought he was a stage door johnny! I didn't hear from him again for three months until I got a cable saying 'Please fly over to discuss new Cole Porter musical' so I came in four days time from Paris to New York, auditioned in New York in the afternoon, took a plane out to California, overnight—it took sixteen hours then—auditioned for Cole Porter, went back to New York that evening, signed the contract and then went back to Paris for my show. It was like a fairy tale story. I never thought I would come to the States to work."

After a tryout in Philadelphia, *Can-Can* opened in New York to rave reviews making Lilo an overnight sensation. Her co-stars were Peter Cookson, Hans Conried, Gwen Verdon and Erik

Jon B. Araneo

Lilo in her New York apartment with author

Rhodes and the show ran for 912 performances, a record in those days. "Somebody is still buying the album too because I still get a little check once in a while. And it can't be my mother, she doesn't live here!"

After *Can-Can* finally ended, Lilo appeared at smart supper clubs in the U.S. and her native France, making lots of money and one big mistake. "*Irma la Douce* was written for me, but the theater they wanted to do it in was very tiny and my salary would only have been the French equivalent of about $8.50 and I had been accustomed to dollars so I thought I would pass this one up. What a mistake! But you know what? I played it here, later, for years and years on the circuit, big towns, little towns—name it! It always reminds me of Noel Coward who told me he turned down *My Fair Lady* because he thought *Pygmalian* had had it!"

On New Year's Eve in 1961 she and her husband, the Marquis Guy de la Passadiere, were caught in Havana in Castro's revolution! We were on the town with Rubirosa and Ambassador Earl Smith, people like that, cha-cha-ing at George Raft's when it started. I thought it was firecrackers." Lilo promptly enchanted the machine gun-toting soldiers and has several photos with them to prove it—one even autographed. It took her a while to get out of the country but she kept busy cooking in the Hilton Hotel kitchen.

She hasn't worked since 1967. "I was in a show called *Pousse Cafe* and we had a tremendous, resounding flop. I vowed I would never set foot on a stage again, which I meant at the time, but now I sometimes think, 'How dumb was I,' but it's too late." She has, however, appeared in two recent Claude Lelouch movies, *Happy New Year* and *And Now My Love,* "but only for thirty seconds. When I want to go home I call them and say 'pay me and I come for thirty seconds.' I have a marvelous time." Her husband imports French movies and Lilo herself loves to go to them. They've been married since 1952 and are extremely happy—but who wouldn't be with the most fascinating Frenchwoman since the Statue of Liberty.

Babe and Stan Laurel
in an early comedy

BABE LONDON

The fraternity of actors is a marvelously close-knit clan that's often unexplainable to us 'civilians'. Friendships started on a movie set or a stage may lapse for years once the production's finished, yet the camaraderie remains. When Babe London, the comedienne of the silent screen who shared celluloid with everyone from Charlie Chaplin to W. C. Fields, married Phil Boutelje in March of 1975 at the John Ford Chapel on the grounds of the Motion Picture Country Home in Woodland Hills, California, that camaraderie was very much in evidence. Mary Astor was there in a rare public appearance as was another screen veteran, Viola Dana, and it was indeed a day for celebration and renewed friendships as the bride and groom repeated their vows.

Babe's career never reached the heights of Miss Astor's or Miss Dana's yet on that sunny day in March all past name-above-the-title considerations were forgotten as the wedding party rode the decorated electric tram from the main building to the chapel. The smiles and toasts were totally real, belying Hollywood's reputation for being an insensitive town and while that myth may persist, it surely doesn't exist in the world of the old pros.

Babe has been living at the Home for the past fourteen years—"I was ill, my family was all dead and I thought I better go out there before I fell on my face"—and had known Phil a year before they married. "I'd been married twice before and we both said we'd never do it again but God changed our minds." Phil had worked for thirty-five years at Paramount Studios, eventually heading up the Music Department and earning two Oscar nominations, for *The Great Victor Herbert* (1939) and *Hi Diddle Diddle* (1943), before his retirement. In his youth he'd played the organ in a local movie house and many's the night he played accompaniment for the Christie Comedies of the Early Twenties—one of whose stars was Babe London!

Mary Astor, Phil Boutelje, Babe and Viola Dana at Babe and Phil's wedding reception

From those, including *Winter has Come* (1924) and *Hula Honeymoon,* filmed on location in Hawaii, she went on to star with Chaplin in *A Day's Pleasure* to *All Aboard* (1927) with Johnny Hines and Anna May Wong, to *The Fortune Hunter* in '28, to *Our Wife* with Laurel and Hardy. The sequence where the three of them plus their luggage try to get into an Austin auto is a classic. Along the way Babe also bounced her comic charms off Fatty Arbuckle and Buster Keaton, and co-starred with W. C. Fields and Chester Conklin in the second version of *Tillie's Punctured Romance.*

After movies, she tackled vaudeville but strong ties remained as evidenced by her reaction to Mack Sennett's funeral in 1960. "I was sitting there next to Louise Fazenda, looked around—all the remaining Keystone Cops were honorary pallbearers—and thought 'this is the passing of the Silent Screen' and I decided to paint it—The Vanishing Era *by* one of The Vanishing Era." Fifty-eight of her portraits of the comics and stars of that era now hang at the University of Wyoming. When Merv Griffin did a tribute to the Silent Screen, he called Babe and once, before she met Phil, she guested on *The Dating Game.*

At this writing, Babe is seventy-three years old and her husband eighty. They live in a small cottage on the grounds of the Motion Picture Country Home which, by the way, is supported by public and industry donations. He's battling arthritis in one hand but has recovered enough "to play beautifully, it's like a miracle. We have a private patio next to the cottage and Phil plays mood music for me on his organ while I paint." His composition, *China Boy,* is part of the famous *Benny Goodman Carnegie Hall Concert* album, and pro that he is, he put together the wedding music "just like he'd score a movie. As the tram pulled up to the chapel the song was *Get Me To The Church On Time.*"

"We're both very creative and we complement each other. It's just wonderful. We're working on a project now combining his music and my art. I can't tell anymore about it other than that it's a humdinger." And when Babe says it, you believe her.

A pleading Danny Thomas with Seldon Leonard and Marjorie from *The Danny Thomas Show*

MARJORIE LORD

Televison's model wife on the *Danny Thomas Show*, Marjorie Lord, like Donna Reed, Pat Breslin of *The Jackie Cooper Show* and Marjorie Reynolds of *Life of Riley* fame, combined the wisest attributes of the All-American Mrs., molding them into a warmly feminine portrait that may not have had much to do with real life but which was just the ticket for her video family. Actually she was Danny's second TV wife. Jean Hagen —most famous for her silent movie star part in *Singin' In the Rain*—was the first, with Marjorie taking over the household reins in 1957, four years after the show's debut as *Make Room for Daddy*. She was so good at it though that when the show finally ended in 1964 she found herself hopelessly typecast as Danny's wife.

Marjorie's dramatic training came at the Sarah Dix Hamlins Finishing School in San Francisco (where she was born on July 26, 1922) but she didn't get much of a chance to use it until her family moved to New York City. Once there she auditioned in earnest and won the role of the ingenue in *The Old Maid*, replacing the girl who'd opened in the part. That was in 1935 and after its run she played in various summer stock companies coming back to Broadway in the hit *Stage Door*, followed by *Springtime for Henry* in 1940, and shortly thereafter *The Male Animal*, another hit— and also where she met her first husband John Archer, the *Male* lead.

Movie director Henry Koster saw Marjorie in the show and optioned her talents for Universal Studios—the beginning of a haphazard movie career which kicked off with *Forty Naughty Girls* in 1938, hardly a title role! Her fresh good looks were utilized strictly for support over the next few years in items like *Timber, Moonlight in Havana* and *Sherlock Holmes in*

110

Marjorie Lord
as she looks today

Washington among others. In 1943 she left Universal to star with Jimmy Cagney in *Johnny Came Lately,* her first big role, and followed it with Duvivier's *Flesh and Fantasy* the same year. Marjorie worked for all the studios through the Forties, stopping at United Artists in 1947 for *New Orleans* and at Paramount for *Riding High,* a Dorothy Lamour vehicle in 1950, but television was to bring her her greatest success. Marshall Grant, who'd produced several of her Universal epics, was starting his own production company, Grant-Realm, to produce the Lucky Strike cigarette TV show and Marjorie was the first actress he signed. She appeared for him with hubby Archer in *The Real Thing* and *Confession on New Year's Eve,* but off screen things were less successful and they divorced in 1953 with her keeping their children, Anne and Gregg. She decided to stick to televison and during the next few years chalked up credits on everything from *Four Star Playhouse* to *Fireside Theater.* Her one excursion back to the movie cameras was for 1954's *Port of Hell.*

1957 saw Marjorie with two new husbands—producer Randolph Hale in real life and Thomas in the series renamed simply *The Danny Thomas Show.* Tiny Angela Cartwright was added to the cast and teen-ager Sherry Jackson began to be slowly written out, but Marjorie's replacing another actress in a well-identified part wasn't entirely a bed of roses. "When I started the show it was like starting a real second marriage. There was a lot of ghosts to fight just as any person marrying for the second time has to fight." Audiences—and Marjorie—got over the wife swap though and she reigned happily until the show's demise in 1964.

Unfortunately her All-American Mom was so good that "producers only see me as Danny's wife." Luckily with reruns of the show she's never complained too loudly and in 1966 returned briefly to the screen as Bob Hope's wife in *Boy, Did I Get A Wrong Number.* Still happily married, she occasionally tours in summer stock and yes, she usually plays a mother.

111

Bessie sporting the patent leather curl, a minor rage of the Twenties

BESSIE LOVE

Bessie Love was one of the most 'discovered' actresses in movies. D. W. Griffith, Thomas Ince, Paramount Pictures and Metropolitan Pictures (later part of MGM) all "Columbused" her—as press releases at the time put it—at one point or another in the helter skelter days of early Hollywood. Bessie was initially celebrated for playing child roles and after many of them got her first featured part in Griffith's *Intolerance* (1915) when she was seventeen. She grew up some more the following year as a Swedish maid in *The Flying Torpedo* and went on to become one of the Twenties' most popular stars in pictures like *The Aryan* (1916); *A Sister of Six* (1917); *Nina The Flower Girl* (1917); *The Purple Dawn* (1920); *Forget Me Not* (1922); *Human Wreckage* (1923) and *Dynamite Smith* (1924). Unfortunately those parts were all cut from the same poor-little-girl cloth and vivacious Bessie got discouraged with her film luck in 1927 and left the screen to star in the San Francisco company of *Burlesque*. It was a wise move for when Talkies came in shortly afterwards she'd built a new reputation as a singer/comedienne and moved right back into the movies in Metro-Goldwyn-Mayer's *original Broadway Melody* (1929) with a whole new career before her.

Though born in Midland, Texas in 1898, Bessie, then Jaunita Horton, grew up in Los Angeles, a sprawling patchwork of orange groves and unpaved city streets. The reason she was discovered so often was because in those days the studios were little more than barns, and pictures were made so quickly that one week she'd be at Triangle and the next at Paramount. Happily though everyone's verdict was the same—Bessie had the stuff that box office attractions were made of.

After the success of *Broadway Melody*, MGM put her into a string of early musicals like *The Hollywood Revue of 1929, Road Show* (1930) and *Chasing Rainbows* (1930). In 1929 her

112

Bessie in London recently

good friend Mary Astor teased her into admitting her secret six month engagement to William Hawks, an actor she'd originally met five years before and with whom she'd had an on-again, off-again romance which finally ended in marriage in December of 1929. They had a daughter Patricia, now an actress, and remained married until 1935.

After she separated from Hawks, Bessie upped and left Hollywood to settle in London, joining other expatriate stars like Bebe Daniels and Ben Lyon. Her movie appearances over there, in things like *Atlantic Ferry* (1942); *Journey Together* (1945); and *Touch and Go* (1955), saw her gradually grow away from top stardom to becoming one of the busiest and most popular character actresses.

In 1958 she wrote a play, *The Homecoming,* about a Hollywood star who returns to America after a long sojourn in England. Based on a visit she herself made in 1951, it opened in Perth, Scotland and was poorly received, although Bessie, as its star, was deemed "delightful and completely natural." In 1961 she played Vivien Leigh's maid in *The Roman Spring of Mrs. Stone,* a tragic tale of an aging actress. Unfortunately when it plays on television now, Miss Love's scenes, all part of a theater sequence that comes before the opening credits of the film, are usually cut.

For a good actress, though, there are always parts, and Bessie had a lot of them. In 1964 she was in *The Wild Affair,* and four years later tellingly played Vanessa Redgrave's mother in *The Loves of Isadora,* often perplexed by her rebellious daughter's actions yet always steadfast despite them. In 1971 she appeared in *Catlow,* a Western with Yul Byrnner and in 1973 got her best role in years in the lavishly produced London stage version of *Gone With The Wind.* She played Aunt Pittypat in it, the fluttery relative constantly scandalized by niece Scarlett O'Hara. In real life, though, she's not fluttery at all, but a total professional who has spanned every generation of the movies so far and has no intention of stopping now.

Earl with a gown he designed for 1933's *Cavalcade*

EARL LUICK

"One night I woke up and the television was still on and a woman was walking across the screen. I thought her dress looked familiar and as I looked closer I knew why. It was Jean Harlow wearing an outfit I designed for her in one of her first pictures, *Public Enemy,* with James Cagney." When Earl Luick talks about his experiences in the golden days of Hollywood, his talk is peppered with the names of the great glamour queens of the time— Loretta Young, Dorothy Mackail, Joan Blondell, Ginger Rogers, Diana Wynyard, Maureen O'Hara —all ladies whose costumes he designed for various pictures during a career which stretched from De Mille's *King of Kings* in 1925 to Betty Grable's *Springtime In The Rockies* in 1942.

Luick landed in Hollywood from his home town of Eugene, Oregon in 1922 as an admitted movie fan who quite simply wanted to work in the business. He moved into a boarding house filled with aspiring actors and for a time thought he might like to be one himself. He learned just how difficult that would be though after getting a job as an extra—by standing on a rock so he'd look taller!—in Douglas Fairbanks' *Robin Hood.* For one full day he stood atop a plaster of paris parapet dressed in a suit of armor in the broiling California sun. Not wanting to chance losing his street clothes in the huge extras' dressing room, he'd put the armor on over them. By day's end all desire to become an idol of the silver screen had perspired away.

Naturally talented in design, he got a huge break several years later by landing a job to work with Adrian and Gwen Wakeling designing the immense wardrobe for Cecil B. DeMille's *King of Kings.* One of the biggest hits of 1925—it's still shown often today—it helped get him a job at Warner Brothers where among many other films he designed the clothes

114

Earl Luick in 1975

for *Public Enemy* (1930)—yes, he's the man who did the fur-trimmed robe for Mae Clarke that got spattered by Cagney's grapefruit—and George Arliss' *Disraeli*. He was there when Joan Blondell first came West and on front office orders designed a foundation that would make her buxom figure more sylphlike. Said Blondell when she saw it, "Listen, Buster, my can got me into pictures and my can's going to stay in pictures!"

One of the greatest designing experiences in Luick's crowded career was 1933's *Cavalcade,* which he refers to "as the *Upstairs, Downstairs* of its time." The research and zeal with which he captured the Edwardian period as inspired by Noel Coward's play is still considered a highwater mark in movie design. That same year he designed *Zoo in Budapest* with Loretta Young and Gene Raymond, "who must have studied early method acting since he continually stalked around the studio in the panther character he played in the film."

At 20th Century Fox in the early Forties, Luick experienced firsthand the changes the movie industry was undergoing and after designing *The Black Swan* with Tyrone Power and Maureen O'Hara and *Springtime In The Rockies* with Betty Grable, John Payne, Cesar Romero and Carmen Miranda, both in 1942, he left the movie business for a career on New York's Seventh Avenue. Partially completed when he left were two more big pictures, *Coney Island,* again with Grable, and *Hello Frisco, Hello* with Alice Faye. The credit for those went to the man who followed him in his job as studio designer. An innovator, he left many techniques behind him that helped his successors, including processes to photograph clothes in Technicolor, a problem in movies' early days.

After several years in New York's garment industry, Luick went into the antique business and today runs one of the smartest shops in the city. He splits his time between New York and a delightful house in East Hampton. A charming and gracious man, he remembers Hollywood and the days when he worked there—at one time being named to the *Best Dressed Men In America List*— with humor, but feels that the secret to a full life is change. He doesn't regret leaving Lotusland; he is working on a book about it though, just to set the record straight.

115

Jock Mahoney in cowboy garb, 1955

Jack Kuster

JOCK MAHONEY

Hollywood has always had a place for the Big Men, those super-virile types who inevitably ride rough-shod through adventure movies clad in tight buckskins or chaps, or even a few Indian feathers (a Fifties favorite, Hugh O'Brien, got his start that way). Occasionally, like Jock Mahoney for instance, they even get a crack at that high water mark of movie masculinity, Tarzan.

Between Jock's birth as Jacques O'Mahoney (thanks to his Irish-French-Cherokee Indian parents) in Chicago in 1919 and his takeover as the screen's 13th Tarzan in *Tarzan Goes to India,* were forty-three years of a life which aptly readied him for the vigorous requirements of his movies roles.

Weighing in at 200 pounds ever since his teen-age years as a star athlete at the University of Iowa, Jock covered a lot of ground before he finally hit Hollywood. There was a stint in the Marines where he was quickly made a fighter pilot instructor, and afterwards he taught swimming, horseback riding, and had a brief whirl as a dance instructor.

When he did get to Tinseltown in 1950, it wasn't the tinsel he was interested in but a career as a movie stuntman—those rough and ready talents that have been the foundation of many a matinee idol's reputation since the movies first moved—and with his 6' 4'' physique and ruggedly chiseled face, he had no trouble getting started.

After years of doubling for screen heroes, Jock got his first real role in 1956 with *Away All Boats,* followed by a bit part in the Rock Hudson starrer *Battle Hymn,* and, that same year, got star billing in *Showdown at Abilene,* a modest oater which featured Martha Hyer. Next came the lead in a science fiction

116

Jock with old *Range Rider* co-star Dick Jones at Stuntman's Ball

epic, *The Land Unknown,* 1957, and Jock was firmly established as one of Universal Studios' strong silent types with, hopefully, some of the stuff that stars like Randolph Scott were made of.

He married starlet Margaret Field and they had a daughter whimsically named Princess Melissa. Margaret's two children by a previous marriage lived with them in their sprawling ranch house. In 1958 Jock was down the cast roster in *A Time To Love, A Time To Die* (the movie that introduced John Gavin), but he came up again with a popular television series *Yancey Derringer.* (He'd also been briefly in another, *Range Rider.*) In *Derringer* his trademark was the pistol packed in his hat and audiences liked it for several seasons.

He took over the role of Tarzan in 1962 with *Tarzan Goes to India* after having supported a previous tree-swinger, Gordon Scott, in his last time out on the vine in *Tarzan The Magnificent,* in 1960. (Between Scott and Mahoney came Denny Miller, a one-timer in a straight MGM remake, *Tarzan the Ape Man,* which flopped.) Jock's Tarzan was a more contemporary version with the forty-three year-old star bringing a new maturity to the part, different from what had ever been done before. Filmed in India, Jock got plenty of chances to utilize his physical skills, getting his elephant speed up to 35 mph at one point. "They can go forty when they're really scared!" The film was a hit and in 1964 he swung again in *Tarzan's Three Challenges.*

Divorced and remarried, Jock's career has been an iffy one in the Seventies. He's popped up on *Streets of San Francisco* and other TV-ers, but his last feature movie was a low-budget item called *Tom* which has never been released. Though he maintains a California address, he's seldom there.

Dorothy and other Fifties blond, Tab Hunter, on the town in Hollywood

Pictorial Parade

DOROTHY MALONE

Dorothy Malone is an example of the kind of actress who started off in B movies—mostly two-week Westerns with plenty of pinafores and pitiful dialogue—and stayed there primly and properly until the right role came along to change not only her hair color but her image as well. Overnight, with the release of 1956's Texas soap opera *Written On The Wind*, she went from reliable second leads to movie stardom as the lustful, hard-drinking Texas heiress determined to chalk up a past if it killed her! She was so good that on-screen she was able to temporarily tempt Rock Hudson away from Lauren Bacall, and off-screen to walk away with the Best Supporting Actress Oscar.

In a way her role in *Wind* was a homecoming since she was raised in Texas (she'd been born in Chicago as Dorothy Maloney on January 30th, 1924). When she was three her family moved to Dallas and in high school she won stage acting honors and scholarships enabling her to go to Hockaday Junior College and eventually to Southern Methodist University. An athletic girl, she was on the swimming and diving teams but managed to be in enough college productions to be onstage the night an RKO Studio scout was in the audience. He gave her her ticket to Hollywood.

The next year was spent on the studio lot studying dancing and diction—but getting nowhere within camera range. Finally they debuted the 5'7", brown-haired beauty in *The Falcon and the Coeds* and also cast her in Eddie Cantor's line-up in *Show Business* (1944). Warner Bros. stepped in then and signed her up for *The Big Sleep* (1946) with Bogie and Bacall in which she gave audiences a sexy peek at what was to come ten years later. The studio was impressed and started building her as a sweet young thing in pictures like *Night and Day* (1946); *Janie Gets Married*, the same year; *One Sunday Afternoon* (a remake of *Strawberry Blonde* with Malone in the Olivia DeHa-

Dorothy as she looks in her latest film, *Abduction*

villand part) (1948); and *South of St. Louis* in which she was a girl fought over by rival ranchers Joel McCrea and Randolph Scott.

The early Fifties saw her cast in things like *Convicted* (1950); *Slade* (1953); *Pushover* (1954); the one that made Kim Novak a star, *Young at Heart* (1954); and *Battle Cry* (1955), as one of the girls waiting for her man to get home from the war.

In 1955 she got the co-starring role with Liberace in his screen debut, *Sincerely Yours*. It laid a very big egg, his candelabras not withstanding. Career-wise Dorothy was in trouble and when she was offered *Written on the Wind,* she grabbed it. The producers dyed her hair a bright blonde and dressed her appropriately as the emotion-driven daughter of an unsavory Texas clan. Bob Stack played her troubled brother, Bacall his wife, and Hudson everybody's best friend.

Hollywood immediately cast her as a bad girl again opposite Jimmy Cagney in the biopic of Lon Chaney's life called *Man of A Thousand Faces* (1957). As in *Wind,* she wound up properly burned out and chastened by the film's end. The same fate awaited her in her next film too, the bio of Diana Barrymore, *Too Much, Too Soon* (1958), with Errol Flynn outstanding as her father John. She was reteamed with Hudson and Stack in *Tarnished Angels* but it wasn't much, and she turned sweet again as Stack's wife in *The Last Voyage* (1960), a sinking ship saga. The picture sank too despite the producers' efforts to make it a biggie by buying the old liner *Ile de France* and destroying it for the film's climax.

In 1959 Dorothy was married for the first time to French actor Jacques Bergerac, a former Mr. Ginger Rogers. They had two daughters but divorced in 1964, the year she began the *Peyton Place* TV series. In 1969 she was married again briefly but it was annulled. In 1971 she wed Huston Bell, a businessman, and until recently they lived in Dallas. Dorothy's back in Hollywood now and there's talk about a new TV series. She's made a new film called *Abduction*, and maybe things are looking up for her again.

119

Enid as a brown-haired sweetheart of the silent screen

ENID MARKEY

When Enid Markey agreed to appear in *Tarzan Of The Apes* with Elmo Lincoln way back in 1918, it's doubtful that she realized she was starting a movie tradition. She had been a star since *The Darkening Trail* with William S. Hart in 1915 and if she thought the role of the ape man's girlfriend was a little offbeat, it wasn't any more so than some of her other roles had been, having already appeared as a Hawaiian princess in *Aloha Oca*, an Indian maiden in *The Aztec God*, and a Mexican cabaret dancer in *The Fugitive*. ("I did that whole picture with a rose between my teeth, dancing constantly.") When she did it, the "Me Tarzan, You Jane" line was only a subtitle but like Vivien Leigh after *Gone With The Wind*, the fame of the role has stuck down through years that have seen her do everthing from playing the manicurist in the original Broadway production of *The Women* in 1936, to being victimized by Tony Curtis in *The Boston Strangler* thirty-two years later. The enormous success of *Tarzan* and its follow-up, *The Romance of Tarzan* (in which she got out of her tailor-made duds and into a leopard skin) prompted a five-year contract offer but Enid wanted to act, not swing from trees, and despite the advice of everybody she knew, left Hollywood and headed for New York.

A native of Dillon, Colorado, she'd first gone to Hollywood with her mother to become a stage actress (California was closer than New York) and enrolled herself in the Egan Drama School before she'd unpacked her bags. She did a bit in a movie but didn't think much about it until later when she was contacted by producer Thomas Ince, who was unabashedly attracted to her long black curls, huge dark eyes and stark white skin. Ince put her into *Darkening Trail* with Hart and overnight she became a leading lady—even though at the end of *Trail* she sailed off

120

Enid's latest portrait

into the Klondike sunset clinging to a cake ice! Until she left in 1918 she was one of the busiest girls in Hollywood.

Landing in New York after quitting Lotusland and its synthetic jungles, she promptly got the lead in the classic comedy *Up In Mabel's Room* as the crybaby bride. A long-running hit, it made her the first screen queen to make the transition to Broadway star.

For the next forty-four years she was a constant face on the Mainstem, starring in plays like *Barnum Was Right* (1923); *The Blonde Sinner* (1926); *Here Goes The Bride* (1928); *The Women* (1936); *Ah Wilderness* (1941); *Mrs. McThing* (1952); *Only In America* (1959), and her last, 1963's *The Ballad Of The Sad Cafe*.

In 1960 she co-starred with another veteran actress, Doro Merande, in *Bringing Up Buddy* with Frank Aletter, a CBS comedy which cast her as fluttery Aunt Violet. She was happy to give the series grind a whirl but couldn't help remarking that compared to silent movies, it was a picnic. "In those days they expected an actress to also be able to do her own stunts. In this, the most strenuous thing I do is lift a teacup."

In 1942 Enid married businessman George W. Cobb Jr. and they set up housekeeping at the Algonquin Hotel, that bastion of showfolks. After he died in a car crash in '48, she stayed on there but spent the summer months at a Fire Island beach house. "I guess some of the Tarzan atmosphere did stay with me. When I took the house it was completely isolated in a very primitive seaside setting. Now there are other houses around but for years I kept up the primitive spirit by not having a telephone."

In February of 1973 Enid broke her hip and spent a good deal of time in a hospital and later in a nursing home. When she left it she was walking without crutches and has recovered completely, as she has from two cataract operations. She resides in New York with friends, John and Marjorie Schell, but still summers at Fire Island. Happily she's maintained her independent spirit, not to mention her bubbly laugh. The Tarzan memories, though, are, to her, frankly becoming a bit of a bore.

121

Massey at his best—the sneer
you loved to hate!

RAYMOND MASSEY

Oddly enough Raymond Massey achieved his greatest fame
by playing both pitch-black villains and Abraham Lincoln! He
only played Lincoln once in *Abe Lincoln In Illinois* (1939) but
his larger than life realization of the man made it seem as though
the Civil War president himself had been captured on film,
an unforgettable portrait. Canadian-born (Toronto, August 30,
1896), Massey's acting career took him initially to London
where, before he got his first decent part, he played end man
in minstrel shows donning blackface at the drop of a line. New
Yorkers first saw him in a stage version of *Hamlet* imported
here in 1931, and America at large got its first gander at the
tall, saturnine actor that same year when he starred as Sherlock
Holmes in *The Speckled Band.* Noble characters both, yet
Hollywood soon sensed his photographic quality of villainy,
and beginning with *The Scarlet Pimpernel* in 1934, he began
a memorable career as perhaps the Thirties' most slippery
character, rivaled only by Basil Rathbone, another serious stage
actor, who also got Hollywood-pegged as a heavy.

Over the next few years Massey was constantly working and
happily much of what he did is still around; the best of its
kind, story, production *and* star-wise, were: *Fire Over England*
(1937) with Vivien Leigh and Laurence Olivier; the elaborate
Prisoner of Zenda (1937) with Madeleine Carroll, Ronald Coleman and Mary Astor; *The Hurricane,* (1939) Sam Goldwyn's
epic with Dorothy Lamour, Jon Hall and Thomas Mitchell,
with Massey the steely-eyed island governor; and of course,
Abe Lincoln In Illinois. (He proved just as effective as an American fanatic, John Brown, in *Sante Fe Trail* the following year.)

The Forties brought World War II and with it an entirely new
cast of characters for Massey to frighten with his villainy. As a
Nazi undercover agent, he scared the wits out of Nancy Coleman

Eddie Colbert

Raymond Massey today

in *Dangerously They Live* (1941) until John Garfield came along to rescue her, and did so again in *Desperate Journey* in 1942 despite the concerted efforts of Errol Flynn and Ronald Reagen.

DeMille—always used to the best—cast him as a white slaver in 1942's *Reap The Wild Wind,* giving him scenery aplenty to chew and toothsome Paulette Goddard to terrorize. He did both in his usually distinctive manner. A rare foray into comedy was 1944's *Arsenic and Old Lace,* playing the role Boris Karloff had originated on the stage. He and Peter Lorre were creepily hilarious in the zany tale of two old ladies, their crazy brother, and their nephew, played by Cary Grant, who tries to cover the effects of their deadly elderberry wine.

In *Mourning Becomes Electra* (1947), he was Roz Russell's father and met his match in that lady for making the most of what was already too much Eugene O'Neill. It flopped, but not because the cast didn't try hard—and maybe that was the trouble. Joan Crawford got *Possessed* over him in 1947 and Patricia Neal didn't fare much better as his daughter in *The Fountainhead* two years later.

The Fifties saw the Massey face mostly swathed in desert turbans—*David And Bathsheba* (1951) with Susan Hayward and Gregory Peck; *The Desert Song* (1953); and *Omar Khayyam* (1957). But there were also some goodies mixed in *Battle Cry* (1955); *Prince of Players,* as Edwin Booth Sr. (1955); and *East of Eden* that same year.

As crochety Dr. Gillespie in the long-running TV series *Dr. Kildare* (1961-65), he became one of television's most familiar faces. It was an enormous hit thanks as much to him as young Richard Chamberlain, and it brought him to the attention of a whole new teen-age audience. Since it ended, his appearances have been relatively few—a notable exception was 1968's *McKenna's Gold*—but his son Daniel Massey, from his second marriage (to Adrianne Allen), has worked hard to keep up an already well-distinguished name. Virtually inactive due to a severe arthritic condition, Massey now walks with a cane. Married since 1939 to Dorothy Whitney, he lives in Hollywood, the thick hair whiter now, but the overall demeanor as rockjawed as ever.

Tim with a young fan in the early Forties

TIM McCOY

"Old cowboy stars never really die—they're too tough and egotistical to slip out of the public's eye. They only fade away by riding off into the sunset for the last time." Veteran cowboy star Tim McCoy said that in 1973 but since then he's changed his mind and ended his fifty-year career as a Western star. "I'm eighty-four, I guess I've earned the right to rest a little," he says now. "I'm living in the Mexican hacienda I built here in Nogales and I'm relaxing for the first time in years." Since it's a recent decision, it's still too early to know if he really likes it or instead misses the life of horses and hoopla that he's known so well for so long.

Tim decided what he liked to do best as a child in Saginaw, Michigan where he was born in 1891. "Those were the horse and buggy days and the horses were all brought from the West by real cowboys," and as soon as he was old enough, Tim wanted to be one of them. After college, he followed his childhood dream to the then wide-open spaces, settling in Lander, Wyoming. "Cattle still drifted on the ranges then and I found work on a ranch pitching hay. But when they found out I could already ride and rope, I became a working cowboy."

Indians still roamed then too and in the Wind River area he came in contact with the Arapaho and Shoshone tribes, learning their language so well that the Arapahoes eventually adopted him, naming him High Eagle. His interest in the Old West has never slackened, and today, at his sprawling ranch near Nogales, Arizona, Tim maintains a vast library of Indian lore and personal souvenirs.

124

Still firm-jawed at eighty-three

World War I broke into his cowboy life, and he served as a cavalryman in Europe, winning several medals in the process and rising to the rank of colonel. After the war he served with General Hugh Lenox Scott in the Dakotas and Oklahoma and his life was falling handily into place until the day he crossed paths with a movie company on location to shoot *The Covered Wagon* (1926), one of the first big westerns. Tim did some stunt work for them as well as playing a part and was immediately hooked on acting. So impressed were the producers that they starred him in their next western, *War Paint* (1926), and cast him opposite a very young Joan Crawford.

Over the next forty years, he was featured in a total of 97 movies, his last on-screen appearance being in 1966 when he co-starred in *Requiem For A Gunfighter* with Rod Cameron. Do movies *really* tell it like it was in the Old West? "The West depicted by films," he says, "is a living, breathing American myth. Even those long drawn out fistfights of John Wayne's are absurd when compared to the short but violent brawls of the real cowboys. Why, no normal man could withstand such punishment in real life."

Married twice, he had two sons and a daughter by his first wife, whom he divorced in 1945. Later that same year he married a Danish journalist, Inga Arvad, who happened to be the first reporter to interview him after he returned from service in World War II. In that war too he distinguished himself in combat—minus horses this time—and in the early Fifties he won an Emmy for an educational television show he'd researched.

His favorite cowboy of them all was the late Buck Jones, killed in the tragic Coconut Grove fire in Boston in 1942. According to Tim, he was "the best all-around western film star of us all. He had the looks, the voice, the charisma—everything it takes. He died while trying to rescue people from the fire—it was typical of him." High praise from the man whom many regard as the granddaddy of them all, from himself right down to Clint Eastwood.

Gardner McKay with starlet
Diane McBain in 1960

GARDNER McKAY

A *new* Robert Taylor? Well, that's what the *Life* magazine cover called him in the summer of 1959 when it declared that after America got a gander at Gardner McKay in the new TV series *Adventures in Paradise,* all memories of Taylor, Tyrone Power and Errol Flynn would be washed away by his good looks and smoldering sex appeal. In the best tradition of Hollywood hoopla the network threw all its weight behind their new star in an attempt to have him firmly established in the minds of the masses by the time the series debuted. Unfortunately it didn't work. Instead of smoldering, Gardner mostly sleepwalked his way through his glamorous role as skipper of the yacht *Tiki;* an adventurer with an even keel and a weather eye out for the ladies. Critics took the show and him over the coals, one saying succinctly, "No *Tiki,* no watchee!"

Gardner was born in Manhattan on June 10th, 1932 to a well-to-do family. His father, Hugh Deane McKay, was an advertising executive and during Gardner's growing-up years the family was transplanted to Paris. By the time he finished a two-year stretch at Cornell University, Gardner had moved a lot more, chalking up a total of twelve schools he'd attended. Admittedly a poor student, his aim was for photography and in 1956 he received world-wide exposure when, as a passenger on the *Ile de France,* he shot the rescue pictures of passengers from the sinking *Andrea Doria.*

His great good looks and awesome physique (6'5" tall, 195 lbs. and size 14 feet!) embarrassed him and though he hated the idea of male models, he worked as one for a while. He got into acting but only guest shots on shows like *Boots and Saddles* and *Death Valley Days.* Ironically it was a razor commercial he did that caught the eye of Dore Schary who picked him for *Paradise.*

His publicity pictured him as a loner who, though often seen dating nubile starlets like Ann-Margret, Diane McBain and

Gardner at a recent
Hollywood screening

Suzanne Pleshette, preferred the company of his sheepdog Pussycat. Interviewers walked away shaking their heads at what they called his own brand of English and a 20th Century Fox producer was quoted as having said, "Figuring out what Gardner is saying is like trying to get a firm grip on whipped cream." But then who wouldn't stumble a little after a publicity buildup like his?

In June of 1961 he was slapped with a paternity suit by a Hollywood waitress and he admitted they had once been intimate friends. There were reports he made a hefty payment for the child's support.

Actually despite critical jeers his series lasted three years on TV but when it's run ended, so did Gardner's career. Surfeited with glamour girls, he fled to South America for five years with migrations to France and the Far East. When he came back the best he could get acting-wise was a small part in *The Pleasure Seekers* in 1965, a top-heavy sequel to *Three Coins in the Fountain*. In 1968 he was briefly considered as Marilyn Monroe's co-star in her ill-fated *Something's Got to Give*. He hasn't been on screen since 1967, when he did *I Sailed Around the World With An All-Girl Crew*—a *Tiki*-like comedy that had him awash with starlets *and* Terry-Thomas.

The Seventies have seen Gardner blossom in several directions. His play *Sea Marks,* produced in Hollywood in 1974, was well received by *Variety*—a far cry from their first McKay critique—and another effort, *Me,* was presented on the *Hollywood Television Theatre,* again to good notices. One of his mobile sculptures is owned by New York's Museum of Modern Art and the days when he once spoiled a massive Western battle scene—"I couldn't move, a horse was standing on my foot!"—are long gone. Still a bachelor, he's an avid horseman and skin diver. He lives quietly and alone in Hollywood and there's no *Life* magazine cover anywhere in sight. He's a survivor of Hollywood's toughest game—publicity.

Hayley and Maurice Chevalier on the set of *The Castaways*, 1961

HAYLEY MILLS

Walt Disney had a knack for discovering talent in unlikely places, as he proved yet again in 1959 when he saw tiny Hayley Mills in a suspenser called *Tiger Bay*. It starred her father, John Mills, and a new German heartthrob, Horst Buchholz, but Disney saw only Hayley, and in her, the talent of a Temple, only not so sweet, and the wistfulness of a Withers, only not so noisy. He saw a little star and he grabbed her under contract for $30,000 a year (quickly escalating to $75,000) and dusted off a part that had helped Mary Pickford corner the market on heartrending over forty years before, *Pollyanna*. Surrounding her with pros like Jane Wyman and Nancy Olson, he pulled out all the production stops to create a charming piece of American flimsy, with Hayley spreading around her juvenile sunshine with a captivating pertness that had mothers all over the world wondering, "Now why can't my kid . . . ?" She even won a special Oscar for it too.

The youngest daughter of the well-known Mills family (her mother is writer Mary Hayley Bell and her sister Juliet later became half of *Nanny And The Professor*) she got her chance to co-star with father John in *Tiger Bay* (1959) after its director, J. Lee Thompson, saw her mugging on the set one day. He changed the lead from a little boy to a little girl and the twelve year-old was in business. After *Pollyanna,* she played twins in Disney's *The Parent Trap* (1961) with Brian Keith and Maureen O'Hara, and then went back to England for 1962's *Whistle Down The Wind,* from a story by her mother about some children, led by Hayley, who mistake an escaped convict for Christ. Both films were so successful in England that she was named top box office draw that year. She was so hot, in fact, that the producers of *Lolita* tried to get her for the role of the pint-sized nymphet but Disney quickly quelled that idea. Lolita indeed! Not when he had a winner like *In Search Of The Castaways* (1963) lined up for her with Maurice Chevalier.

Hayley with hubby Roy
Boulting and their son Crispin

1963 saw her in *Summer Magic* but she was growing fast and attempted her first mixed-up-kid role a year later in *The Chalk Garden* which didn't fare well with either critics or audiences. In *The Moonspinners* (1965) she was better, keeping pace with Joan Greenwood, the throaty-voiced English comedienne, and, with Pola Negri, coaxed out of retirement by Disney for a few small scenes. *The Truth About Spring* (1965) wasn't as interesting as its producers thought it would be but she finished her Disney tenure in 1965 with a big hit, *That Darn Cat.*

In an effort to help her over her awkward period, Hayley's mother wrote *Sky West and Crooked* (1966) for her, concocting the role of a mentally retarded girl who falls in love with a gypsy, but it didn't work. Critics began referring to them as the poor man's Redgrave family and Hayley wisely repaired to Hollywood for the successful *Trouble With Angels* with Roz Russell as the Auntie Mame-ish Mother Superior. That same year, 1966, she made *The Family Way* for producer Roy Boulting, a film that promised a 'new' Hayley, even to a brief nude shot. It was successful abroad but not in the U.S., as wasn't her next, *Pretty Polly* (1967) a Noel Coward yarn about a girl who arrives in India a virgin but doesn't leave that way.

Boulting made another film with her in 1968, *Twisted Nerve*, a nasty story about a psychotic, played by Hywel Bennett, who stalks Hayley with less than pleasant intentions. It was a mild shocker in itself but when coupled with the news that Hayley and the then fifty-five year-old producer Boulting were living together, it got very shocking indeed. They were married in 1970 and since then she's tried hard to make a full transition to serious acting parts, even trying Ibsen—*The Wild Duck*—in repertory, a version of *Peter Pan* in London, and a film in South Africa called *The Diamond Hunters*. The Boultings and their young son Crispin live in a lovely house in Belgravia Square, but in the hearts of many she'll always be the funny little girl with the crooked grin who tomboyed her way from one end of the Disney studio to the other.

129

Aurora and a very well-known duck

AURORA MIRANDA

For some reason Hollywood has always looked slightly askance at the younger sisters of established stars, those bright-eyed girls, often with the same name, who glide into town after Sis has already had her first starring role. Pier Angeli was followed by Marisa Pavan, her twin, and after Brigitte made her hit, Mijanou Bardot came to Hollywood to carve a piece of the pie for herself (but after pictures like *Sex Kittens Go To College*, went back home). Perhaps the most exotic double-take of all, though, was Carmen Miranda of the fruit-filled hats and her sister Aurora.

Carmen was born in 1904 (in Portugal, *not* Brazil as was commonly believed) and Aurora came fourteen years later after the family was firmly entrenched in South America. Carmen was already a star of sorts before she left Brazil, a veteran of several movies and a radio show on which her sister, an up-and-comer, often appeared. Carmen got to California via Broadway (her famous debut number *South American Way* from *Streets of Paris* in 1939 was inserted into Betty Grable's movie *Down Argentine Way*—which was filmed entirely in New York), and so did Aurora, opening there at Manhattan's Copacabana nightclub singing something called *Paso Do Kangero*—The Kangaroo Walk. Carmen's number led to a long-term contract in Hollywood but although Aurora's English wasn't good enough for the same kind of luck, she went there anyway in 1941.

Once in Hollywood, Aurora quickly signed up with linguist Signor Z. Yaconelli, an Italian, to help her perfect her *English!*

Jack Kuster

A recent shot of Aurora Miranda

Since sister Carmen had been her manager in South America one can only presume it was her idea to bring in Yaconelli. (Aurora herself doesn't remember whose idea it was.) In any case, American moviemen still didn't grab her—except for one, the inimitable Walt Disney.

Disney was preparing his *Three Cabelerros,* a partly live, partly animated feature that colorfully extolled the glories of South America. Who better to represent her 'home' country of Brazil than the available Miranda—Aurora? The segment was called simply *Brazil* and was introduced by a talkative parrot named Jose Carioca who transports none other than Donald Duck through a tour book's pages and right into the glories of Baia, the country's oldest city. Aurora appears out of the almost psychedelic background as a cookie seller extolling her oven-warm wares in a wildly wacky number called *Os Quindins De Yaya.* She and a group of native dancers weave their way through the streets of the city with a peripatetic Donald bringing up the rear. And since the lyrics of the bouncy tune were primarily *yayas*—Spanish for cookies—it didn't matter a whit whether Aurora knew English or not. At the end of the sequence, she turns her back to the camera and grabs Donald in an exuberant kiss, transporting him to the heights of happiness and herself into Disney history.

According to Disney expert John Canemaker, the film was completed by the end of 1944 but due to a war shortage of Technicolor materials, wasn't seen by the public until 1945. In retrospect Aurora enjoyed it all immensely but adds, "I did not like to kees the duck!"

She appeared in *Phantom Lady* (1944) with Franchot Tone, and with Tito Guizar in *Brazil,* but those were the only films she made. She soon decided to return home to Brazil after marrying Lockheed aeronautical engineer Gabriel Richaid. Their marriage has been a long and happy one and they live in the plush suburb of Rio de Janiero called Copacabana. Recently she gave permission for Broadway producers to begin work on a musical based on sister Carmen's life and to be called, appropriately, *Miranda, Miranda.* After all, there *were* two of them!

131

Barbara in a typical publicity shot—this time she's "Miss Thanksgiving"!

Pictorial Parade

BARBARA NICHOLS

In the 1960 comedy *Who Was That Lady,* Barbara Nichols had a memorable scene that possibly sums up her whole career. Playing one of two dumb blonde playmates of philandering husbands Dean Martin and Tony Curtis (the other playmate was the late Joi Lansing), she's eating dinner in a Chinese restaurant when she starts to choke on her food. She coughs, swallows, grimaces, and then gasps in her babytalk voice, "A piece of lousy swordfish—and it got stuck right here!" pointing an index finger straight at one of the most spectacular cleavages of the Fifties.

But it didn't start out that way because little Barbara Nickerauer, born in Jamaica, Queens, New York in 1932, originally wanted to be an actress, not a sex symbol. She got the urge after appearing in several Woodrow Wilson High School productions while a student there, but made use of her undeniable beauty by modeling after school for a local department store. She won her first beauty contest while a sophomore and went on to pick up titles like *Miss Loew's Valencia* (A Queens, N.Y. movie house), *Miss Long Island Duckling* and *Miss Dill Pickle* for one wacky National Pickle Week.

Luckily Barbara knew a good thing or two when she saw them and after graduating from high school decided her looks were her best—and fastest—passport to fame, and set off to join the chorus line at a Dominican Republic nightclub during the heyday of the Trujillos. She was seventeen at the time, and her 5'5½" frame weighed in at 125 pounds.

By 1953 Barbara had landed her first Broadway role in a revival of *Pal Joey,* playing a chorus girl, and 1954 saw her—as did millions of others—as *Esquire* magazine's calendar girl. A TV role got her spotted by movie producer Frank Rosenberg who signed her for *Miracle In The Rain* (1956)—and Hollywood had a new not-so-dumb blonde.

Barbara as she looks today

Eddie Colbert

It was the age of the Blonde Bombshells and every studio had at least one contender waiting in the wings for Marilyn Monroe to drop the crown. For several years Barbara was one of the town's busiest, appearing in *Joy Ride* (1956), *Beyond a Reasonable Doubt* (1956), and a biggie, *The King and Four Queens* (1957) with Gable and Eleanor Parker. As one of the queens in question, it was perhaps the closest she ever got to a title role.

Barbara interspersed lots of television with her movie work (*George Gobel Show, Untouchables,* etc.) but kept busy big-screen-wise in *Pal Joey* and *The Pajama Game* (with Doris Day and John Raitt), and was a very hot item for Tony Curtis to handle in *Sweet Smell of Success,* all in 1957. A natural queen of the cheesecake covers, Barbara was never hesitant about showing off the talents that made her famous but she could also act, as proven in *That Kind of Woman* in 1959 with Sophia Loren and Tab Hunter, and in 1960's *Dark at the Top of the Stairs* for which she got plenty of Oscar talk.

Tiring of her constant image as the blonde with the heart of gold, Barbara went to Broadway opposite George Gobel in *Let It Ride* in 1961, but it was a short trip and she was quickly back in Hollywood doing more of the same kind of roles—*The World of Henry Orient* (1960); *Where The Boys Are* (1961) as a submerged stripper; *House of Women* (1962), a prison saga; and *Dear Heart* (1965).

Like most glamour girls, Barbara has had a difficult battle making the transition from perennial starlet to mature actress. Her part in the almost-classic *The Loved One* in 1965 ended up on the cutting room floor and there haven't been many since. She showed up on TV's *Emergency* series last year as an overweight stripper who overdoses on diet pills.

Still a bachelor girl, Barbara feels her image of the tough gold-digger has hurt her chances of finding Mr. Right—although she's still looking for him at the many Hollywood parties she's seen at!

133

MAUREEN O'HARA

The flame-haired temptress of a hundred Technicolor swash-bucklers, Maureen O'Hara has exhibited admirable staying power in the public's mind. Thanks to latter-day John Wayne movies, she never had to resort to tiny character parts in B movies but left the screen smiling, almost as radiant as when she first lit it up in 1939's *Jamaica Inn*.

Maureen Fitzsimmons was born in Dublin, Ireland (where else?) in 1920 and swept into the Abbey Players Theatre at age 14, quickly winning every prize for excellence they offered. Singer Harry Richman kicked off her movie career with a role in his *Kicking the Moon Around* in 1938 and she was making another in London when the project was scratched. What she'd filmed though was seen by Charles Laughton who snapped her up for *Jamaica Inn* and brought her along with him and wife Elsa Lanchester when he went Hollywood for *The Hunchback of Notre Dame* (1939). Her Irish beauty might not have been the ideal for the gypsy girl in that flick but she did it anyway—and well enough for RKO Pictures to buy up her British contract.

1941 was the year that made the difference when John Ford picked her for *How Green Was My Valley*. It was voted Best Picture of the Year and pushed Maureen into the star ranks. She'd left husband George Brown behind her when she came to America, and in 1941 that marriage was annulled. She married producer Will Price shortly after. Her contract was shared between RKO and 20th Century Fox who'd made *Valley*, with 20th starring her in *To The Shores of Tripoli*, 1942; *Ten Gentlemen From West Point*, 1942; and *The Black Swan* (1942) as a haughty lady won over by buccaneer Tyrone Power. That was the start of the trend that would result in her labeling as Queen of Technicolor and though she came back to Earth in films like *Sentimental Journey* (1946); *Miracle on 34th St.* and *Sitting Pretty* in 1948, it's her image from *The Spanish Main*,

A casual Maureen on a recent Hollywood stopover

(1945); *Sinbad the Sailor* with Doug Fairbanks Jr. in 1948 and *Bagdad* in 1949 that sticks.

At Sword's Point in 1950 (though not seen until 1953) found her as Athos' daughter teamed with Cornel Wilde as Artagnan, Jr. and that year her husband directed her in *Tripoli,* with John Payne versus the Barbary pirates. Her first movie with John Wayne was *Rio Grande* and a year later in 1952 they made a classic, *The Quiet Man,* as endearing a portrait of Ireland, its people and its customs, as has ever been filmed. She shone as the feisty village girl as interested in her "things"—furniture and dowry—as in her new husband. *Flame of Araby* in 1952 was a downer, as was *Against All Flags* (1952) with an aging Errol Flynn. John Ford came to her rescue again with *The Long Gray Line* in 1955 but Universal almost sank her for good as their dimpled and, naturally, Technicolored *Lady Godiva* (1955).

About this time O'Hara was cover-storied by *Confidential* magazine for some alleged balcony antics in a Hollywood movie house. She sued and won and if anything the publicity only fortified her image of the independent beauty. In 1954 she and Price divorced shortly after the birth of their daughter.

In 1957 she made *Wings of Eagles* with Wayne, but it was warmed-over Ford and she wasn't good again until *Our Man in Havana* in 1959 with Alec Guinness. In the part originally set for Lauren Bacall, O'Hara was excellent in the Carol Reed drama. She went the mother route for Walt Disney in 1961's *Parent Trap*—a giant hit—and became resident wife to aging male stars in *Mr. Hobbs Takes a Vactaion* (1963, James Stewart); *Spencer's Mountain* (1963, Henry Fonda); *McLintock* (1964, John Wayne); and *The Rare Breed* (1966, Stewart again).

Her third marriage to pilot Charles Blair has been an exciting and thoroughly satisfying one. She makes her home in the Virgin Islands where he heads up their Antilles Air Boats Company (with a fleet of 22 planes) and recently they flew their latest addition, a World War II vintage Sunderland, from Australia to California. Last on screen with Wayne in 1971's *Big Jake,* she'd come back if the part were rich enough to tempt her away.

135

Nancy in 1957

NANCY OLSON

Sunset Boulevard is regarded by many as the greatest film about Hollywood and the movies that has ever been made, and their case is a good one. Gloria Swanson, as the aging megalomaniacal star Norma Desmond, is stunningly powerful in a role many thought was almost autobiographical, and William Holden, as her handsome young writer/lover, is superbly at sea in her machinations for a return to stardom until he unwittingly becomes the catalyst that triggers her famous news-camera 'return'. Another excellent reason for the reputation of the film was a young, bright-as-a-new-penny actress named Nancy Olson, who played the part of a struggling studio scriptwriter who falls in love with Holden. She walked away from the film with a Best Supporting Actress nomination. Swanson was nominated for Best Actress, Holden for Best Actor, and Erich Von Stroheim, Best Supporting Actor for his touching portrayal of Swanson's former director/husband. In true Hollywood tradition, they all lost! The golden statuettes of the industry's approval walked into other living rooms that night in 1951 but that loss hasn't kept the film itself from its deserved acclaim. It should have marked the beginning of a great career for Olson, also deserved, but that never happened, mostly because she didn't want it to.

Sunset Boulevard was produced by Paramount Studios to whom Nancy was under contract. A studio talent scout had spotted her in a college play in California where her family had moved after the retirement of her father, a distinguished Milwaukee doctor. (She was born there in 1928.) She was a good actress as she proved in her first movie, also starring Bill Holden, *Union Station* (1950), a crackling story of a kidnapped blind girl and the chase to rescue her. Holden was then the studio's top male star and after *Boulevard*, they were

Nancy Olson as she looks today

teamed yet again in 1951's *Force Of Arms* and *Submarine Command*. *Command* was standard military stuff with Olson left behind for Holden's sub, but it helped her land a tangy part in the 1952 remake of Edna Ferber's *So Big*. Playing a smallish role as an independent artist, she comes on near the film's end but makes a crackling impression. That same year she crackled a bit more opposite John Wayne in *Big Jim McLain*. She got folksy again in *The Boy From Oklahoma* in 1954 with Will Rogers Jr., but sparkled briefly in 1955's *Battle Cry*.

In 1950, Nancy had married lyricist Alan Jay Lerner (they had two children, Liza and Jennifer) and commuted to Hollywood for most of her career. After their divorce in 1957, she moved from their 270-year-old colonial mansion in upstate New York into New York City where she forgot films for a while to concentrate on the stage, starring with Tom Ewell in *Tunnel Of Love* and with David Wayne in *Send Me No Flowers*.

In 1960 she returned to Hollywood to play Jane Wyman's housekeeper in Disney's *Pollyanna* and stayed right on the lot for *The Absent-minded Professor* (1961) and its sequel, *Son of Flubber* in 1963. As Fred MacMurray's wife in both, her maturing wholesomeness and sharp wit were in perfect contrast to his stock-in-trade bumbling. She worked for the Disney studio again in 1969 in *Smith!* with Glenn Ford, a contemporary story about Indians and their problems.

The six years between pictures had been rewarding ones though, and included a marriage to Capitol Records president Alan Livingston and a son Christopher, now eleven. The Livingstons, including the daughters by her marriage to Lerner, live in a beautiful mansion in Beverly Hills, and she can now be choosy about working or not. Last seen in *Airport '75*, she's determined not to do the type of roles so many actresses are doing just to keep her name in lights. "I'm ready to work, but it has to be worth it," she says with that flashing Olson smile.

137

Silvana on a New York visit in 1955

Jack Kuster

SILVANA PAMPANINI

The cult of the Starlet, Genus European, has been around almost as long as there have been photographers to shoot them. In the Fifties, with the advent of Ekberg, Loren, Bardot and Lollobrigida, they proliferated like crabgrass in an untended yard—almost as good as the real thing unless you were a gardener. Magazines like *Vue* and *See,* not to mention the early issues of *Playboy,* vied for their pinups. In those days a foreign name still exuded a quality of lusty fun which homegrown girls just didn't project, a sense of naughty wickedness which titillated but didn't threaten the double standard of the American Male. Silvana Pampanini, with her close-cropped black hair and abundant figure, was a leader of the bikini brigade, and while her career as an actress was mostly press releases and premieres, she was, for a time, a safe American dream, available at every corner newsstand for a quarter.

A former *Miss Italy,* Silvana had wanted to be an opera singer but unfortunately wolf whistles had drowned out her tremulous contralto so, taking the cue, she became an actress. A ripe twenty-five when she first hit Hollywood in 1953, she got off on the wrong foot when she was quoted as saying that American men were "too old and decrepit" as lovers. Starlet Dawn Addams hinted that perhaps she just wasn't meeting the right ones because although "Silvana might be the Marilyn Monroe of Italy, for America she's a little too plump." Odd, considering Pampanini's hobbies were listed as ballet dancing, swimming, bicycling and horseback riding. The only sedentary one in the bunch was piano-playing.

In 1955 President Peron himself welcomed her to Argentina on a stopover en route to the Uruguayan Film Festival and she jumped right into the South American spirit—and frontpages—by mambo-ing off the plane. After that she said she planned on going to New York to meet her Mr. X, "a wealthy young Manhattan

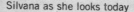
Silvana as she looks today

Jack Kuster

businessman'' and then on to Denver to meet President Eisenhower. Wishful thinking or not, the 37-23-36 starlet's quotes were certainly grist for the tabloids, not to mention Earl Wilson. She also took time out to up her grading of U.S. men, saying "All I've met have been fine and admirable.''

In May of 1956 she was sued by Greek producer Ergas Morris over some $49,000 worth of furs and jewels he gave her in hopes of eventually marrying her. Pampanini dismissed his claim to the goodies, saying they were only the normal tribute given to a star by a production company, and went back to work on *Don Juan's Night of Love.* (She won the suit in 1962.)

American TV audiences got a long look at her when, on *I've Got a Secret,* she got her signals crossed and sat looking into a live camera for a full minute waiting for her cue. Back home she spent most of her time in court being sued by the wife of a Milanese gentleman who sold her his next door property at too low a price just to get her to live there, and by a Mexican producer who claimed she didn't show up for work on his movie. Not to be outdone, she sued an Italian Duchess whose dog allegedly bit her leg. Said the Duchess, "Beniamino (the dog) bites everybody.''

One thing about Silvana was that she was always ready, willing and certainly able to spread a good thing around, managing to get herself engaged to an American comic, George DeWitt, during a two-day stopover in Havana in March of 1959. They met one afternoon in the swimming pool and the press agent announced the engagement shortly thereafter.

Actually she's never married and she's yet to make a good movie. In 1962 she was in *Guns of the Black Witch* with American actor Don Megowan, and in 1966 was in *A Day In Court*—which was *not* autobiographical. Recently she made a Mexican adventure called *Princess of The Canary Islands,* and in Latin countries, is still considered a sex symbol of sorts. She lives in Rome and a magazine there recently did a color layout on her life today, which is just as sumptuously Fifties as always.

Fess in the classic
Davy Crockett pose

Pictorial Parade

FESS PARKER

During the Fifties, television took over much of the hero-making that the movies used to do and one of that medium's greatest and most promoted idols of all time was *Davy Crockett* —King of the Wild Frontier. A Walt Disney inspiration which debuted in Walt's *Disneyland* Show in 1955, he threw the entire machinery of the Disney empire behind Crockett after the huge success of three hour-long episodes which defined the life and legend of the frontier scout. Overnight Fess Parker became the King of Kids as well as the aforementioned Wild Frontier, and songs were recorded that sold almost as many millions as did the copies of his famous coonskin hat!

Fess Parker—and that's his real name, by the way—was born in Texas on August 26, 1926 and stayed there all his life, eventually going to the University of Texas where he majored in Business Administration. His career seemed pretty well plotted out until one day he met the late character actor Adolph Menjou, who after hearing him pluck out a song or two on his guitar, suggested he give acting a try. Since Parker liked singing and strumming better than the account books, he took his advice.

He left Texas and headed West, Hollywood-style, where he quickly found out that an acting career took more than just good looks and a strong voice. The rangy lad (6'4") studied acting and got his first break in 1952's *Untamed Frontier*. It wasn't much of a part but it was a beginning. He had small parts in half a dozen other pictures but it wasn't until *Them* (1954) that he got lucky. A sci-fi flick about ants attacking Los Angeles, none other than Walt Disney himself saw it and also Parker. At the time he was casting the part of Crockett and once he'd seen Fess, it was accomplished! Actually it was a good break for both of them since Fess virtually had his bags packed for a Texas return and his by-passed business career.

140

Fess and wife Marcie at a recent Hollywood screening

Crockett swamped the nation that summer and next to the hoola hoop, was every kid's favorite distraction. The merchandising around the character was monumental and Fess Parker became inextricably one with the image of Davy. Disney eventually strung the TV episodes together into a movie which also did huge business—the kids couldn't get enough of him. When he came out with a sequel, *Davy Crockett and the River Pirates* the following year it was almost as successful.

Disney kept Fess busy over the next few years in movies like *The Great Locomotive Chase* (1956); *Westward Ho The Wagons,* with another TV-hero George (Superman) Reeves; 1957's *Old Yeller* with Dorothy McGuire; and 1958's *Light In The Forest* with Carol Lynley and James MacArthur.

Fess was getting pretty tired of the good-guy image by now—all his parts in all those flicks were virtually interchangeable and the appeal, while still a popular one, was getting a bit boring for him as an actor. Knowing he was best in some sort of saddle, though, he stuck to the West but a tougher version of it in *The Hangman,* a 1959 *very* rough and ready Mike Curtiz production which teamed him with an aging Robert Taylor and nubile Tina Louise. Jack Lord was in it too as a baddie. That same year he also made *The Jayhawkers* with Jeff Chandler, a violent Western pitting Fess against Chandler in a battle for power and French starlet Nicole Maurey.

Parker gave up his bachelorhood in 1960 when he married Marcie Rinehart. They had a son, Fess III, a year later and have since added three more children to the family. In 1962 he appeared in Don Siegel's gutsy *Hell Is For Heroes* with Steve McQueen, and tried a TV series of the Jimmy Stewart classic *Mr. Smith Goes To Washington.* It flopped and he returned to his ranch in Santa Barbara where he and his family still live. He's invested well over the years in such diverse interests as a plastics factory and mobile homes. Last on-screen in *Smoky* (1966), he does occasional TV shots, and Marcie says in real life he's easy to live with "if you leave him alone."

141

Jean in a classic publicity still in 1950

JEAN PETERS

Jean Peters had one of the most memorable lines in screen history when in 1953's *Niagara,* she watched Marilyn Monroe wiggle across the Cinemascope screen in a tight red dress and remarked to her eyeballing husband, "To wear a dress like that you've got to start laying plans when you're thirteen!" Not that Jean wasn't an eye-filler herself; she was, as proven on screen in pictures like *Three Coins In The Fountain,* and off when she married the world's most reclusive bachelor, Howard Hughes, only to disappear from the screen and become a sunglassed face in the tabloids, caught on the run from airline terminals, living the classic life of the bird in the *very* gilded cage.

Ohio-born Jean went straight to Hollywood after graduating from college with the title Miss Ohio State. It wasn't a credential outstandingly different from that of thousands of other girls, but luckily Jean got the break most others never come close to and was signed by 20th Century Fox, who promptly presented her opposite the screen's leading lover, Tyrone Power, in *The Captain From Castile,* an epic outing of 1947. Her role as the simple farm girl who helps nobleman Power escape the wrath of the Spanish Inquisition made her an overnight star.

Her next one, *Deep Waters* (1948) with Dana Andrews, threw her into just that in a muddled story of a triangle—Andrews can't decide between Peters or his fishing boat.

In 1951's *Anne of the Indies,* Jean played a lady pirate with entertaining gusto and the following year shared equal billing with Marlon Brando in the arty-but-unsuccessful *Viva Zapata!* directed by Elia Kazan. Luckily *Niagara* came along with a good part as the woman mistakenly menaced by Joseph Cotton, Monroe's supposedly-dead husband. The climax where the couple heads for the falls in a stolen cabin cruiser is still breath-catching on the Late Show. (Naturally Monroe got all the ad copy in this one with tag lines like "See TWO of Nature's Wonders for the Price of ONE!")

Jean Peters, today a Beverly Hills matron

Her movie image was fast shaping up as that of the perfect wife but she cracked that with her part in *Three Coins In The Fountain,* one of 1954's biggest hits. That year she went back to wifely duties—in a teepee—with Burt Lancaster in *The Apache.* Her last film was her best—*A Man Called Peter*—and she walked away from her career with an Oscar nomination for her role as Catherine Marshall . . . and into Hughes' privately constructed world of fabulous wealth and dense secrecy.

Their romance had actually begun in 1947 when he was still a very visible man on the Hollywood scene. For years she saw no one else but then upped and married businessman Stuart Cramer, who went on to marry Terry Moore, in 1954 only to divorce him two years later. She and Hughes were secretly married on March 13, 1957 and a Golden Curtain quickly dropped around them. There were rumors that she only saw the billionaire on weekends and spent the rest of her time alone in her Beverly Hills mansion. He'd discovered Las Vegas and preferred living there, manipulating his empire and, at one point, buying the local television station so he could choose what pictures would run on The Late Show, which he constantly watched.

Hollywood and the world were surprised when, in 1970, the Hughes office announced that Peters would seek a divorce. No grounds were given, nor the date when the proceedings would formally occur, but shortly afterwards she resurfaced on the Hollywood scene with 20th Century Fox production chief Stanley Hough. On June 18, 1971, her divorce was granted and two months later she became Mrs. Hough.

Comeback-wise, Jean has only worked a bit, most notably in a television production of *Winesburg, Ohio* in which she was excellent as the depressed mother. She and Hough live in Beverly Hills in a house reportedly given them by Hughes. When asked what it was like, she said that being married to Howard Hughes "was and shall remain a matter on which I have no comment."

143

On the set of *The Egyptian* with gossip queen Hedda Hopper

EDMUND PURDOM

Edmund Purdom may never have become a star if Mario Lanza and Marlon Brandon hadn't helped him. Not that either knew it at the time, but they were completely responsible for his two biggest films, *The Student Prince* and *The Egyptian*. The year was 1954 and Lanza was in deep personal trouble at his home studio, MGM. Work had begun on *Prince,* starring him and Ann Blyth, but after he finished recording the soundtrack, he abruptly walked out on his contract and Purdom got the part. The six foot Englishman looked every inch the role and was so persuasive that moviegoers overlooked the fact that every time he opened his mouth to sing, Mario Lanza's voice came out! Almost the same story landed him *The Egyptian* that same year when, ready to go with sets built, costumes made, and the lights practically turned on on the lavish sets, Brando ankled the part because he disliked the script. 20th Century Fox was out one star, but after a quick and frantic search, Purdom got the part—and several million more dollars worth of publicity. Dubbed 'the Epic Saver', he had all the requisites for a long-term career but unfortunately began believing his own publicity. It wasn't long before he joined the ranks of American 'names' seeking work in Italian spectacles—pallid takeoffs on the kind that made him famous.

The son of an English drama critic, Purdom began his acting career in 1945 when he was nineteen, cutting his teeth in English repertory famous for their classical training. He first came to the U.S. in 1952 with Laurence Olivier, to appear with him in two Broadway plays. Studio scouts took one long look at his supremely handsome face, heard his resonant voice and the offers came pouring in—six of them, one from every major studio in Hollywood. He appeared impressively as Lt. Lightoller in 1952's *Titanic* but signed a long-term contract with MGM who utilized him very well in their *Julius Caesar,* which ironically starred Marlon Brando as Marc Antony. MGM was

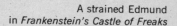

A strained Edmund
in *Frankenstein's Castle of Freaks*

wondering what next to do with him when Lanza walked out, firmly washing up his own career in the process, and they put him into quickly redesigned costumes as *The Student Prince.* As soon as he finished it, they lent him to 20th for *The Egyptian,* matching him gamely against Michael Wilding, Peter Ustinov, Jean Simmons, Gene Tierney, Victor Mature and every DeMille extra who was looking for a job in the mammoth story of Sinuhe, the physician who learns about life the hard way—due in large part to his dealings with Bela Darvi as Nefer, the courtesan who teaches him "the finer perceptions of love."

Both films were moneymakers but not hugely so, and his next at MGM was a real bomb—*The Prodigal* with Lana Turner. Her rhinestone bras notwithstanding, the heavy-handed epic was too long and too talky, causing one reviewer to comment that the finale—when Lana Turner jumps into the sacrificial pool of fire—didn't come a moment too soon! With three huge pictures behind him, Purdom acted like a star even if the box-office didn't back him up, and he and MGM started to clash over properties. He did *The King's Thief* in 1956, but was billed fourth after David Niven, Blyth, and George Sanders. After a few more outbursts, the studio let him go and six years later he was in Italy starring in things like *The Nights of Rasputin.*

In 1962 he married fiery Linda Christian, most famous as Ty Power's one-time wife, but within the year they were squabbling in Italian headlines. In '65 he appeared in *The Yellow Rolls Royce* (The Rex Harrison-Jeanne Moreau episode) but most other flicks, like *The Beauty Jungle,* never made it across the Atlantic. One of his most recent outings was with Rossano Brazzi and the late Michael Dunn in something called *Frankenstein's Castle of Freaks.*

He has a twenty-three year old daughter, Lilan, by a long-ago marriage to dancer Anita Phillips and has recently left his Roman roost to give Hollywood another go-round. His return was greeted by a few gossip column items but not many offers although the looks remain almost as good as in the past.

145

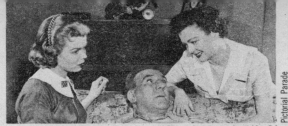

Marjorie, as usual, soothing William Bendix's ruffled feathers in *Life Of Riley*

MARJORIE REYNOLDS

With the possible exception of Alice Cramden on *The Honeymooners*, no TV-wife in the Fifties lived closer to the paycheck than did Marjorie Reynolds in *The Life of Riley.* Her TV hubby, the great William Bendix, worked in an aircraft factory and the show's mass appeal was to other blue collar families who lived the same way. No lavish houses and "yes, buy that new dress·if you really want it" for these folks. The fun centered around the misadventures of scrambleheaded Bendix with patient Marjorie always handy with a shoulder for him to lean on. She started out as a blonde hoofer and ended up etching as fine a portrait of the All-American Mom as any actress has before or since.

Marjorie started acting in high school back in her hometown of Buhl, Idaho and went directly to Hollywood when she graduated. Since no one could pronounce her real name of Goodspeed, she changed it to Marjorie Moore and got a job as a dancer—"Hoofers, we called them"—on the Paramount lot. In 1936 the pretty blonde married Jack Reynolds so she took his last name for her professional one, debuting it in 1937's *Murder In Greenwich Village.*

That was only one of a long string of B pictures—"mostly Westerns, as I remember"—that required her to look properly scared, or properly smiley but always properly pretty. In 1940's *Up In The Air,* she eased into more popular roles and in 1942 landed a plum as femme lead opposite Bing Crosby and Fred Astaire in *Holiday Inn.* It landed her a seven-year Paramount contract and remains her personal favorite of all her films. She was with Crosby again in *Dixie* in 1943 and also that year did her stint in Paramount's wartime spirits-lifter *Star Spangled Rhythm* which showcased every star on the lot.

In *The Time Of Their Lives* (1946) she held her own opposite the antics of Abbott and Costello in a charming tale of two Revolutionary War spies (Reynolds and Costello) whose ghosts

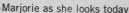
Marjorie as she looks today

are condemned to a plantation until their innocence is finally established almost two hundred years later. It's a Late Show delight, thanks greatly to Marjorie, even though "I was pregnant at the time and in it I had to wear pants and climb trees and things. I just wanted to get it over with."

After many more films, Marjorie decided to try television and got the role of Peg Riley in the revamped *Life Of Riley.* (There had been an earlier version in 1949 which had starred Jackie Gleason and Rosemary De Camp.) It was a smash hit with the Riley family rounded out by Lugene Sanders as Babs and Wesley Morgan as Junior Riley. They were all aided and abetted by their next door neighbors played by Gloria Blondell (now living in Pacific Palisades) and Tom D'Andrea. The fun lasted from 1952 until 1958.

During the series hiatuses, Marjorie appeared in some movies too; *The Silent Witness* (1954), *Mobs Inc.* (1955), and afterwards in *Juke Box Rhythm* in 1959. In 1952 she divorced her first husband and a year later married businessman John Haffen. Her daughter, Linda Reynolds, has been both a secretary at Fox studios and an airline stewardess.

The Silent Witness in 1964 was Marjorie's last picture—"Now that you mention it that title does sound familiar"—and she considers herself semi-retired although she's recently done some television commericals. Two serious back operations over the past few years have limited her activities, "and I still don't feel like jumping up and down." They were disc fusions and have taken a long time to get over. When she can, Marjorie works at the UCLA Medical Center as a volunteer, which she greatly enjoys. Thanks to almost continual reruns of the Riley series, she's often recognized, which delights her. "At the time the series wasn't that exciting—I remember being in the kitchen a lot peeling carrots. I remember spending more time with my TV family than my real one." She still sees Lugene Sanders but they've both lost touch with Wesley Morgan, "such a bright boy." And a lucky one to have had Marjorie Reynolds' attention all those years!

147

Erik in top hat and tails, 1935

ERIK RHODES

In 1934 a classic piece of Hollywood magic happened when RKO Studios produced the movie version of the stage hit *The Gay Divorce*. They added an 'e' to divorce coming up with *The Gay Divorcee*—and were smart enough *not* to subtract any of the three male leads from the Broadway production: Fred Astaire, Eric Blore and Erik Rhodes. Astaire became the most famous dancer, Blore perhaps the most perfectly pompous butler, and Rhodes the most charming gigolo in all of Hollywood. Since Rhodes was then constantly cast as the suave Continental, people would invariably be suprised upon meeting him at the lack of his inch-thick movie accent. "They tried to explain the currency to me but since I was born and bred in Oklahoma, I know an American buck when I see it!"

Born in El Reno, Oklahoma, he moved as a youngster to Oklahoma City and went on to graduate from the state university. After winning a scholarship given by Metropolitan opera singer Marion Talley, he came to New York to concentrate on studying opera and the theater, but instead found himself in musical comedy. *The Gay Divorce* was his first big break.

The film version was actually his second movie (he'd made one in London while appearing there in *Divorce*) but he felt the latter would be a big one. "We knew the studio was spending a great deal of money on the production to launch Fred and Ginger Rogers as a starring dance team. (They'd second-leaded it in *Flying Down to Rio* in 1933.) It was a gamble but when it became such a success, we all got on the bandwagon together." *Top Hat* in 1935 was an even bigger success and "for a while we were an RKO family."

Though he didn't make any more films with Rogers and Astaire, Rhodes was busy in pictures like *One Rainy Afternoon* in 1936 with Francis Lederer and Ida Lupino; *Woman Chases*

Erik and his wife Emmala
in their Park Avenue apartment today

Man (1937) with Miriam Hopkins and Joel McCrea; *Criminal Lawyer,* also 1937, with matinee idol Richard Dix; and freelanced at MGM in 1938 for *Dramatic School.* He was cast in that one opposite Paulette Goddard.

His last feature was at Warner Bros. in *On Your Toes,* (1939) and for weeks he studied ballet for his Scheherazade sequences with Vera Zorina. In 1940, after six years in Lotusland, he left for a three and a half year stint in the Army, and afterwards decided to go back to New York and try to break the popular mold the movies had put him into. He didn't return to Hollywood until twelve years ago when he guested on a *Perry Mason.* "The studios were truly dream factories in the old days—worlds unto themselves. I felt like Rip Van Winkle when I saw them last, all almost empty."

The years since his Hollywood retreat have given Erik the chance to finally—and fully—explore his talents. He sampled the wild days of live television in 1950 with six months on the *Gloria Swanson Show* and starred on Broadway in *Can-Can* with Lilo in 1956, *Shinbone Alley* in 1957 with Eddie Bracken and Eartha Kitt, and a year later shared the stage with Lena Horne in *Jamaica.* He's trod the boards of every major summer theater in the United States from Colorado to St. Louis to Jones Beach (where he made his entrance in *Song of Norway* on a miniature Swedish steamboat!) in such diverse roles as the king in *The King and I,* to an encore as the courtly gentleman in *Barefoot in the Park.* In the early Sixties he was hilariously reunited with his old RKO pal Edward Everett Horton in the national company of *A Funny Thing Happened on the Way to the Forum.*

Married three years ago to Emmala La Branche, the widow of sportsman George La Branche, they last year attended a revival of *Gay Divorcee* at a small New York theater. At the end of the film the audience recognized Erik and gave him an ovation which resulted in "a real nostalgic crying jag. My wife and I broke out crying—we had a marvelous time. It gave me great pleasure to see those wonderful people on film again and remember the fun we had working together." A fun that will last as long as there are movie lovers!

149

Arriving in New York in 1938

LENI RIEFENSTAHL

The world will always call Adolph Hitler a criminally insane megalomaniac but there was, undeniably, one area in which he was brilliant—the manipulation of the minds and ideology of the German people, fanning them into the frenzied legions who came close to engulfing the globe in World War II. He recognized genius in others and surrounded himself with the best minds he could find, including that of a young blonde movie actress-turned-director named Leni Riefenstahl. In her he saw the perfect tool to set forth his ideas and desires; he put the entire German Film industry at her disposal when he commissioned her to direct the classic propaganda film of perhaps all time, *Triumph of the Will,* in 1934.

At the time she was one of Germany's top film stars, having reached her peak just two years before as star and director of the lyric *The Blue Light.*

Born August 22, 1902 to Berliners Bertha Amalie and Kaufmann Riefenstahl, Leni had planned on a career as a dancer until a leg injury forced her to channel her talents into acting. She starred in a series of outdoor epics—*Der Grosse Sprung,* (1927), *White Hell of Pitz Palu* (1929), and *Storm on White Mountain* (1930), among others—and combined a Garboesque beauty with a not inconsiderable athletic ability. Her films invariably had her framed by windswept mountains and stormy skies as a symbol of the purity of the outdoors as opposed to the decadence of big city life. *The Blue Light* was her first directorial experience and while it wasn't a smash hit in Germany, it was everywhere else. When it finally opened in New York in 1934, the *Times* critic called it a "highly fascinating fantasy." Again she played the unspoilt mountain girl who comes down to the city to enchant the big town. She also enchanted Hitler.

150

With a Nuba baby recently

He liked the film so much that he personally asked her to shoot *Triumph*, the gigantically organized paean to Nazi will-power centered around the famous Nuremberg Rally in 1934. (The week-long spectacle was carefully staged for the cameras with one million 'extras' brought to the rally.) He told her to make the film as an artist, which she staunchly says is the way she did it. Instead of giving her artistic status, it has been her downfall. In 1938 she also filmed *The Olympiad*, a poetic documentary of the sports competition but also calculated to show off the German people as a super race. Her childhood training at a Berlin art school enabled her to imbue the proceedings with an allegorical strength that further delighted Der Fuhrer.

When the German downfall engulfed her country, she did not escape it and was subjected to a 'de-Nazification' trial that made her name synonymous with those of the party's leaders. Rumors that she and Hitler were lovers and that she was, in fact, half-Jewish—stories started by envious Nazi officials during her years as Hitler's favorite—came back to haunt her.

In 1974, the Tellerude Film Festival invited her to attend and planned to award her for her undeniable contributions to moviemaking. The announcement brought forth a storm of protest and the sleepy Colorado town became, overnight, an arena of protest and dissension. (So much so that another guest, Gloria Swanson, was irked that not enough attention was being paid *her*—"There has been plenty of scandal and rumor about me. Why don't you ask me about that?") Riefenstahl used the opportunity to tell interviewers that life for her had not been the picnic people believed it to be. After the war she lost her officer-husband—"love went kaput"—her mother, her possessions and her freedom as an artist. She has not made a film since 1945's *Tiefland* and it's unlikely she ever will again.

In fact, in light of her contributions to the Nazi machine, it's doubtful that she'll ever outlive the controversy that surrounds her. For the past few years she has lived in Africa among the little-known Nuba tribe and has written and photographed a book about their simple society far removed from the everyday tribulations of the real world.

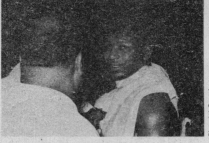
Sugar Ray in his prime

SUGAR RAY ROBINSON

Sugar Ray was one of the classiest gents to ever slip on a pair of boxing gloves and his record as a champion is one of the most distinguished and interesting in ring history, with his hopscotching from title to title and class to class, culminating in his winning of the Middleweight Championship from Jake Lamotta in 1951. When he finally left the ring in 1965, some of his legend had been tarnished (the last few years were exhibition bouts for the money—and not much of it) but any tarnishing of his reputation was personally done and he had one hell of a good time doing it!

His life is the stuff movies are made of—a Depression-torn youth which saw him uprooted from his Detroit birthplace (March 23, 1921) and transplanted to the streets of New York after his parents divorced when he was twelve. Odd jobs shining shoes, running errands for the neighborhood grocer and selling seaweed he'd collected from the Harlem River to help support his family, left him little time for an education, which he wasn't much interested in anyway. He left school before graduating, after deciding he wanted to be a fighter, and started hanging out at the Salem Crescent gym. It was there he was discovered by George Gainford, who with moneyman Curt Hoffman, shepherded him into amateur bouts—89 of them, all of which he won.

In 1939 he won the Golden Gloves Featherweight title and made his professional debut in October of 1940 in a lightweight bout against Joe Echavarria in New York. That same night he saw his idol, Welterweight champ Henry Armstrong, floored by Fritzie Zivic, and determined to avenge his defeat. He did so twice, winning a decision over Zivic in '41 and three-months later knocking him out in their famous ten round bout in January of 1942. His induction into the Army in '43 barely stopped him as he served as a sergeant in Joe Louis' boxing troupe, giving exhibitions in camps and hospitals. He was honorably

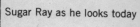
Sugar Ray as he looks today

Eddie Colbert

discharged in '44 after "ineptitude for military service" charges but he left with the reputation as being the fastest glove in the ring.

His career slipped right into high gear and in December of '46 he won the Welterweight crown after a fifteen rounder with Tommy Bell and defended it the following year against Jimmy Doyle. He won that too but Doyle died the day after the fight from ring injuries and Sugar Ray quickly stepped forward to turn over 80% of his purse to the family. His reputation as a generous 'swinger' was growing and he lived up to it. When he left for Europe for a triumphant five weeks of boxing, he sailed on the *Liberté* with his blonde wife Edna Mae and an entourage of sixteen including his barber and masseur. Europe idolized him.

He fought Jake LaMotta on Valentine's Day of '51 in the Chicago Stadium and took LaMotta's Middleweight crown after thirteen gruelling rounds, surrendering his own Welterweight crown in the process. He was acclaimed as the first black middleweight champ in twenty-five years but a year later he retired and his title went to Carl (Bobo) Olson, until he regained it in 1955. Over the next few years he remained a ranking boxer but also tried for a toehold in show business, appearing on television and in Las Vegas. It didn't work out too well.

By 1961 he was broke, having gone through some four million dollars. His marriage broke up but in Vienna in '62 he met Millie Bruce whom he married in 1965. After his final retirement he worked again as an actor but the parts were small: *Run For Your Life*, the Ben Gazzara series; *The Odd Couple*, supporting Mickey Rooney and Tony Randall at Caesar's Palace in Vegas; a detective role in Frank Sinatra's *The Detective;* and an even smaller bit in the ill-fated *Candy* in '68.

In 1973 he was elected to the Sports Hall of Fame and today he and Millie live quietly in Los Angeles where he looks after the business interests he was able to salvage. They are comfortably off and anyone who sees him knows instantly who he is. The class is still there.

Jimmie on an early publicity tour

Jack Kuster

JIMMIE RODGERS

Acknowledged as one of the fathers of country music (he was one of the first to spread that down-home word to the pop record charts with *Honeycomb* in 1957), Jimmie Rodgers was described as "a dark-skinned singer with brown eyes and black wavy hair, stands 5'11", weighs 145 pounds and owns the quietest pair of hips ever seen on a guitar player." Born in Camas, Washington, September 18, 1933, the road to international fame has been a rocky one for him, to say the least. The setbacks—like his near-fatal accident—have been major but he's managed to come through smiling, and today has the slick, been-through-it-all look of the seasoned trouper he's become.

He began singing and building up his repertoire of country-folk songs during his four-year hitch in the Air Force, adding to it the songs he learned while working as a logger around his native state of Washington. He married his high school sweetheart, Coleen McClackey, on January 4th, 1957—a good start to a great year that saw *Honeycomb* make him a star, followed quickly by some of the biggest hits of the Fifties, *Kisses Sweeter Than Wine, Oh, Oh, I'm Falling In Love,* and *Secretly.* His soft style was a nice contrast to the sexy shouting of Elvis Presley and his pack of imitators, and he was the hottest singer around, guesting on such TV variety shows as *Ed Sullivan* and *Steve Allen.*

He even got a crack at a show of his own, appropriately called *The Jimmie Rodgers Show,* but the NBC network outing only lasted from March to September of 1959. His recording of the theme from the movie *The Long Hot Summer* made up for it though—another smash hit. In fact it was so successful that an independent movie company made him an unheard of deal to sing *their* title song, something called *Seven Is For Sinners,* for a percentage of the movie's eventual profits.

Jimmie as he looks today
in his nightclub act

MGM signed him for movies and in 1961 he starred in *The
Little Shepherd of Kingdom Come.* Directed by Victor McLag-
len's son, Andrew, it was the story of a boy who fought for
the North in the Civil War and his subsequent return to civilian
life, and featured Luana Patten, Chill Wills and silent screen
idol Neil Hamilton.

The movie didn't lead to the career that MGM—and Jimmie
—had hoped for, and as the Sixties came on, his hit records
became fewer and fewer. Towards the end of 1967 he made
headlines when he was in a mysterious auto accident. He was
found near his car by police, who said he'd been struck by
a blunt instrument. It was a very serious injury and a controversial one as there were claims that the police, thinking originally
that the singer was drunk, had added to his injury. In 1968
he underwent a delicate brain operation and for a time it was
thought that he'd live out his life as a human vegetable. Happily
he recovered remarkably well and was able to resume his career.
A collapse on stage in Albuquerque, New Mexico the following
year proved to be only a temporary setback.

Before the accident he and Coleen, who by now had two
daughters, had separated and were subsequently divorced. In
1970 he remarried and currently—another two daughters later
—he and wife Trudy are celebrating their fifth anniversary.

They live in Los Angeles now and Jimmie is presently
involved in making another film, a family musical called *The
World Through The Eyes Of Children,* which he not only stars
in but has written and co-produced as well. When he completes
it he has another film in mind and is so involved with picture-
making that he's temporarily shelved his singing career in favor
of it. He still writes and performs music though, frequently
at March of Dimes Telethons. Grateful for his own recovery
he's an inspiration for those who still have a struggle ahead
of them.

155

Roland when
one of Hollywood's handsomest men

Pictorial Parade

GILBERT ROLAND

You'd never guess it by looking at him, but Gilbert Roland's career stretches back to the days when Valentino was the screen's number one hearthrob and the Latin Lover was very much the rage. He was one of the few stars to make the transition from Silents to Talkies, pulling down major roles right up to the Fifties, with even a brief spurt of new interest in the Sixties when he appeared in a couple of made-in-Spain Westerns.

The dashing swashbuckler downed his Latin Lover mantle with all the right credentials. Born Luis Antonio Damaso De Alonso in Chihuahua, Mexico in 1903, his first desire was to become a bullfighter like father and grandfather, but he then decided to answer Hollywood's open call for suave, Continental types. When barely out of his teens, he debuted in his first picture, *The Plastic Age,* in 1925. He hit big the next year in the venerable tearjerker *Camille* with Norma Talmadge, and was on his way.

Over the next few years he was in several pictures and made the transition to sound opposite Clara Bow in 1932's *Call Her Savage*—which they did, but not for long. Her career waned while his swelled, notably the following year in the Mae West romp *She Done Him Wrong.* His dark good looks nicely accented la West's buxom charms and if there had been any questions about his future, she answered them! That year he also co-starred with another famous blonde, Constance Bennett, in *Our Betters* and *After Tonight*—shortly after which he became her third husband. (They had two daughters, Lorinda and Gyl.)

Bennett was Queen of the Screen in those days, greatly overshadowing him, and with the Latin Lover finally dying an ignoble death, Roland had to work hard to keep up. He did, though, in films like 1937's *Last Train From Madrid* with Dorothy Lamour; *Juarez,* in 1939, with Bette Davis and Paul Muni, and in Errol Flynn's lusty *Sea Hawk* in 1940.

156

Gilbert Roland today

Throughout the Forties Roland specialized in those rough-and-tumble second leads, long after he and Bennett divorced: *Isle of Missing Men* (1942); *Captain Kidd* (1945); *Pirates of Monterey* (1947); *Riding the California Trail* (1948); *We Were Strangers* (1949), and *The Bullfighter and the Lady*—at last fulfilling his childhood ambition, on screen, at least—with Robert Stack and Joy Page in 1951, among others.

In 1953 he got a chance to act as Gaucho, the aging movie star in *The Bad and the Beautiful,* helping co-star Gloria Grahame win her Oscar; he played the man who tempts her away from stolid Dick Powell. It was a triumph for all concerned and he shortly left for Spain to make *That Lady* with Olivia DeHavilland, both trying gamely to recapture their romantic images of years past. It was lushly made with Paul Scofield in the cast, but it quietly flopped.

In 1959 he married again to Guillermina Cantu and appeared in *Guns Of The Timberland* with Alan Ladd and Jeanne Crain. His billing slipped from star to co-star to featured player, but the performances still had the clear masculine stamp they'd always had. He was good in 1960's *Taras Bulba* and better as an Indian chief in John Ford's 1964 Western epic, *Cheyenne Autumn.* Dolores Del Rio appeared in it with him.

In recent years Roland has kept busy handling his business interests and his ranch in the San Fernando Valley. Occasionally he'll pop up among the cast lists of action-oriented TV shows and in 1968 made *Any Gun Can Play* with Edd Byrnes in Spain. With his own daughters grown, he's done his best to help others less fortunate and has been highly praised for his work with the underprivileged in Los Angeles. He feels that he's gotten the best that America has to offer and wants to try and help others to make the same grade. He is, and deservedly so, one of Hollywood's most-liked gentlemen.

Peggy when
one of Hollywood's cutest child stars

PEGGY RYAN

In the late Thirties, Peggy Ryan was one of the cutest little tricks on the screen, delighting audiences right along with Deanna Durbin and Judy Garland, with her funny-faced grin and light-footed way with a time step. Like those others, she was for a time an MGM kiddie star but unlike Judy, got out before the going got rough. (Deanna switched to Universal in 1936 for *Three Smart Girls,* leaving Judy at Metro to fill her shoes with a vengeance!) Peggy too made her biggest pictures for Universal, teaming up with the irrepressible Donald O'Connor in a series of lighthearted musicals that began with 1942's *Private Buckeroo.* When she left movies after 1953's *All Ashore* at age 29, she'd chalked up 26 of them as a performer!

The vaudeville team of *The Dancing Ryans* knew a good thing when they had one after baby Margaret O'Rene was born to them on August 28, 1924 in Long Beach, California. They worked the baby into the act by the time she was three years old, and when she was five, they OK'ed her first motion picture, *The Wedding of Jack and Jill.*

She was only twelve when Universal (after her brief tenure at MGM spent mostly in the famous Red Schoolhouse with Judy, Mickey Rooney, Freddie Bartholomew and Deanna) signed her to a long-term contract after seeing her on stage in something called *They Can't Get You Down.* That studio's success with Durbin had them scouting high and low for other talented young ladies and Ryan tapdanced right into their arms. Her first picture for them was 1937's *Top Of The Town* after which they let her ripen on other studios' time, lending her to MGM for *The Women Men Marry* (1937); to RKO for *The Flying Irishman* (1939) about Wrong Way Corrigan's famous trip; to Republic for *She Married A Cop* (1939); and to 20th for *Grapes of Wrath* (1940) and *Sailor's Lady* (1940). After a couple more they brought her home for *Private Buckeroo*

Peggy grown-up

Tony Drake

with Donald O'Connor. They quickly became Universal's answer to Garland and Rooney and over the next few years starred together in fourteen musicals! They worked like crazy making them; *Give Out Sisters* (1942), *Get Hep To Love* (1942), *Mister Big* (1943), *Top Man* (1944), *When Johnny Comes Marching Home* (1944), *Chip Off The Old Block* (1944), *Follow The Boys* (1944), *This Is The Life* and *The Merry Monahans* (1944) were some that made them stars.

In her off-hours—which weren't many—Peggy chalked up a reputation as the engagement ring starlet, having had four of them by the time she reached nineteen! Of O'Connor she said, "He was always right on the beam, givin' out with that old double talk as fast as I could dig him." Of the ex-fiances, "Each time I thought I was in love but I guess maybe getting engaged with me is just what other girls call 'going steady.'"

She took one ring and kept it when she married actor James Cross on St. Patrick's Day, 1947. They had a son, James, but divorced in 1952. By then her movie career was virtually over. Child parts hadn't ripened into more mature roles, but she kept busy on the nightclub circuit in a song and dance act with Ray McDonald, whom she eventually married. At Columbia she made *All Ashore* with Mickey Rooney, Dick Haymes and McDonald but after that it was mostly TV. (She had been, by the by, a guest on the premiere shows of both Ed Sullivan and Milton Berle in the late Forties.) They had a child, Kerry McDonald, but grew apart career-and-other-wise, eventually divorcing. In 1958 Peggy sailed for Hawaii for a vacation and while there met Eddie Sherman, a columnist for the *Honolulu Advertiser.* The vacation turned into a romance, the romance into marriage—on board the liner *Lurline,* June 11, 1958—and the marriage into a new life away from Hollywood.

The Shermans have a child, making three altogether for Peggy, and their marriage is a secure one. Peggy lives in Hawaii and for a while guested on *Hawaii Five-O* as a semi-regular. She's happy now though and has no plans to 'comeback'.

159

Sheila as a movie ingenue in 1940

SHEILA RYAN

In 1944's *Something For The Boys,* Sheila Ryan shared leading-lady duties with Carmen Miranda, Vivian Blaine and Cara Williams in the light-hearted, Cole Porter-scored musical about the misadventures of some soldiers' wives put up in an old plantation house. Perry Como, Phil Silvers and Michael O'Shea were some of the 'boys' but Sheila held her own in the lineup very well. After all, she hadn't been *Wampus Baby Star* for nothing. Joan Leslie was also one of the 'stars' that year (1938), but it was Sheila's bit that brought down the house of hardened professional judges. Her monologue about a budding movie hopeful before and after stardom hits started out 'before' with a sweetly simple "I hope you like me" innocence while 'after' had her quickly transformed into a fur-draped celluloid goddess dropping "Daaarlings!" left and right. It was catchy enough to help her land a small role in the original Henry Aldrich flick, 1939's *What A Life* with Jackie Cooper.

Katherine Elizabeth McLaughlin was born on June 8, 1921 in Topeka, Kansas, but was brought up in Los Angeles from age three months on. She wanted to be an actress since her first play at Hollywood High, and in fact was still a student there when the Wampus honor came along. She'd been awarded an art scholarship, but turned it down in favor of acting and started in the business for real almost as she picked up her diploma. Katie McLaughlin changed her name to Sheila Ryan— at least she kept it Irish.

Her first roles were in Westerns at Republic Studios which kept her busy but hardly made her a threat to Deanna Durbin. She met and married a young actor named Eddie Norris, but they didn't stay together very long. (He, by the way, now lives in Malibu and is in the real estate business.) She got lucky when 20th Century Fox signed her to their standard $250-per-week contract and her publicity focused on how well she

160

Sheila Ryan today

managed to stretch it and still look like a movie star. (She'd had a bit of practice looking good on a budget and had been voted by her senior class in high school as Best Dressed Junior Miss.) Publicity also played up her dates with other young contract players on the lot like Bob Stack, Cesar Romero and John Payne. Meanwhile her screen roles were in things like *Careful, Soft Shoulders, Gay Caballero* (1940) *Lone Star Ranger* (1941), *Women In The Wind* (1942), and finally a biggie, *The Gang's All Here* (1943) with the Queen of the Lot, Alice Faye, as well as Payne and Carmen Miranda. In one sequence of the Busby Berkely-directed musical, she danced with Tony DeMarco of the DeMarco dance team. Meanwhile studio publicity mills continued grinding out puff stuff like when she was selected by a group of football coaches and makeup men (in undoubtedly one of their rare moments of togetherness) as having one of "the perfect figures in the world of sports and movies."

She married cowboy star Allan "Rocky" Lane but they divorced in 1946, the same year she made *A-Haunting We Will Go* and *Lone Wolf In London.* Two years later she was good in a low budget circus-murder outing, *Caged Fury,* with Buster Crabbe.

The Fifties started with a new marriage to Gene Autry's sidekick Pat Buttram and a co-starring role with them in *Mule Train* (1950). She was busy out of the saddle too in *Jungle Manhunt* (1951); *Mask of the Dragon* (1951); and *Fingerprints Don't Lie* (1951), but finished her career back among the sagebrush in 1953 with Autry and Buttram in *Pack Train.*

In 1954 the Buttrams had a daughter, Kathleen, and though Sheila did a bit of early television, she pretty much dropped out of sight. They live in Northridge, California but Sheila herself in recent years has become something of a recluse. One fan waited seven years to meet her. When he did get in though she was glad to see him. Rumored to be very ill lately, she's no longer seen out with Buttram on his endless round of testimonial dinners. Perhaps she's had all the chicken à la king she cares to have!

161

Dr. Jonas Salk in the research laboratory of Muncipal Hospital, Pittsburgh, Pennsylvania, shortly after his world-shaking discovery

DR. JONAS SALK

As a kid who grew up in the Fifties, I vividly remember the summer of 1955 when, thanks to the genius of Dr. Jonas Salk, a vaccine was developed which eliminated the fear of the crippling disease of polio. Before its discovery, the cares and cautions of mothers everywhere made drinking from a playground fountain tantamount to suicide because of possible exposure to the dread disease. However, once the Federal government approved the commercial production of Salk's killed-polio-virus vaccine, he became their hero overnight. As children lining up for the shots, we may not have agreed, but a large cloud was indeed lifted from the nation and from the future of children all over the world.

Today, Salk's vaccine is no longer produced in the United States. In its place most doctors use the Sabin, live oral vaccine, and Dr. Salk is not sure that the switch has been for the better. He feels that though polio "is now under control where vaccination has been practiced," the virus has been completely stamped out only where his killed-virus vaccine is used exclusively—"Sweden, Finland, Holland, the province of Ontario, Canada." Of the live vaccine now used he says: "I can't confidently recommend to anyone that they be vaccinated with it without recognizing that risk is entailed." He contends it causes "several cases of paralysis a year" and reintroduces polio into the population.

Though slightly disillusioned now, Salk is philosophical about his work and achievements. The son of a garment worker, he was born in New York City on October 28, 1914, and initially envisioned a law career. He switched to medicine though, and his keen, analytical mind soon told him he'd made the right choice. In 1946 he discovered an improved influenza vaccine and three years later began his research into polio basically because "it was just another job to be done in a field in which I was interested." The acclaim he received beginning in 1955

Dr. Salk with his wife, Francoise Gilot, the artist

mattered little to him. When asked who owned the patent on his vaccine he replied, "the people. Could you patent the sun?" After countless honorary dinners and lectures, he quipped, "Sometimes I wish I had developed a preventative for Chicken a la King!" Once the limelight died down a bit, though, Salk returned to the life of a dedicated researcher.

Most recently he has turned his attention to investigating the potential of the human brain and expounds his somewhat controversial theories about that subject in a book entitled, *The Survival Of the Wisest*. He feels that in order for the world to survive in the years ahead, it needs to develop, and concentrate on, the fifty percent of the population who are most intelligent. He feels a conscious effort should be made to select the most "sensible" among us and encourage them to flourish and multiply. He also figures that a democracy with only 50% "sensible" voters would be enough to maintain the best degree of government. A radical theory? Perhaps, but as a scientist he feels his job is not to determine any moral issues of an idea but rather it's obvious efficacy.

In 1970 Salk surprised his colleagues and the world at large when he married French artist Francoise Gilot, a former mistress of Pablo Picasso and the mother of his two children, Claude Ruiz and Paloma. After the engagement, Claude told newsmen, "My mother met Dr. Salk through friends in California. I know they are going to be very happy together and both my sister and I are delighted about it." Paloma met Salk in Paris at a 1970 art exhibit of her mother's work where she commented, "This is only the second time we have met," adding drily, "but, after all, mothers are allowed to get married."

The Salks now live a quiet life near his lavish Salk Research Institute outside San Diego, California. He prefers his privacy and now that he's regained it after years in the spotlight, is anxious to keep it. Which may be for the best since the mind that conquered polio may well be able to conquer other ills if given the time and the atmosphere in which to do it.

163

NATALIE SCHAFER

Natalie has played *so* many chicly dizzy society ladies in *so* many movies that she's lost count. She could have been a major star had she taken up Louis B. Mayer's MGM contract offer in 1945 but instead chose independence—which has resulted in a hilarious assortment of well-coiffed women that has kept her busy longer than any one studio possibly could.

She knew she was meant to be an actress as soon as she realized that she could get her own way by carrying on. Born in Red Bank, New Jersey in 1912, she started drama courses almost as soon as she started school. When she was finished with her formal education she made straight for the stage and after a year or so in Ina Claire-type roles ("Ina played them on Broadway, I got them afterwards.") got her first Broadway role in 1927's *Trigger*. After *Adam Beats The Drum* with Mary Boland, (1930) and a few more like *The Great Barrington* with Otto Kruger (1931), she was given the part that changed her life in *The Rhapsody* with Louis Calhern. She played his mistress in it (Calhern's wife was also in it) and shortly thereafter life began imitating art. She and Calhern began a "tempestuous" affair, of which she says, "I was scared to death. And when he divorced his wife to marry me, I couldn't believe it!"

It was a perfect union in every respect but one: Calhern had a drinking problem. "Other than that he was perfectly marvelous and we remained great friends until he died, even though we didn't stay married too terribly long."

In 1936 she starred in *Lady Precious Stream* on Broadway and in *Susan and God* in 1938 with Gertrude Lawrence. In 1940 she co-starred with Calhern in *Royal Family*. After *Lady In The Dark* (1944), she got her call from Hollywood.

"I went out to play Lana Turner's mother in *Marriage Is A Private Affair* in 1944 and afterwards Mr. Mayer wanted me to sign for seven years. I said no, that if I started by playing

Having a laugh with author in her Park Avenue apartment

Jon B. Aroneo

mothers, I'd end up playing Clifton Webb's! Well I went out again to play Lana's sister in *Keep Your Powder Dry* the next year and he called me in again, saying what a brilliant career I'd have, how flexible I was, etc. I said no again because I was in love and the man was in New York. He said, 'We'll bring him out,'' and then I told him the man's wife might object and, well, he hit the ceiling! He said how he thought I was such a lady and how few there were in pictures and finally told me to get out of his office.''

But Mayer's wrath couldn't stop a talent like Natalie's and over the next few years she worked constantly—''I was always the star's best friend; Hedy Lamarr's, *(Dishonored Lady,* 1947*)*, Joan Bennett's *(Secret Beyond the Door,* 1948), Greer Garson's, Claudette Colbert's—everybody's. That's why I loved my part in *The Snake Pit* (1948). Suddenly I had a chance to play a woman without makeup, pregnant—I had to fight to wear a sandbag so that I could walk like a pregnant woman. I loved it!''

Her archly stylish wit continued to keep her busy right through the Fifties in pictures like Joan Crawford's *Female On The Beach* (1955), *Anastasia* (1956)—as a rich American who adores impoverished nobility—and sparkled briefly in Susan Hayward's *Back Street* in 1961—''a marvelous girl and a fine talent.''

When she was offered *Gilligan's Island* in 1963 she accepted the idea of a series because ''the script was so awful I didn't think it had a prayer. I burst into tears when it was sold. Originally my part was a very proper Pasadena lady, but I asked to meet the writers, bought them each a copy of *Dulcie,* and made her a scatterbrain. We had a marvelous time''—and so did America for the next three and a half years. She doesn't watch the reruns any more ''because I don't get paid any more residuals.'' She does voice-overs for the cartoon version though, and between stage appearances in things like *The Front Page,* squeezed in *The Day Of The Locust.* ''I play the madam of a whorehouse—a very respectable madam I mean!'' And if anyone could pull it off, Natalie could—and did!

Jacque Sernas on his first trip
to Hollywood, 1955

Jack Kuster

JACQUES SERNAS

When Technicolor, Vista-Vision and Stereophonic Sound
were at their glorious peaks in the mid-Fifties, Hollywood
studios utilized them to showcase beautiful young people on
whom they'd pinned their hopes for stardom. Warner Bros.
launched one of their periodic campaigns with a lavish version
of one of history's most romantic tales, *Helen of Troy*, casting
in the lead roles two of Europe's most promising young talents,
Rossana Podesta as Helen, and Jacques Sernas as Paris. They
were chosen after a world-wide talent hunt which caused the
hearts of thousands of young hopefuls to beat a little bit faster.
As the man who wooed and tragically won the beauteous Helen,
Sernas performed more than capably but the picture itself,
despite the lavish attention to details (including Hollywood's
biggest wooden horse), laid an egg at the U.S. box office.
Supported by Stanley Baker and Sir Cedric Hardwicke, Sernas
and Podesta did their beautiful best but it just wasn't enough.
The film is mostly remembered now for the brief appearances
of a brown-haired Brigitte Bardot who scampered through a
few scenes as Helen's maid.

For a while Sernas was a movie Golden Boy. He was born
in Kaunas, Lithuania on July 30, 1925, to a wealthy family
and was educated in Paris and in the United States. All that
ended when World War II broke out. The Nazis confiscated
his family's holdings and Sernas joined the French Resistance,
a patriotic act that earned him one and a half years in Buchen-
wald.

When the war ended he had to take whatever jobs he could
get, supporting himself variously as a waiter, a night watchman
and a ski instructor. He studied for a medical career but in
1945 got a chance to make a movie with France's leading male
star, Jean Gabin, and took it. It was *Miroir* and he played a
boxer. A few years later he got his first lead in *Lost Youth*,

As he appears in *Children of Rage* in 1975

which nabbed him the Italian Silver Ribbon Award making him a very hot star in the process. In 1951 he was so busy that he worked on two films simultaneously: *Mill On The Po* and *The Wolf of Sila*.

After almost two dozen films, Warners spotted him and brought him to Hollywood in 1955, Americanizing him temporarily to Jack Sernas. They starred him in *Jump Into Hell,* a parachute yarn, and while he didn't threaten their other blond, Tab Hunter, they publicized him as much as possible, fan-mag matching him with available Warner starlets. He surprised them though when he met and married Maria Stella, a *Paris-Match* reporter.

For *Helen of Troy* the studio originally tested him for the role of Aneas, Paris's companion, but gave him top spot instead. The film was shot in Europe, premiering in 1957 in fifty countries simultaneously. Audiences abroad liked it even if most Americans remained somewhat cool. The studio, then heavy into television, cast him on many shows, notably *Captain Without a Country* opposite Inger Stevens, and a Matinee Theater episode, *The Pursuit of Happiness,* but he never made another major American movie.

When his contract was up he went back to Europe and worked constantly. His chiseled good looks and classic body were perfect for the Italian shoestring epics and he made a lot of them—*Sign of The Gladiator* (1959), *The Nights of Lucretia Borgia* (1960), *The Loves òf Sallambo* (1962), and two Steve Reeves epics, both 1963. The best acting he ever did was in Fellini's *La Dolce Vita* in 1961. He played an aging movie idol trying to borrow against his next picture salary, but few in the huge American audiences who saw the film recognized him as the golden Prince Paris of just a few years before.

Today Sernas lives in Rome and still works although his parts fall now into the character actor category. He was recently seen in *Children of Rage,* billed as "also starring in alphabetical order. . . ."

Wini in a typical movie pose as a Broadway hostell. The man with the big eyes in Phil Regan.

WINI SHAW

In the difficult days of the Depression-struck Thirties, the public turned to the motion picture screen for relief, and luckily there was a genius named Busby Berkeley at Warner Bros. Studios who knew precisely how to give it to them. While he often focused on social problems—as with Joan Blondell's heartrending *Remember My Forgotten Man* number from *Forty-Second Street*—his primary gift was taking the public's mind off their troubles, substituting gorgeous chorus lines and intricate dance numbers for the monotonous regularity of the bread lines! Pictures like *Gold Diggers of 1933, Forty-Second Street* (1933), *Footlight Parade* (1933), *Dames* (1934) and others gave a weary America coin-covered chorus girls *(We're In The Money)*, dancing violins *(The Shadow Waltz)*, shipshape cadets *(Flirtation Walk)*, and pyramids of bathing beauties *(By A Waterfall)*. Stars like Dick Powell, Ruby Keeler, Joan Blondell, Ginger Rogers, and even Jimmy Cagney cut their teeth in Berkeley's musicals—as did another star, Wini Shaw. In *The Gold Diggers of 1935* she sang *The Lullaby of Broadway,* and neither the street or the movies have been the same since!

The number—a story in itself—opens with a tight close-up of Wini's face, a white dot in the darkness, which melts away to expose the "hip hooray and ballyhoo" of the world's most famous street, complete with its denizens of every size, shape, and color. The bustling streets, a ballroom crowded with frenzied dancers all cavorting till "early in the morning" because "Manhattan babies don't sleep tight until the dawn," was all captured in the strikingly dramatic number that was the finale—and the high point—of the film. At the scene's end, the carousing gold digger, Shaw, is separated from her boyfriend of the evening and hurtles over a balcony to her death. As her face

Wini on a recent New York
night on the town

again appeared full-screen to dissolve away again, even Depression-weary audiences were affected by the on-screen drama.

Born Winifred Lei Momi Shaw (San Francisco, California, February 25, 1910), the singer broke into show business at age eleven when she joined her family's Hawaiian vaudeville troupe. Of Hawaiian/Irish/English ancestry, her first number was a Kanaka chorus. In 1925 she married orchestra leader Leo Cummins and they quickly had three children, Elizabeth, James, and John, before the marriage ended in 1929. He helped steer her towards the big time and she was well-known when she made her first film in the early Thirties for Fox, *Wild Gold*. During those years she appeared in many movies including, in 1934, *Three On A Honeymoon* and *Gift of Gab*. As Winifred Shaw she was in Warner's *Sweet Adeline,* the excellent *Front Page Woman* and in *Sons 'O Guns,* and also appeared, vocally at least, in others as the voice behind the stars in many a production number.

After *Gold Diggers of 1935,* Wini starred in *In Caliente* (1935), singing another song that's perhaps her true signature tune—*The Lady In Red.* That was her billing when she eventually returned to vaudeville. Her last movie was 1937's *Melody For Two.* After her Hollywood sojourn, the stage welcomed her back with open arms and she starred at Ben Marden's *Exhibit of Beauty* on the heights across New York's Hudson River—one reviewer said that "besides being 'shockingly' beautiful, she also sings" — and at Miami's famous Olympia Music Hall.

In 1955 she married Bill O'Malley and it has been a long and happy union. The live quietly in Sunnyside, Queens in New York and she's very active in the Catholic Actors Guild. In 1971 she suffered a stroke which temporarily cut down her activities but when I caught up with her she was very much up and about, singing along with old chum Roberta Sherwood at the latter's nightclub return in New York.

As you can see, the face has hardly changed since she warned people not to listen too closely to the "lullaby of Old Broadway."

Roberta in the Fifties

ROBERTA SHERWOOD

When Roberta Sherwood burst on the national scene in 1956, people didn't know quite what to make of her. She was a forty-three-year-old housewife who'd been singing since her childhood but no one had heard her very much except around Miami, Florida, belting out old standards and accompanying herself on a cymbal and wire brush. Thanks to Walter Winchell that all changed overnight and she became a 'name'—the first middle-aged woman to hit it big, which in the un-Liberated Fifties was quite extraordinary.

Born in St. Louis, Missouri in 1913, she broke into vaudeville in her father's minstrel act after her mother's death, when she was seven. A splendid monologist, her father recited poems like *The Face On The Barroom Floor* while Roberta and her sister sang and danced their way through numbers like *I Had Somebody Else Before I had You and I'll Have Somebody Else After You're Gone.* In 1932 she went on her own and one of her first bookings was at Miami's Silver Slipper—certainly one of the luckiest she ever got. The club's manager was Don Lanning, some seventeen years older than she and a Broadway veteran of several Twenties musicals. He taught her a few more tricks of the entertainment trade and before long she became a fixture around the Miami club circuit. After seven years of that, though, she finally agreed to give up her career to marry him. She did, with three sons to follow.

When the children were old enough to handle the news, Roberta went back to the bandstand in her husband's club. All was going splendidly for the husband-wife team when tragedy struck. Lanning was operated on for lung cancer and came out of it an invalid. With a mortgage on their home and a family to maintain, Roberta got a job at a small club for a small salary—$150.00 a week. She might have stayed there too, but for Walter Winchell, who happened in one night in 1956. He was struck by the plucky lady's way with a song

After a performance at New York's Spindletop with son Jerry Lanning

and spread the good news via his gossip column and radio show. It wasn't long before she found herself starring at the Eden Roc Hotel for $1,700 a week, shortly afterwards invading New York's Copacabana.

Singing things like *Up A Lazy River, Smoke Gets In Your Eyes* and *You're Nobody Till Somebody Loves You*, she was a hit in Gotham even if her image as a be-spectacled woman with a sweater thrown around her shoulders was a far cry from nightclub chic-sters like Lena Horne and Hildegarde. She TV-debuted on *The Jackie Gleason Show* and did virtually every other show too, including Edward R. Murrow's *Person to Person*. Her recordings became hits, and Las Vegas was only a short step away. There she introduced a piece of business other stars have been copying ever since—her entrance from the back of the room, down through the crowd and singing all the way. "One night John Wayne was there and we shook hands as I went by but he got up out of his chair and kept on coming. Everybody wants to get into the act!" She also starred as George M. Cohan's mother in a TV special called *Mr. Broadway,* with Mickey Rooney and June Havoc in 1959.

Though her bigtime career got somewhat lost in the shuffle of the Sixties' changing entertainment tastes, Roberta hasn't been idle. She appears in Las Vegas in small rooms and when she isn't working, lives in Sherman Oaks, California. Her three sons have all done well; Don currently works at the Dunes Hotel in Vegas, and Bob's a drummer—"and a great one. But he's too expensive for me!" Son Jerry starred with Angela Lansbury in Broadway's *Mame* and has the looks and voice to make a long and successful career an easy prediction.

Recently she made her first New York appearance in eight years at Van Rapoport's *Upstairs at the Spindletop,* bringing back all the tunes and camaraderie that made her famous. The two-time grandmother with golden blonde hair now even brought back the old cymbal, beating it with the same relish that made her a star as she happily sang *Just The Kind of a Girl Men Forget*—but obviously everyone remembered!

171

Pictorial Parade

PRINCESS SORAYA

The romantics of the world sighed loudly in March of 1958 when the Shah of Iran, Mohammed Reza Pahlavi, divorced his beautiful young wife of just over seven years, Princess Soraya, because of her inability to bear him a son to carry on the royal succession. Their marriage had been a love match that equalled anything in the *Arabian Nights* but love alone was not enough to satisfy the Iranian people or the Shah's advisors. He reluctantly let her go and she began a life as an international nomad, a tragically beautiful figure who still drifts from one posh watering spot to another in quest of a full life.

Soraya had been the Shah's second wife. His first was King Farouk's sister, Princess Fawzia, whom he'd wed in 1939 when he was twenty. Though they had a daughter, Princess Shahnaz, Fawzia too was unable to produce a male heir and they were divorced in 1948. He then began a search for another wife which eventually took him outside the list of international royal possibilities and into the arms of Soraya Esfandiary the daughter of a noble Iranian family. She was eighteen and he was thirty-two and their wedding was a cause of joyful celebration in Iran, but as the years wore on, their personal happiness was marred by her infertility, an insurmountable obstacle to overcome. Soraya's father, Prince Esfandiary, became the Persian ambassador to West Germany and it was to his embassy in Bonn that she went in early March of 1958 when rumors first surfaced that their marriage was ending. At first the Shah considered taking a second wife but days later, on March 13, Soraya's uncle, Prince Assad Bakhtiar, arrived in West Germany with the Shah's final decision: it would be divorce. It happened almost overnight; she went to sleep the Queen of Iran and woke up Princess Soraya. (Had she had a son, she would have been named Empress, as was her successor, Farah Diba.)

She was twenty-five then, and, chaperoned by her princess-mother and younger brother Bijan, began her life of wandering.

Sorayo today, off to another party

In November of 1959 when the Shah's engagement to art student Farah Diba became public, he wrote her saying she would never have to care about her future financially or otherwise and that Iranian embassies all over the world would help her at any time. She said simply, ''The Shah has told me not to worry.''

Within the year her name began to be linked with a succession of out of work nobility, playboys and film stars—Prince Alonzo de Bourbon, grandson of Spanish King Alphonso XIII; Prince Raimondo Orsini; Maximilian Schell. In 1963 she and Schell made headlines in Istanbul, Turkey when they landed in jail, briefly, after an altercation with a photographer. Schell got a black eye out of it and Soraya just got embarrassed. German auto king Gunther Saks von Opel, later married briefly to Brigitte Bardot, was another suitor.

When in 1965 producer Dino de Laurentiis announced he would make a movie star out of her, the Shah was rumored to be against it but Soraya went ahead anyway, beginning work on an historical epic appropriately entitled *The Empress* in Athens, Greece. Production halted though when the producer could find no big male star who would take second billing to her. (As former Queen, Soraya thought she deserved top spot.) Undaunted, de Laurentiis went ahead with another, *Three Faces Of A Woman,* an episodic 'woman's' picture about the trials and tribulations of a beautiful woman. Taking it all very seriously, Soraya told newsmen who flocked to the Venice shooting site, ''I am no longer a princess. I am now just Soraya, an actress.'' Critics heartily disagreed, however, and her film career ended as abruptly as it had begun.

Soraya's home base is Rome, where she maintains a beautiful house, but actually she's as often there as she is in Paris, London, or any other Beautiful People gathering place. In the past two years she's been linked to film director Franco Indovini, who directed a segment of her movie, and a 27-year-old Frenchman, Claude Kahouza. It's doubted she'll ever marry again and once, when asked if she had any ambition, she answered, ''My ambition is to learn from life.'' She's still learning.

Kay and discoverer
Joe Venuti in 1948

Pictorial Parade

KAY STARR

Though she hit it big in the blues and ballads field primarily, Kay Starr's roots were strictly downhome Southern. The dark-haired songstress with the big voice was born in Dougherty, Oklahoma in 1923, but before she was four years old had become a resident of Dallas, Texas. As little Catherine Starks she stayed there long enough to start high school but then moved again with her family to Memphis, Tennessee. She left behind her a singing spot on station WRR in Dallas which had earned her $15 a week. When she got to Memphis, she changed her name, upped her price, and landed another job at WREC singing with the studio orchestra. It was at that station two years later, when she was fifteen and part of a cowboy outfit called the Light Crust Boys, that jazz violinist Joe Venuti discovered her and signed her to sing with his orchestra. She had to finish high school before she could take Venuti up on his offer full-time but after graduating at seventeen, she did, trouping through a thousand one night stands over the next few years. Glenn Miller heard her during this period and set up a recording test at Victor Records, but stardom was still a long way away.

She joined Bob Crosby's orchestra and doubled as vocalist and emcee on the first radio show sponsored by Camel cigarettes, but even with Johnny Mercer's help as a writer, the show didn't make it. In 1943 Kay joined up with Charlie Barnet and his band, and toured for two more years until she developed a serious throat ailment and had to go into temporary retirement. For a full year she scarcely spoke let alone sang but never seriously thought about not coming back to the business. In school she'd flirted with the idea of becoming a fashion designer but her years on the bandstand convinced her that the flirtation

Kay as she looks today

was over. She was sure of one other thing too, and that was that she wouldn't be returning to the bandstand.

Instead she took a chance and struck out as a single, her new voice sweeter and with a haunting roughness around the edges. After landing a deal with Capitol Records, she recorded *I'm The Loneliest Girl In The World* and had her first hit. She appeared on bills with The Andrew Sisters, Connie Boswell, and even The Three Stooges but shortly segued from 'also starring' to full-fledged billing as a single at Slapsie Maxie Rosenblum's Hollywood nightclub.

The hits kept coming for Kay after that: *Bonaparte's Retreat, Frankie and Johnny,* her own version of Sunny Gale's *Wheel of Fortune,* and a popular re-do of the classic *Stormy Weather.* In 1953 the owners of the Flamingo Hotel in Las Vegas presented her with a diamond-studded cigarette case engraved "To Kay 'Never A Vacant Chair' Starr" after her record-breaking four-week run there.

Rock and Roll Waltz was another big hit, and in 1956 she went dramatic on television's *Producer's Showcase* with Louis Armstrong and Dick Haymes in *The Lord Don't Play Favorites* as the owner of a small traveling circus. When rock and roll really took over, Kay found herself in a bind. While her star billing remained tops, the money offers didn't until, in 1960, she decided to limit herself to the best of the bunch and work only about ten weeks a year. She was quoted as saying that an average offer of $5,000 a week hardly covered the cost of her band, costumes, hairdresser, etc.

Since that decision, Kay's stuck to her guns and works only when she really wants to. Six times married, the songbird's current husband is businessman Delmar Guenther and they live in Beverly Hills, California in great style.

Credit: Christopher Young

Pat backstage after a performance of *Flower Drum Song,* 1960

PAT SUZUKI

In the old days having a starring role in a Broadway hit meant a ticket to Hollywood. People like Ray Bolger, June Allyson and Erik Rhodes all started there before flashing their faces on the silver screen, but in the Sixties that one-way-ticket syndrome had virtually vanished. Broadway was just another street in New York and what happened there didn't matter much in the power towers of the West Coast. In fact it didn't matter much in New York either once your hit had run its course, as talented Pat Suzuki can tell you. Pat starred in the glorious Richard Rodgers musical *Flower Drum Song* in 1960 and for a while was one of the shiniest lights on the Great White Way. But since then, she admits, "I haven't been able to get arrested."

The Japanese-descended songstress became somewhat of a household word one night in 1959 after being discovered in a Seattle, Washington nightclub by Bing Crosby. Der Bingle helped get her on the *Jack Paar Show,* where the tiny (4'11") Oriental doll sang her heart out and laughed her way into Paar's notably fickle affections. Luckily composer Rodgers was watching too and that's how she got *Flower Drum Song.*

It opened to rave reviews and was just what the theater needed, a happy show. It was so good in fact that the show itself was snapped up for the movies—but not the star. Pat's part, in the 1961 less-than-grand version, went to Myoshi Umeki, the girl who had died in Red Buttons' arms in the weepie *Sayonara* five years before. Hollywood's version of the Chinese picture bride was lavishly overproduced and had a fair-to-poor reception at the box office, but it really didn't matter to Pat by that time.

Married to President John F. Kennedy's photographer, Mark

On a recent windy afternoon in New York

Shaw, she had a son, David, in 1961. When Shaw died in 1970 they were already divorced but had happily been able to remain friends. Without his support though—"I haven't had any family to push me"—things went from bad to worse. The girl who grew up on a farm in Cressy, California began to find out just how tough New York can be, but she stayed and stuck it out. There were some offers for her services though, and as unlikely as they seemed she took them, playing a French girl in the Montreal and Toronto version of *Irma la Douce,* and Orientalizing the role in *The Owl and The Pussycat* originated by the late black star Diana Sands. She starred in New York with George Takei at the American Place Theater in *The Year of the Dragon* but not enough people saw it either there or when it was filmed and shown on public television. Singing offers were mostly in clubs like Greenwich Village's *Trude Heller's,* once a vanguard of the Swinging Sixties but recently more a showcase for new acts or a refuge for old ones.

But Pat's not discouraged. She jokes about the fact that like any novice in the business she lines up in agents' offices for a part in a TV commercial, but feels "you never leave the arts be you writer, composer, musician or actor. It's always your love. It's what makes you cook. You have to use your spirit, your optimum resources," adding ruefully, "it strengthens your character."

Age-wise she admits, "I was twenty-one plus when Bing Crosby discovered me. I'm twenty-one plus now—I've reached the age of reason."

For a while the tiny singer struggled with a weight problem but that's behind her now—literally, not figuratively. In May of 1975 she appeared in Las Vegas for the first time in years and while not exactly a headliner, did good business in one of the hotels' lounges. Old friend Merv Griffin gave her a spot on his TV show and she sang with the same zest of fifteen years ago. As to why she hasn't been back on Broadway since her *Song* ended: "The truth? Nobody asked me. But they will." And she may just be right about that.

Phyllis at her comeliest in 1951

PHYLLIS THAXTER

Ladylike could perhaps be the best adjective to describe Phyllis Thaxter's image on the wide screen. She had that quality in her debut movie, 1944's *Thirty Seconds Over Tokyo,* as Van Johnson's wartime wife, and she still had it in her last big screen outing twenty years later, 1964's *The World of Henry Orient.* In between she starred in some dozen and a half films, always precisely pretty and classily dependable. Usually holding down wife roles, the hubby in question (like Ronald Reagan in 1952's *She's Working Her Way Through College)* might be temporarily vamped away (in that instance by burlesque queen Virginia Mayo), but he always returned in time for THE END.

Like Gene Tierney and later, Dina Merrill, Phyllis came to acting from a very stable and very social background. She was born in Portland, Maine on November 20, 1920, where her father was a state Supreme Court judge. A natural actress, she talked her family into letting her play in the Ogunquit, Maine summer theater and eventually got good enough to try Broadway. One of her first real breaks was as Dorothy McGuire's understudy in the hit play *Claudia,* where an MGM talent scout saw her and signed her up. *Thirty Seconds Over Tokyo* didn't give her that much to do, focusing as it did on America's first attack on Japan, but it was a big hit, big enough to get her her first lead in her next film, *Betwitched* in 1945. Playing a schizophrenic girl who murders in one personality and forgets it in the other, she got good reviews and excellent support in it from Edmund Gwenn and Henry Daniell. That same year she was in the glossy remake of *Grand Hotel,* retitled *Weekend At The Waldorf.* Another popular hit, the credit went mostly to Ginger Rogers, Lana Turner and Walter Pidgeon. Her next biggie was *Sea of Grass,* perhaps the most unsuccessful of the Spencer Tracy-Katherine Hepburn pairings. Made in 1947, she did her best opposite Robert Walker but it was a lost cause.

Phyllis at a recent Hollywood screening with director Ralph Nelson

She continued at MGM for several more pictures like *Living In A Big Way* (1947), *Tenth Avenue Angel* (1948), and *Act Of Violence* (1948) but got really meaty roles only after moving over to Warner Bros. Film historian Christopher Young maintains that she deserved a Best Supporting Actress nomination for her work in 1950's *The Breaking Point,* a remake of Hemingway's *To Have And Have Not* which teamed her with high voltage actors like John Garfield and Patricia Neal. After a modest Western, *Fort Worth* (1951), they put her opposite Burt Lancaster in *Jim Thorpe—All American* (1951) in which she suffered long and often as the Indian athlete's wife. The highly realistic *Come Fill the Cup* came next that year and she was excellent in the drama about an alcoholic newspaperman's (Jimmy Cagney) battle with the bottle.

After several more at Warners, she freelanced at Columbia for the very steamy—and often very funny—*Women's Prison* (1955) which teamed her with as hard-boiled a bunch of dames as ever set foot inside a movie jailyard—Ida Lupino, the sadistic matron; Jan Sterling, the whore with the heart of gold (who quips to the butch matron who takes her earrings away, "Wear 'em with green honey, they did wonders for me."); Mae Clarke, the sympathetic guard; and Audrey Totter, the dumb blonde with a husband in the jail next door. Oh how she suffered in that one!

Married in 1944 to James Aubrey, the man who much later changed MGM from Hollywood's greatest studio to a TV production company singlehanded, she divorced him in 1962 after having two children, Susan and James, Jr. Her daughter changed her name to Skye Aubrey and works often on TV. In fact, one of Thaxter's most recent acting outings was co-starring with Skye in a TV-movie about a real-life kidnapping.

Since 1963 she's been quietly married to Gilbert Lea, the head of Tower Publishing Company and they live quietly in her home state of Maine most of the year. As precisely pretty as ever, she's gracious but not chummy to her fans.

179

Todd in 1954

Jack Kuster

RICHARD TODD

Richard Todd was the kind of movie actor who should never have grown old. His apple-cheeked youthfulness, so evident in his 1949 screen hit *The Hasty Heart,* was his primary asset and in later years when he did pictures like the dim remake of *The Portrait of Dorian Gray* (1972), it was too obviously gone. It certainly wasn't his fault, but it was sad nonetheless.

Brought up in a proper British Army family, though Dublin-born in 1919, Todd was raised in India and in England. He joined an acting repertory group in Dundee when he was twenty but left it to serve His Majesty in World War II, seeing service in both parachute and commando divisions. When he was mustered out he returned there to star for eighteen months in the stage version of *Hasty Heart.* In 1948 he made a film called *From Them That Trespass* but it wasn't until *Heart's* cinematic reincarnation a year later that his real movie career began. It was a sensation, linking him with Hollywood actors Patricia Neal and Ronald Reagan in the poignant drama of a dying soldier. It—and he—was deemed sensational and Warner Bros. imported the film to America where it was enthusiastically received.

Heart's director, Vincent Sherman, helped Tott to shine in that one, as was obvious when his next film, Alfred Hitchcock's *Stage Fright,* was released in 1950. As good as he is, Hitchcock had his hands full with Todd and later admitted the film came off badly, Marlene Dietrich and Jane Wyman notwithstanding, because "the villain (Todd) was a flop."

Todd made some more films in Britain like *Portrait of Clare, Lightning Strikes Twice,* and *Flesh and Blood,* all in 1950, before Walt Disney signed him for *Robin Hood and His Merry Men.*

Disney gave his career a whole new lease on life, starring him again in *The Sword and The Rose* and *Rob Roy,* both in

Todd in New York in 1975

1954, and both hugely successful with Disney ticket-buyers. So effective was Todd that 20th Century Fox got interested and signed him to a long-term contract, kicked off with *A Man Called Peter,* an inspirational account of the life of Peter Marshall, which co-starred Jean Peters. He went back into costume opposite Bette Davis in 1955's *The Virgin Queen* and also that year starred in *The Dam Busters,* a British-made WWII opus with Michael Redgrave. He stayed in military uniform for *D-Day, The Sixth of June* with Robert Taylor the following year.

In 1958 he surfaced in Otto Preminger's disasterous *St. Joan;* a thriller called *Chase A Crooked Shadow* with Anne Baxter; and his last film for 20th Century Fox, *Intent To Kill* with Betsy Drake. In 1961 he did make an attempt to break the pretty-boy mold by playing a failing cosmetics salesman in a seamy little picture called *Never Let Go* with Peter Sellers. It failed for both of them and he traveled to South Africa for a 'Western' called *The Hellions* and popped up in Zanuck's *The Longest Day,* all that same year.

In 1965 he was very good opposite Maureen O'Hara and Rossano Brazzi in *The Battle of the Villa Fiorita* but was then off screen until *Operation Crossbow* in '69. That year he divorced his first wife Catherine to marry a model some twenty years his junior but even the spate of headlines it caused (he had been named by his new wife's former husband as correspondent in their divorce suit) didn't rekindle much professional interest.

The Seventies have seen Richard return to the London stage in revivals of things like *The Constant Husband,* and also appear in minor films such as the pale remake of *Dorian Gray* with Helmut Berger.

He and his wife live on a dairy farm in Sussex, and except for occasional tours like his recent Australian one in *Sleuth,* he's content to stay there enjoying the role of gentleman farmer. He's earned the right.

181

Colleen in the 20th Century studio parking lot in 1951

Jack Kuster

COLLEEN TOWNSEND

Religion and movie stardom aren't a particularly compatible mixture career-wise and Colleen Townsend's living proof of it. The beautiful brunette walked away from stardom when it was just within her grasp in 1950's *When Willie Comes Marching Home,* and though initial reaction was that her conversion from 20th Century Fox to a higher calling was a publicity stunt, she soon proved it wasn't when she broke her contract and married divinity student Louis Evans Jr., her childhood sweetheart. Though she was only twenty-two at the time, Colleen had been in movies for quite a spell, starting out in 1944 at Warner Bros where she appeared in *The Very Thought of You* and as a child bride in the popular *Janie.* By age sixteen she'd been let go and labeled a has-been by the movie press, and though the way back was a hard one, she'd almost made it when she made her ultimate decision to quit the business.

A California native, (Glendale, December 21, 1928), Colleen had been signed by Warners when she was only fifteen and her two pictures for them might have been the extent of her career if 20th Century Fox hadn't re-discovered her in 1947 and placed her into their star-building contract program. Her first work for them was in 1948's *Scudda Hoo, Scudda Hay,* a Lon McAllister epic with June Haver, which had McAllister, then a popular teen-age hearthrob, torn between Haver and his two mules. Anne Revere and Natalie Wood were also in it as was another young contract player, Marilyn Monroe. Colleen and Marilyn shared a rowboat for one scene but in the final print they are so far out from shore you can't see their faces. In such ways are careers born, or in Colleen's case, reborn.

That year she also appeared in *The Walls of Jericho* with Cornel Wilde, Anne Baxter, Linda Darnell, Kirk Douglas and a passel of character pros including Henry Hull, Ann Dvorak,

Tony Drake

Colleen still very lovely today, outside her Church in Sumner, Maryland home

Marjorie Rambeau and Barton MacLane. It was rather heavy-handed Americana but she went on from it to something better in *Chicken Every Sunday,* again 1948. A turn-of-the-century comedy about a get-rich-quick schemer (Dan Daily) and his understanding wife (Celeste Holm), it was a delightful movie and for a while 20th execs had her slated for *Green Grass of Wyoming.* Instead they gave her the lead in *When Willie Comes Marching Home* (1950), again with Daily, and featuring one of the studio's latest sex imports, Corinne Calvet.

About a West Virginia lad who finally goes off to World War II after originally being thought 4-F, Townsend plays the girl he leaves behind—and returns to after a French Underground episode with Calvet—and plays it beautifully with all the simple touches of the thousands of girls who went through the real thing. Right in the middle of publicity for the picture, Colleen broke the news that *Willie* would be her last movie and that henceforth she'd devote her life to religion. Coincidentally the Ingrid Bergman-Roberto Rossellini scandal was breaking at the same time, which gave newspaper editors plenty of headline fuel—the Chicago Tribune getting top prize for its article which had the caption 'Bad' over Bergman's picture and 'Good' over Colleen's!

She and Evans were married in March of 1951 and she quietly disappeared, only to be discovered by newspapers a year later working in a peace colony in California called Agape, from the Greek word meaning spiritual love. Evans was ordained a minister in the Presbyterian church and by 1958 had a parish of his own in La Hoya, California. By that time, the Evanses also had two sons.

They now live and work in Sumner, Maryland, a suburb of Washington, D.C., where he heads up another parish and where Colleen herself is a minister. She hasn't for a moment regretted her decision to leave stardom behind and is totally fulfilled leading the useful life she lives today. It must agree with her since she's still very beautiful.

183

The royal family. Seated are Queen Marie Jose and King Umberto II; behind them, left to right: Prince Alexander of Yugoslavia, his wife, Princess Maria Pia, and Prince Victor Emmanuel. Not present is Princess Maria Gabriella.

UMBERTO II, Former King of Italy

Out-of-work royalty has been somewhat of a drug on the market ever since the first World War started unseating them, and through the years, the titled nomads have drifted from one country to another in search of the welcome they no longer found at home. One such is Umberto II, King of Italy for barely one month in the Spring of 1946, who has finally found some sort of restful permancy outside the Portuguese resort city of Estoril in the village of Cascais.

His story is a sad one yet an almost predictable one, what with the changing codes of government of the 20th century. Born the son of King Emmanuel III, who ruled Italy from 1900 until 1946, Umberto was brought up to rule a Kingdom that was fast outgrowing his credentials. A quiet man, as Prince of Naples he worked to help the crippled and retarded children of his country and did his best to uphold his family's image and traditions until the day he assumed the throne. It did not happen as he had expected it to, though.

Mussolini, Italy's Prime Minister since 1922, was calling the shots in those days—adding to the King's titles the questionable one of Emperor of Ethiopia after his conquest there in 1937—and under his rule the monarchy became increasingly an in-name-only affair. Political pessures forced Emmanuel III to abdicate the throne in 1946 and seek asylum in Egypt with his friend King Farouk, leaving his son facing a plebescite election that would decide whether or not he would have a

Pictorial Parade

Former King Umberto with the Duchess of Bedford at a birthday party given by J. Paul Getty in 1972

throne to sit on. Unfortunately, after only a month as king and occupant of the Quiurnal Palace, he found he didn't. Umberto had encouraged the vote to stabilize his throne but the populace, by only a narrow margin of five-to-four—voted to end the rule of the House of Savoy.

The results of the election brought forth a virulent reaction from Monarchists, who didn't believe it was an honest one, and violence broke out over the country including several threats on Umberto's own life from the opposite factions. Rather than plunge the already war-torn country into further disorder, he chose to leave the country with his family and seek asylum elsewhere. At first he wanted to settle in Switzerland but the Swiss were not willing to accept him even though they agreed to take his wife, Queen Marie-Jose, and child. The family chose Portugal instead, and he's hardly left there since 1947 when he journeyed to Egypt for his father's funeral.

Friendly with Don Juan of Bourbon, the father of the current successor to the Spanish throne, he assisted at Juan Carlos' first communion. The city of Estoril is host to many former members of royalty, including Umberto's sister, the former Queen Giovanna of Bulgaria. She lost her throne in 1946 also and left there several years after the mysterious death of her husband, King Boris. She often shops in the local market with a lady-in-waiting carefully filling up her shopping cart.

The natives of Cascais see Umberto daily during his long strolls through the town and along the beach. Tourist officials regard him as a local fixture, often pointing him out to visitors. If they in turn stop him to speak, he's invariably polite and agreeable.

He lives simply, unlike his old friend Don Juan who enjoys an art-filled mansion which he shares with his wife Princess Maria Mercedes. Umberto seems to enjoy his life and the regulated lifestyle which is far removed from the few not-so-glorious days when he sat perched on the throne of Italy. He'd like to be buried in his home country when the time comes but has given up hope that he'll ever be able to resume his duties as monarch.

Sexy Mamie at the height of her fame

Christopher Young

MAMIE VAN DOREN

For all her voluptuous platinum blonde beauty—and there was plenty of it!—Mamie Van Doren inevitably portrayed that movie staple, the Girl From the Wrong Side of the Tracks. Not that she wanted to stay there, no indeed. Mamie was forever using her charms to elevate herself, but somehow her screen characters always maneuvered on a level that led straight to *Girls Town*—the title of a 1959 Universal epic which epitomizes Van Doren on the screen. As Silver Morgan, she arrives at that institution, meets the Mother Superior and immediately gets off on the wrong foot with "Mother is a dirty word to me!" When advised that dinner is at six sharp, she casually enters her request for roast beef, rare, a baked potato, and fresh asparagus on the side. "You'll have hash and like it!", says the Mother Superior, and though Mamie's career was mostly that, she did indeed like it.

The sexy look-alike for Marilyn Monroe had come a long way from her birthplace in South Dakota in 1933 as Joan Lucille Olander, until the time agent Jimmy McHugh discovered her and sent her to drama school. After a stint as a band singer, he helped her get a part in 1954's *Forbidden* with Tony Curtis and Joanne Dru (Vol. 1) and she took it from there, making the powers-that-be at Universal sit up and take notice—not to mention the males in the audience. The studio then put her in *Yankee Pasha* (1954), letting her give Rhonda Fleming a run for the glamour, money *and* pasha Jeff Chandler. Next she supported Jeanne Crain (Vol. 1) and George Nader in *The Second Greatest Sex* in 1955 and got her first taste of star billing in *Running Wild* (1955), a B-budgeted tale of car thieves and their women. The die was permanently cast and so was Mamie!

In 1955 she married bandleader Ray Anthony and while he went on to co-star with her in several pictures, Taylor and

Mamie at a recent Hollywood costume party

Burton they weren't. They had a son named for Perry Como, and were divorced in 1959 with Ray taking custody of the child.

In the late Fifties Universal made a series of films pegged for the teen-age market and without exception they were lurid melodramas and starred types like Jackie Coogan, John Barrymore Jr., Fay Spain and Pamela Mason, with Mamie their chief sex symbol. The titles speak for themselves—*Born Reckless, Girls Town, The Beat Generation*—all 1959 releases, and *Sex Kittens Go To College* with Tuesday Weld and Brigitte Bardot's little sister Mijanou. (For TV it's been retitled *Beauty and the Robot!*) The clinker of them all though was *The Private Lives of Adam and Eve* which threw Mamie up against Mickey Rooney's Adam in a soap opera-dream sequence outing which had little to do with history or reality.

Like Mansfield and to a degree Monroe, Mamie's appeal was primarily of the Fifties Bombshell variety and when the Sixties dawned her career was in trouble. TV talk shows were her main showcase, although in 1966 she did make something called *The Navy Versus the Night Monsters* and journeyed to Germany for a 'sauerbraten Western'. Romantically she's always been a favorite headline maker with men like ballplayer Bo Belinsky, whose career slumped noticeably when he met her, and country-rock singer Johnny Rivers. She married another ballplayer, Lee Meyers, who died in an auto accident, and her third marriage to a Texas oilman lasted a mere four weeks before it was annulled.

Mamie put together a cabaret act in the Mid-Sixties and headlined in Las Vegas and later in London, where she briefly considered living.

Lately she's been taking to the stage in the old Jayne Mansfield comedy *Will Success Spoil Rock Hunter?* and as usual the romantic notices—with her much younger co-star—have been as good if not better than the critical ones. They began their tour in a Florida dinner theater and after their first stage kiss Mamie purred, "We both knew we weren't acting anymore." Well, acting may not be what Mamie ever did but whatever you want to call it, she's done it with glamour.

Monique in the late Fifties

Pictorial Parade

MONIQUE VAN VOOREN

Most of the blonde Sex Symbols of the Fifties were ultra-bosomed babytalk ladies from Monroe on down to Mansfield, on further down to Sheree North, Joi Lansing, Barbara Nichols and dozens of others. But Monique Van Vooren is an exception to that top-heavy club she belonged to. Her babytalk had a foreign accent and she survived it!

It's been a long road since her birth in Belgium in the early Thirties and her arrival in the United States as an exchange student in 1950, one that's seen her blossom and re-blossom as one of those media-made celebrities whose name has somehow always managed to stay on the right invitation lists. Her photograph has appeared in every publication on the stands but her most ardent admirers would have to think twice to name a movie or TV drama she's appeared on.

Monique's first break in the acting game was in Broadway's *Almanac* and subsequently she became a television staple as the resident glamour girl on panel and game shows like *To Tell The Truth*. Actually she's always been a bigger name abroad than here, having forged a second sexy career in French movies in the Fifties and early Sixties. She got a good crack at American audiences though in 1959's *Happy Anniversary* opposite urbane David Niven and ever-cute Mitzi Gaynor. And, yes, she was the temptress in that teapot.

Monique personally thinks of herself as much an actress as a famous face and fabulous body. Over the years she's studied acting with the likes of Stella Adler and regularly hits the regional theater rounds in actress-needed parts like Princess Cosmonopolis in *Sweet Bird of Youth.* What she really wants though is "to create a part and tear up the stage."

Her birthday is March 25th, which makes her an Aries, and every year she celebrates it by taking down her Christmas tree. Monique likes holidays.

Monique as she looked in her recent Broadway musical

Somewhat of an international wanderer when not on-stage somewhere, Monique has survived all the labels from Jet Setter to Beautiful Person although she still qualifies with her addresses alone—an apartment in Rome and a villa on the coast of Sardinia near the Aga Kahn's Emerald Coast housing development for the super rich. "It has wonderful views of the sea and a bathtub for twelve," she admits candidly. She also admits it's regularly populated—the villa, not necessarily the bathtub—with friends like Rudolph Nureyev, Rex Harrison, Italian movie queen Sylvana Mangano, and other 'name' names.

A veteran of a Brussels convent, Monique's voice retains a sexy hint of an accent that only adds to her Dietrich-like charms. She doesn't smoke or drink yet despite her lack of bad habits she nonetheless attracted the interest of Andy Warhol two years ago when he was casting his *Frankenstein* in Rome. She starred in it as a constantly undraped and unsatiated lady. Warhol flew to Kansas City to see her sing and dance in *Can-Can* and then signed her for his Broadway musical *Man On The Moon* in early 1975.

Like so many of Monique's projects it proved more publicity than performance and closed almost as fast as it opened. Authored by John Philips of the old Mamas and Papas singing group, it starred his wife Genevieve Waite and there were rumors of backstage-biting with Monique quoted as saying that Genevieve was getting almost every number in the show—"And even Ethel Merman never took them all!"

Divorced from her second husband, and mother of a twenty-one year old son, Eric, whom she refuses to talk about, Monique's currently heading back to the chic nightclub circuit. She doesn't mind her playgirl image because, "I play!," and as for being a sex symbol, she doesn't mind that either—"Liberated I have always been." And probably always will be.

189

VERA-ELLEN

One of the last star products of the spectacular MGM musicals Vera-Ellen went about her dancing business with a seriousness that belied her apple-cheeked image on the screen. After all, she started out as a dance instructor and realized early in life that dancing was what she did best—something that took Hollywood several years to find out. When she danced, Vera-Ellen was a dream—but as for acting? Suffice it to say that she smiled very prettily, and often. She wasn't the exclusive creation of MGM but her films for that studio have been the ones that have kept her name and fame alive since she danced off the screen in 1957's *Let's Be Happy*.

And her movie stardom wasn't an overnight thing. Before she landed her first role in 1945's *Wonder Man* she had parlayed her train ticket to New York City for a Dancing Teachers of America convention to get on the *Major Bowes Amateur Hour*, had a short career as a Radio City Rockette, danced at Billy Rose's Casa Manana nightclub, and was on Broadway in three hits: *Very Warm For May, Panama Hattie* with Ethel Merman, and *By Jupiter* in 1942, as Minerva. It was a year later, while she was high stepping in *A Connecticut Yankee* that one of Samuel Godlwyn's talent scouts saw her and brought her to Hollywood.

Born in Cincinnati, Ohio in 1926, she'd been a fragile child and her parents decided that dance lessons would build her up. They did indeed and several million timesteps later she demonstrated just how much in *Wonder Man*, in a tap-adagio-boogie number with Danny Kaye that got her instant acclaim. Kaye was Goldwyn's big money maker at that time and he was smart enough to back up his funnyman with glamour—most notably Virginia Mayo. Vera-Ellen was the second female lead to Virginia as she was again a year later in *The Kid From Brooklyn.* Goldwyn loaned her to 20th Century Fox for *Three Little Girls in Blue* (she was the third after Vivian Blaine and

Eddie Colbert

Vera-Ellen in Hollywood today

June Haver) and she stayed there for *Carnival in Costa Rica* with Dick Haymes, in which she danced a bit and smiled a lot. Goldwyn then released her from her contract and she at last got a call from MGM who put her in a long blonde wig for the *Slaughter on Tenth Avenue* ballet in 1948's *Words and Music* with Gene Kelly. Her sensational dancing led Metro chiefs to insert a sexy number for her in the Marx Brothers *Love Happy* in 1949 and to make her Miss Turnstiles in the great *On The Town*—accompanied by a seven-year contract.

Studio makeup men quickly transformed her, and with Fred Astaire in *Three Little Words* (1950), she looked fresher and prettier than ever before. She went to England to make *Happy Go Lovely* with David Niven in 1951 but returned to MGM for *The Belle of New York*, a charming but unsuccessful musical, again with Astaire. They loaned her out for *Call Me Madam*, a big hit with her a princess opposite commoner Donald O'Connor and Ethel Merman as Perle Mesta but brought her back for a straight dramatic role in *Big Leaguer*, a flop.

Oddly enough it was Danny Kaye who came to her rescue, starring her with him, Bing Crosby and Rosemary Clooney in *White Christmas*—a smash hit. MGM announced her for leads in *Seven Brides For Seven Brothers* and *Hit the Deck* (both eventually played by Jane Powell) but Vera-Ellen was getting ideas of her own. She wanted to be a nightclub star and chose Las Vegas over the soundstage.

She'd been briefly married in her teens to dancer Robert Hightown but they'd divorced long ago. In 1954 she married a wealthy oilman, Victor Rothschild, and informed MGM at contract time that she wasn't interested in a renewal. After *Let's Be Happy* with Tony Martin she called her career a day and has been adamant about her decision. She's been asked to do revivals of *No No Nannette* but has turned all offers down. Tragedy struck in the late Sixties when her only child died and shortly thereafter so did her marriage. Since then she shows up on the tennis courts, as pretty as ever, and lives with her mother in the San Fernando Valley.

On the set with Ava Gardner during *Showboat* filming

WILLIAM WARFIELD

One of the high points of the movie *That's Entertainment* comes at the end of the *Showboat* sequence when William Warfield sings *Old Man River*. His thunderous tones wrapped around the lyrics of the classic Jerome Kern-Oscar Hammerstein II song, again thrilled the millions of moviegoers who first heard and saw the movie in 1951, plus new millions hearing and seeing him for the first time. Since then Warfield has reached and maintained a top position among concert artists, but, like it or not, *Old Man River* is the song he'll go down in history for. *Showboat* was his only movie, but that wasn't his fault. MGM was so impressed with his performance in it that they planned a production of *Huckleberry Finn,* with a score by Lerner and Lane, to star him, Danny Kaye and Gene Kelly. Unfortunately there was a fallout between Kaye and Kelly and the film was never made.

Warfield began his career after a stint in the Armed Forces during World War II and made his concert debut on a memorable evening in March, 1950 when he stormed New York's Town Hall in a recital that made him an overnight sensation. One of the resultant offers was for a thirty-five concert tour Australia which he embarked upon immediately, and it was while he was singing there that his manager and former Army buddy, Larney Goodkind set him up for *Showboat*— without a screen test!

Metro was at first reluctant to sign an untested singer for the featured role of Joe, but after hearing recordings of him and seeing the rave notices from New York and the ones flooding in from Australia, they were won over. Goodkind knew Warfield was perfect for the part the moment he heard Metro was planning to remake the film, and luckily he was listened to.

When Warfield reported to the studio for the shooting it was only natural for the studio bosses to put him right into music

A thoughtful Warfield today

rehearsals. He didn't argue with them. The first trial run-through of the number was so perfect that it was the track used in the movie, unheard of in Hollywood—or anywhere for that matter. Louis B. Mayer, whose heart has been described as only slightly softer than granite, burst into tears when he heard it, so overwhelmed was he by Warfield's richly hued and emotional rendition. When the film opened it was an immediate smash hit—the biggest box office hit of 1951, in fact—and Warfield's singing at the climax of the film caused audiences across America and around the world to break into spontaneous applause upon its finish. And while Hollywood fumbled the ball with his future, the rest of the world didn't

He starred in a ten-week American tour of *Porgy and Bess*—acclaimed as one of the greatest Porgys of all time—and the State Department snapped the production up for a world tour that included Vienna, Berlin, London and Paris. (He has made six separate tours for the Department, more than any other solo artist, and in recent years has gone to places like Vietnam, Laos and Cambodia.)

In 1952 he married soprano Leontyne Price but it was a stormy union. They separated in 1957 but were not divorced until 1972. 1957 saw him star on television as De Lawd in *Green Pastures* which was so successful—no singing, by the way—that it was done again live in 1959.

New York finally got a chance to see him as Porgy in 1961 when he appeared in *Porgy and Bess* for the New York City Opera, reprising it again with them three years later. A critic wrote that it was a tragedy its composer, George Gershwin didn't live to see him in it.

On March 24, 1975, Warfield sang his 25th Anniversary Recital at Carnegie Hall, concentrating on the music he especially loves, classics like Schumann's *Liederkreis, opus 39* and Purcell's *Arise Ye Subterranean Winds.* His final encore though was *Old Man River.*

Henry and Claudette Colbert in DeMille's *Cleopatra*, 1934

HENRY WILCOXON

In one of the most famous moments in screen history, *Cleopatra*'s barge set sail on a 1934 soundstage—sails billowing, carved oars fanning the air already heavy with perfumed incense, and what appeared to be another regiment of slave-girls fanning what was left. Coiled on a silken dais lay a catlike Cleopatra, her knowing eyes gazing soulfully at her Marc Antony. She, of course, was Claudette Colbert. And Marc Antony? He was Henry Wilcoxon, a square-jawed, 29 year old Britisher on his first Hollywood outing, a fortuitous one for him because *Cleopatra*'s producer, Cecil B. DeMille, was to become the mainstay of his career, even elevating him to associate producer status when he no longer commanded the hero's role.

Henry had cut his teeth in British repertory theater with people like Laurence Olivier, Ralph Richardson, Robert Donat and Dame Edith Evans when a Paramount talent scout spotted him and tested him as a possible contract player. He came to DeMille's attention by accident when DeMille happened into the studio screening room with a reel of horse footage under his arm. While waiting for it to be run he caught the end of Wilcoxon's screen test, and allegedly cried, "Forget the horses. I've found Marc Antony instead!" The film was a huge success (costing, by the way, only $750,000 as compared to the Taylor-Burton remake which came in at over forty million!) and DeMille cast him as Richard the Lionhearted in 1935's *The Crusades*, which featured Katherine DeMille and starred a youthfully blonde Loretta Young.

DeMille and Wilcoxon struck up a friendship—"I wasn't a yes man; he hated those"—and while he worked constantly in pictures like *The Last of the Mohicans*, (1936); *Souls at Sea* (1937); *If I Were King* (1938); *Tarzan Finds A Son* (1939) (as a White Hunter to Frieda Inescourt's huntress); and *That Hamilton Woman* (1941), he was always ready for a call from the master—which came next with *Unconquered* in 1947. (De-

194

Henry Wilcoxon in Hollywood, 1975

Eddie Colbert

Mille was notoriously faithful to his older stars. Julia Faye, who starred as his Queen of Egypt in the original *Ten Commandments* played Samson's mother in *Samson and Delilah* twenty-five years later, and his Jesus in *King of Kings*, H. B. Warner, found a few days' work as an extra in the exodus sequence of the 1956 *Ten Commandments*, to name two examples.)

Fresh out of the Navy, Wilcoxon was glad to be back in the DeMille fold as the fifth star of *Samson and Delilah*—after Hedy Lamarr, Victor Mature, Angela Lansbury and George Sanders— and two years later DeMille suggested he take a stab at co-producing as well. For the next thirteen years he helped shepherd multitudinous casts through *The Greatest Show on Earth, The Ten Commandments* and the last of the DeMille legacy, *The Buccaneer,* a white-washed tale of pirate Jean LaFitte which reteamed *Commandment* stars Yul Brynner and Charleton Heston. Unfortunately it wasn't very successful. DeMille served only as production supervisor and left the direction up to then son-in-law Anthony Quinn. (When DeMille died in 1959 he was working on the life of Lord Baden-Powell, the founder of the Boy Scouts, a project Wilcoxon says is still in the works.)

After DeMille's death, though, Wilcoxon's career slowed down and he turned to television guest shots, not appearing in another film until Universal's weighty *The Warlord* in 1965 with Charlton Heston. He played a scruffy Viking chieftain in a backlot epic that was a far cry from the pageantry and pomp of DeMille.

In recent years he's been seen in *The Private Navy of Sgt. O'Farrell* (1968) with Bob Hope and Phyllis Diller, and got third billing in Richard Harris' *Man In The Wilderness* in 1971. TV-wise he's been on *Marcus Welby,* and was recently seen as an exorcising priest in *The Curse of the Hope Diamond.* Long married to Thirties actress Joan Woodbury [*Forty Naughty Girls* (1938); *Flame of the West* (1946)], they live comfortably in Hollywood where he expects to keep on working as long as the scripts come in.

195

Cornel Wilde in 1955

Jack Kuster

CORNEL WILDE

During the peak of his popularity there were few movie critics who took Cornel Wilde seriously, often referring to him as a male Maureen O'Hara because of his long string of Technicolor costume epics. But when the lean days of the 1950s hit Movieville, he was one of the few stars who was able to keep his career going. He switched from pretty-boy leading man to producer/director and while the results haven't been stupifying, they have kept him in the running.

Of Hungarian parentage, Wilde was born in New York City in 1915 only to be uprooted when his family moved back to Budapest. He returned to the U.S. though and after high school, enrolled in Columbia University where he studied medicine. In his off-hours he pursued an interest in the theater and after a small role or two, switched careers. His prowess with a sword helped win him the role of Tybalt in Laurence Olivier's production of *Romeo and Juliet* with Vivien Leigh, and while it wasn't a great success, it did get Wilde a Warner Bros. movie contract.

They gave him roles in things like *The Lady With Red Hair* (1940) and *The Perfect Snob* (1941), and if you look closely you'll spot him as a Mexican hotel clerk in Bogart's *High Sierra*. Warners then dropped him, and he went to 20th Century Fox to co-star with Sonja Henie in *Wintertime* (1943). Columbia made him a star though when they chose him for the lead role in the overblown biography of Frederic Chopin in *A Song to Remember* (1945). His tousled dark hair framing his classic face kept moviegoers' eyes off the keyboard—which was just as well—and he became an overnight sensation. Fan magazines of 1945 put it succinctly: "Everybody's wild about Wilde!"

Next he was Aladdin in *A Thousand and One Nights* (1945) for Columbia, then returned to 20th for the steamy *Leave Her To Heaven* (1945) with Gene Tierney, then back to Columbia for *The Bandit of Sherwood Forest* (1946) as Robin Hood's son. After *Centennial Summer* (1946) with Jeanne Crain and

196

Cornel Wilde and Clint Eastwood after a round of tennis recently

1947's *Homestretch* with Maureen O'Hara—ironically *not* a costume picture—he grabbed the male lead in *Forever Amber* (1947) opposite Linda Darnell. One of the most intriguing pictures he did during this period was *Roadhouse* with Ida Lupino and Richard Widmark. It still simmers on the Late Show, and holds up very well too.

When DeMille signed him for *The Greatest Show On Earth* (1952) as the French aerial artist with a weather eye for the girls, Wilde's career needed a boost. It was a huge hit and helped people forget *At Sword's Point* with O'Hara and *in* costume. His marriage to actress Pat Knight ended about that time and he married Jean Wallace, a comely blonde who later became his co-star in his independent movies. They first worked together in 1954's *Star of India,* yet another costume outing.

After the plush *Woman's World* in 1954 and a few not-so-plush epics like *The Scarlet Coat* (1955) and the hilarious *Hot Blood* (1956), a 'true' story of contemporary gypsies with Jane Russell awash in gold earrings and swirling skirts, Cornel struck out on his own, figuring he could do no worse for himself than Hollywood was doing. He and Jean co-starred in 1958's *Maracaibo* and a racing yarn, *The Devil's Hairpin,* and ventured into ancient Rome for *Constantine and the Cross* (1960) and into the Middle Ages for *Lancelot and Guinevere* (1963). They were successful enough although far from smash hits.

He experimented too and struck it lucky in 1965 with *The Naked Prey* as a lone, and naked, man against the jungle. His *Beach Red* in 1968 was a bloody war movie and in 1969 he did a good piece of work in the minor classic *The Comic* with Dick Van Dyke, one of the most penetrating exposes of the Hollywood mystique ever done.

After 1971's *No Blade of Grass,* an ecological science fiction thriller, Wilde was off-screen for a while preparing another independent production called *Shark's Treasure.* He and Jean maintain a Hollywood home but keep their bags half-packed for wherever his next career move may take them.

Burt Brazier, Betty Wragge and Marian Barney from *Pepper Young's Family*

BETTY WRAGGE

From 1936 until 1960, Betty Wragge played one of the most popular roles ever in radio soap operas—Penny Young in *Pepper Young's Family*. For over 6900 installments America listened as she grew up, got married, and had children: everything that every *other* young girl was doing, only Betty did it to the carefully orchestrated organ strains of the daytime serial. She got the part by crashing the audition and had to wait until every other little girl had done her bit but patience paid off because she was the one chosen. It's an interesting story.

"We lived on 46th Street between Broadway and Sixth Avenue and my parents ran a theatrical boarding house. One day while my brother and I were playing out front, a man came along and asked us to be in a movie. My mother said OK and that's how it began. When actor Tom Brown's mother wouldn't tell my mother where he went to school, she followed him there one day and shortly enrolled us in it, the Professional Children's School. When I was in first grade I was on Broadway in a play called *Up The Line,* then *Betsy; My Maryland;* and a funny play called *Her Unborn Child* starring Adelle Ronson— one of the first about birth control.

"Around the time of the early radio shows I was asked to audition for a kind of *Our Gang* on the air called *The Goldspot Pals,* named after the man who made Goldspot shoe soles. I was also in Madge Tucker's Children's Hour, *Our Barn,* a variety show where we'd put on little plays and skits. Then I auditioned for a show to be called *Red Adams*—actually I crashed the audition—and got the part of Red's daughter. Burgess Meredith played Red. Because Beechnut gum was the sponsor and there was an Adams chewing gum, the name was changed to *Red Davis* and I became Betty Davis on the show. When Proctor and Gamble became the sponsors about three years later, it was changed to *Pepper Young's Family.* We were on for twenty-four years."

198

 Jon B. Aroneo

Betty in the garden of her New York apartment house

The cast changed over the years with several actors as Pepper but the final one was Mason Adams with his family, Laddie Seamon, Eunice Howard, Marian Barney, Burt Brazier, Tom Chalmers, and, of course, Betty.

Besides her daily *Family* duties, Betty did a few Broadway plays too, notably *Dead End,* in a small part but also under-studying the lead role which she eventually took over. "I was written out of *Family* every matinee day for two years by Mrs. Carrington, the writer of the show." Unfortunately there were a lot of stage roles that Betty had to miss out on because the plays had out-of-town tryouts and she couldn't be written out of *Family* that long!

Shortly after *Family* ended its radio run, the author, Elaine Carrington, died and the show never made what would have seemed a natural transition to television. Betty kept working though, doing TV commercials, touring in plays like *The Sound of Music* with Gloria De Haven, and *Oliver* with Walter Slezak, plus dubbing her voice into Italian movies. "It's funny to watch Gina Lollobrigida or Silvana Pampanini on the Late Show and hear your voice come out! And if you ever see Giana Maria Canale in *Theodora the Slave Empress,* you're really hearing me." She dubbed over fifty of them.

On Broadway she stood by for Ruby Keeler during the long run of *No No Nanette,* and eventually toured with the show in the Patsy Kelly part with Ruby and Cyril Ritchard. "I took it over on a couple of hours notice and pulled it off very well. Mr. Ritchard couldn't believe I'd only just stepped into the part."

She's also popped up from time to time on *The Secret Storm* and *Love of Life,* two daytime soap operas, and in her spare time practices yoga and takes tap dancing lessons. Her daughter, Tina Brook, is a beautiful girl who's acting now and her son, Tom Brook, has done many TV commercials plus several Broadway plays. He's also a promising drummer with one of the largest sets of drums I've ever seen. Recently Betty went to Hyannis, Massachusetts for a radio revival program meeting up again with many of the actors she once shared a microphone with.

199

Jane wearing a chic, late Thirties hat

JANE WYATT

Of all the TV Mothers of the 1950s, perhaps Jane Wyatt is the best remembered and best loved. As the female mainstay of *Father Knows Best* from 1954 until today (thanks to the magic of continual reruns!) she managed to combine just the right amounts of charm, warmth and good, old-fashioned common sense to make her role as Robert Young's wife believably human. She was graceful and level-headed, a mature version of many of the sweet-young-thing parts she first played in Hollywood, proving that such girls do indeed grow into capable women.

She came to the movies after a brief career as a stage actress specializing in ingenue roles. When she got to Hollywood in 1933, she was twenty-two, and the Campgaw, New Jersey native was immediately pegged as a 'nice girl', the kind that Mama would totally approve of. Like Frances Dee and Loretta Young, Wyatt never *took* the man but wisely bided her time until he discovered *her*. And he usually did by the fade-out.

Her second movie after something called *One More River* (1934) was the classic *Great Expectations* (1934) and after its success, her studio had just that for her career. Happily, though, after things like *Luckiest Girl In The World* (1936), they loaned her out from Universal to Columbia for *Lost Horizon* in 1937, and that remains the picture everyone most remembers—and with good reason. Directed by the genius Frank Capra, her role as Sandra, the girl who waits for Ronald Coleman to return to Shangri-La, is a haunting one and she plays it with a precise loveliness that has helped the film reach its classic status. It is a picture everyone has seen at least once and never fully forgotten. Not only was it her high-water mark but Capra's and Coleman's as well. (Actress Margo also is memorable as the woman who leaves Shangra-La only to have her face fall as fast as a bad souffle!)

Eddie Colbert

Jane Wyatt and husband, 1975

Despite *Horizon*'s popularity, Wyatt didn't find it a springboard to full-fledged stardom. She freelanced at Republic for *Girl From God's Country* (1940) and *Hurricane Smith* (1941, but after those and more fluff like *Weekend For Three* (1941) and *Kisses For Breakfast* (1941) at Warner, she got the nice-girl-out-West routine in *Buckskin Frontier* (1943) and *The Kansan* (1943).

Given the opportunity she was very good indeed, as in the moody Cary Grant-Ethel Barrymore starrer in 1944, *None But The Lonely Heart* (as one of the girls who tries to straighten Grant out), not to mention the greatly acclaimed *Gentleman's Agreement* for 20th in 1947.

Jane Wyatt got her first big crack at on-screen motherhood in Samuel Goldwyn's *Our Very Own* (1950) as the mother of Ann Blyth. Adopted mother, I should say, as that was what the story was all about—Ann finds out her real mom (played stunningly by Ann Dvorak) gave her away at birth.

When *Father Knows Best* came along in 1954, it saved Wyatt's career. Though dropped by its original sponsor after its first 26 weeks on the air, the program grew in audience appeal to become one of TV's all-time most popular shows. As small-town lawyer Jim Anderson, Young was the perfect husband and their children, played by Elinor Donahue, Billy Gray and Lauren Chapin, were the kind of kids that every mother wanted.

A mother in real life, Jane has two sons, Christopher and Michael, from her long-time marriage to Edgar Ward. In fact, they've been happily wed for forty years and recently she debuted several of her grandchildren in some television commercials. In 1975 she proved that talent doesn't age, when she played an overbearing mother on Public Broadcasting's *The Ladies Of The Corridor* with Cloris Leachman and a powerhouse cast. Last on the big screen in 1965's *Never Too Late,* she won't say no to a good offer. She lives in Bel Air, California with Ward, where they're often seen on the movie screening circuit.

201

NOSTALGIA

All in Color for a Dime Lupoff & Thompson
$1.50

An Informal History of the Pulp Magazine
Goulart $1.25

Glad You Asked That Gardner   95c

Is That Who I Think It Is? Vol. I Agan $1.50

Is That Who I Think It Is? Vol II Agan $1.50

The Kane Book of Famous First Facts & Records
$1.95

Seven Glorious Days, Seven Fun-filled Nights
Sopkin   75c

Whatever Become of . . .? Vol. I Lamparski $1.50

Whatever Became of . . .? Vol. II Lamparski
$1.50

Whatever Became of . . .? Vol. III   Lamparski
$1.50

Why Did They Name It? Campbell $1.50

Available wherever paperbacks are sold or use this coupon.